The Lord Is Near

Daily Bible Meditations for

2013

Printed in the U.S.A.

The Lord Is Near

Daily Bible Meditations for

2013

Copyright: © 2012 Believer's Bookshelf Canada Inc.
ISBN 978-1-894956-61-1

Published and distributed by:

Believer's Bookshelf Canada Inc.
5205 Regional Road #81, Unit # 3
BEAMSVILLE, ONTARIO
CANADA L0R 1B3
www.bbcan.org
orders@bbcan.org

For distributors in other countries please refer to the back pages.

Knowing the time, that now it is high time to awake out of sleep: For now is our salvation nearer than when we believed."

(Romans 13:11 KJV)

Let your loins be girded about, and your lamps burning.

(Luke 12:35)

Another year has dawned and our Lord's coming has drawn that much closer. May we be found watching and waiting for Him!

With thanksgiving to the Lord we present the 2013 edition of *The Lord is Near Daily Bible Meditations*. We pray that its Christ-centered daily readings may prove to be an encouragement and blessing to the reader. These meditations have been prayerfully selected from writings of past and present authors. When the name of an author is unknown, the title of the publication from which the selection is extracted is shown wherever possible. We thank all who have contributed articles or have helped in the production of this year's calendar.

A careful, sound translation of Scripture is essential to properly understand what God is saying to us. Therefore, J. N. Darby's excellent literal translation* serves as our basic text in these meditations, though we also make use of other sound translations.

May the Lord continue to use this publication for His glory and for the rich blessing of all those who read it.

The Editors
Jacob Redekop, Brian Reynolds, John van Dijk, Eugene P. Vedder, Jr.

Correspondence should be directed to the following address:

The Lord is Near
4 Elwin Cr.
DARTMOUTH, NOVA SCOTIA
CANADA   B2W 3J6
or: **E-mail: contact@thelordisnear.org**

Orders should be placed with your local Christian bookstore or one of our distributors.

*available at reasonable cost from most of the distributors of this calendar

The Lord Is Near

Daily Bible Meditations for

2013

I returned, and saw under the sun, that the race is not to the swift, nor the battle to the strong ... but time and chance happeneth to them all. For man also knoweth not his time.

(Ecclesiastes 9:11-12)

A traveler was walking along a road. His movements were uniform and there was no deviation. He looked straight ahead and gazed on what was beyond. As he went, he saw one person after another drop down along the road and rise no more! This is, figuratively, a description of the passage of time!

You are now walking the road of life in 2013, but you do not know for how long. You may see the buds of spring and not live to see the flowers of summer, or watch leaves fall from the autumn trees and then lie beneath them in the winter. You may begin the year with grey hair or with youthful buoyancy, but you know not how the year will end. Whether your days may be few or many, there remains the question, Are you ready for eternity? God would "teach us to number our days, that we may acquire a wise heart" (Ps. 90:12). To begin the year with God is more important than anything else in this world, no matter what. The Bible says: "Seek ye Jehovah while He may be found, call ye upon Him while He is near. Let the wicked forsake his way, and the unrighteous man his thoughts; and let him return unto Jehovah, and He will have mercy upon him; and to our God, for He will abundantly pardon" (Isa. 55:6-7).

In view of the uncertainty of life, how important it is to be "justified on the principle of faith" and have "peace towards God through our Lord Jesus Christ" (Rom. 5:1)! Having this peace through Christ as our personal Savior will alone enable you to enter upon and experience a truly "happy New Year" now, and to look forward with absolute certainty to a glorious eternity.

J. F. Paulsen

I therefore, the prisoner of the Lord, beseech you that ye walk worthy of the vocation wherewith ye are called, with all lowliness and meekness, with longsuffering, forbearing one another in love; endeavoring to keep the unity of the Spirit in the bond of peace. There is one body, and one Spirit.

(Ephesians 4:1-4 KJV)

All who believe in Christ as dead and risen are sealed by the Spirit and form part of His body. This body is presented as the Church. "There is one body" is as true now as when the apostle wrote it to the Ephesians. This body is indissoluble. Its unity cannot be broken. There is no such thing as "rending the body of Christ."

We are bound to recognize as a great foundation truth the unity of the body. We are not called to form a unity, but to own the unity which God the Holy Spirit has formed. It is as contrary to the truth to set about forming a unity as to set about working out our righteousness for ourselves. God reveals His righteousness on the principle of faith—we believe and possess it. Any righteousness or unity of their own which men try to establish will pass away like the vapor of the morning, whereas that which God has established will remain.

Our motto must be: "First truth; unity if possible, but never at the expense of truth!" The unity of the Spirit is a grand reality, a substantial truth, in the light of which we are called to walk. We are no more competent to form that unity than we are to atone for our sins. It is God's work from first to last. He has revealed His unity; it would be a grave error, would we attempt to work it out ourselves. Christ is the center of God's holy unity; the Spirit is the power to keep it. All other methods to attain unity are false.

C. H. Mackintosh

The Lᴏʀᴅ brings a charge against the inhabitants of the land: "There is no truth or mercy or knowledge of God in the land. By swearing and lying, killing and stealing and committing adultery, they break all restraint, with bloodshed upon bloodshed … My people are destroyed for lack of knowledge. Because you have rejected knowledge, I also will reject you from being priest for Me; because you have forgotten the law of your God, I also will forget your children." *(Hosea 4:1-2,6 NKJV)*

PROPHETS AND THEIR PROPHECIES – HOSEA (3)

The charges the Lord here brings against Israel can also justly be brought against mankind today. Lawlessness is on the increase while courts often sanction wickedness and sin in the guise of human rights. The language used in public and on the media steadily becomes filthier and more profane. Lying, especially in politics and among those in high places, is commonplace. One hears daily of wars, mass murders, and dreadful atrocities. Stealing is no longer merely cheating, breaking and entering, or simple robbery; complex sophisticated schemes to enrich their perpetrators are devised in loftiest financial circles and bring ruin to many. And sex not only sells, but adultery, fornication, and perversion of all kinds, especially among celebrities, are glamorized and celebrated as models for the world to imitate.

People deliberately reject the knowledge of God. They deny or minimize the importance of sound doctrine, while tolerance, even of evil of all kinds, has become society's highest virtue. The consequences can only be tragic. Our holy God must deal in judgment. God cannot accept those who love such things to serve Him acceptably as priests. Tremendously sad effects reach on to the succeeding generations, for God visits the iniquity of the fathers upon the children to the third and fourth generation.

E. P. Vedder, Jr.

Take My yoke upon you, and learn from Me; for I am meek and lowly in heart; and ye shall find rest to your souls; for My yoke is easy, and My burden is light. *(Matthew 11:29-30)*

The yoke of Satan, of sin, is a *heavy* and *grievous* one, but that of Christ is a happy one. Serving Christ is a happy service even when there is a cross to carry or a yoke to bear. We are not treated like dumb, driven cattle, goaded on, but we are *led* most tenderly. Remember that the yoke He puts on His people is the one He bore Himself: "He hath borne our griefs and carried our sorrows" (Isa. 53:4).

The great apostle Paul calls himself a *servant*, literally a slave, of Jesus Christ (Rom. 1:1). This seems to be his boast! Do you know this blessed servitude? True, His yoke is the appointed discipline He employs in training us, but the Lord is no hard taskmaster! Be comforted! It is His tender hand that *puts* it on and keeps it on. He will suit the yoke to your neck and your neck to the yoke. He will suit His grace to your trials. His people need to be in heaviness through manifold temptations to keep them meek and submissive. Never is there more gracious love than when God takes His own means to curb us, to humble us, and to prove us—to bring us out from ourselves, from our desires, from our confidences, and put us under the needed yoke.

No one has ever repented of joyful servitude. Has He ever failed you? Has His yoke ever been too grievous? Have your tears been unalleviated, your sorrows unsolaced, your temptations above that which you were able to bear? Ah, rather have you not found that if you cast your burden upon the Lord He will sustain you (see Ps. 55:22)? Remember, those who take His yoke are encouraged with the promise, "Ye shall find rest to your souls."

J. R. MacDuff

Now before the feast of the Passover, Jesus ... rises from supper and lays aside His garments, and having taken a linen towel He girded himself ... and began to wash the feet of the disciples, and to wipe them with the linen towel with which He was girded.

(John 13:1,4-5)

FEET WASHING (1)

Beginning with chapter 13 and until Jesus was arrested in the Garden of Gethsemane He spoke only to His disciples to prepare them for His departure. As they were sad and troubled, He assured them that He would go to prepare a place for them and then would come and take them to be with Him in the Father's house. He instructed them to love one another as He loved them, and promised to send the Holy Spirit who would abide with them and be in them. He also taught them how to be fruitful, and prepared them for possible persecution.

But before all that, He had to deal with a serious problem—their misunderstanding of what true greatness is. John and James had wanted to be distinguished, and the others were indignant because of it. This shows they all had the same problem—pride and the desire for preeminence. Therefore before His wonderful discourse in the Upper Room, He wanted to teach them that true greatness is in humility. Earlier they had heard Him saying, "Take My yoke upon you, and learn of Me; for I am meek and lowly in heart; and ye shall find rest to your souls" (Mt. 11:29).

The hardest lesson for us to learn is true humility—therefore He gave them a living example. He laid aside His garments and, as a servant, girded Himself with a towel. To wash someone's feet one must kneel on the floor. You cannot sit on a chair or pedestal and wash a brother's feet; or there are apt to be some broken bones. King Solomon said, "Pride goes before destruction, and a haughty spirit before a fall" (Prov. 16:18).

A. M. Behnam

Thinkest thou that I cannot now call upon My Father, and He will furnish Me more than twelve legions of angels? How then should the scriptures be fulfilled that thus it must be?

(Matthew 26:53-54)

The chief priests and temple officials had come to arrest the Lord Jesus. This prompted Simon Peter to attempt a well-meaning but ill-advised defense of the Lord. After cautioning Peter that those who take up the sword "shall perish by the sword," He then asked him two questions: Did he not know that the Father would supply Him twelve legions of angels if He so requested? But if so, how then would the Scriptures be fulfilled?

The first question is staggering in its implications: could He not at any time easily ask His Father for twelve legions of angels for deliverance? A Roman legion consisted on the average of 5,000 men. Twelve legions would be 60,000. But the Lord does not limit it to that, for He says, *more* than twelve legions! When the Assyrian army surrounded Jerusalem in Hezekiah's day, an angel of Jehovah went forth in the night and smote the Assyrians so that by the morning light 185,000 of them were dead (Isa. 37:36). An angel killed 70,000 Israelites and would have destroyed Jerusalem but for David's intervention (2 Sam. 24:15-16). In each of these cases only one of God's angels wrought such destruction! In Revelation 6–7 we read of the destruction that only six angels bring upon earth in the Great Tribulation. The mind staggers at the thought of over 60,000 angels intervening in behalf of their Master! Truly, His angels are "mighty in strength" (Ps. 103:20).

The second question was rhetorical. If the Lord had asked His Father for powerful angelic intervention, how should the Scriptures have been fulfilled that He should go to the cross and suffer for the sins of men! Truly, He is worthy!

B. Reynolds

They called Rebekah, and said unto her, Wilt thou go with this man? And she said, I will go. *(Genesis 24:58 KJV)*

Rebekah exemplifies the Church or bride of Christ. As the earrings and bracelets given her by the servant were a token of Isaac's love, so Christ "having loved His own which were in the world, He loved them unto the end" (Jn. 13:1). The jewels of silver and jewels of gold and raiment typify the fruit of Christ's redemptive work on the cross, for He "loved the Church, and gave Himself for it" (Eph. 5:25).

By her affirmative answer to the question, she virtually severed her earthly ties in order to follow Abraham's servant, a type of the Holy Spirit, across the desert. This reminds one of the verse "Hearken, O daughter, and consider, and incline thine ear; forget also thine own people, and thy father's house" (Ps. 45:10). What animated her in the journey were the things of Isaac, which the servant showed her. Speaking of the Holy Spirit, the Lord said to His disciples who would form the nucleus of the Church, "He shall glorify Me: for He shall receive of Mine, and shall show it unto you" (Jn. 16:14).

Just as Rebekah's family sought to hold her back "ten days" so the world would delay us from going out to meet Him. Notice too, that it was the servant who "took Rebekah, and went his way." So it is with us. We need the help of the Holy Spirit along the way. He has come to abide with us, and in us, forever.

When she saw Isaac, she veiled herself in preparation. The Church will do the same, for we read: "Let us be glad and rejoice, and give honor to Him: for the marriage of the Lamb is come, and *His wife hath made herself ready*" (Rev. 19:7). Finally, as Isaac was comforted to have Rebekah with him, so will Christ be, for "He shall see of the fruit of the travail of His soul, and shall be satisfied" (Isa. 53:11).

R. A. Barnett

I am crucified with Christ, and no longer live, I, but Christ lives in me; but in that I now live in flesh, I live by faith, the faith of the Son of God, who has loved me and given Himself for me. *(Galatians 2:20)*

This is the language of a soul who has learned his utter nothingness, being humbled to see there is no life, no source of goodness, but in Christ Himself. He knows that God sees him as "crucified with Christ." Yet Christ has risen, and it is the power of this resurrection life that operates in the believer, causing the heart to well up in admiration of Him, ascribing every good thought, word, and deed to Christ who lives in him.

Precious attitude of soul! The old life is set aside as worthless; not that it is eradicated, for practically speaking, we have much occasion to be humbled by its sinful workings; but in God's sight it is done away with by the death of Christ. We are to reckon ourselves dead indeed unto sin, but alive to God through Jesus Christ our Lord. This is a matter of faith, not of feeling or experience; though when recognized by faith there will be thankful feelings and consistent experience. It will be made real to the soul.

But it is made real only by faith. One is not only to be justified by faith, but to live by faith, the faith of the Son of God. This is not a creed or a set of rules by which to be regulated: rather faith fixes its eyes simply and only upon Christ. He is its standard: there can be none higher; and a lower one (even the holy, just, and good law of God) can never take His place, for it could never suit the heart of God. It is Christ who loved me and gave Himself for me, He who is the blessed Son of God.

L. M. Grant

If anyone will come after Me, let him deny himself and take up his cross daily and follow Me; for whosoever shall desire to save his life shall lose it, but whosoever shall lose his life for My sake, he shall save it. *(Luke 9:23-24)*

The ordinary thought of self-denial is giving up. There may be many different ideas among the saints as to what is to be given up. Some would think of things like card-playing, dancing, or the theater, or other "worldly things." Others would confine it to a certain season like Lent. However, merely giving up these things tends to foster spiritual pride!

But giving up these things is not our Lord's thought here! His thought is that *self* is to be refused, to be given up! A person may well give up almost anything but, so long as he has not yielded himself, he has not begun to put into practice the first elements of self-denial. When the apostle says, "I am crucified with Christ, and no longer live, I" (Gal. 2:20), he was not thinking about giving up anything but was simply done with himself so that Christ could live in him. Then there were no questions about what to give up.

The ordinary thought of taking the cross is doing something disagreeable. People even talk of prayer and public confession of Christ as taking up the cross, but the cross means death—an end of self!

What relief we obtain when we understand and apply the truth, and in realizing the end of oneself have reached the end of struggling. The person now alive in Christ Jesus can walk in the newness of life that goes with it. And then, the person will find new power for the laying aside of every weight which would hinder that walk.

S. Ridout

Come and let us return unto Jehovah: for He hath torn, and He will heal us; He hath smitten, and He will bind us up. After two days will He revive us; on the third day He will raise us up, and we shall live before His face; and we shall know—we shall follow on to know Jehovah: His going forth is assured as the morning dawn; and He will come unto us as the rain, as the latter rain which watereth the earth. *(Hosea 6:1-3)*

PROPHETS AND THEIR PROPHECIES – HOSEA (4)

In the previous chapters the Lord had been condemning Ephraim, the northern Ten-Tribe Kingdom, for their apostasy in having turned from Him to idolatry. Judah too comes under His censure. He compares their turning away from Him to immorality of the basest sort. He points out that in the difficulties He had brought upon them, Ephraim had turned to the Assyrian King Jareb for help, but that this effort had been in vain. God was dealing with His people like a lion, and none could deliver them.

But here we see that God was expecting His people to turn back to Him. And they know His heart and are ready to turn to Him. A small child spanked by its mother often clings all the closer to her as it cries. It is evident that the father in Luke 15 was expecting his prodigal son to return to Him. In His love he had fully prepared for this eventuality! The best robe, the ring, the shoes, the fatted calf—all was ready. And despite all he had done, the son had no doubt that his father would receive Him.

For us the word in Hebrews 3:13 is of utmost importance: "But encourage yourselves each day, as long as it is called Today, that none of you be hardened by the deceitfulness of sin." We are still living in the wonderful day of God's forgiveness and grace. Let us turn to Him in repentance and confidence of faith. He will heal us, raise us up, and we shall live before His face!

E. P. Vedder, Jr.

The word of Jehovah came unto Jonah the second time, saying, Arise, go to Nineveh, the great city, and preach unto it the preaching that I shall bid thee. *(Jonah 3:1-2)*

Initially, Jonah refused to do what he knew to be the will of God. Has that not been true of all of us? But God brought Jonah to his senses and delivered him! If people would only accept the work of the Lord Jesus Christ for their salvation, how soon they would experience deliverance from bitter lives.

Jonah finally remembered the Lord and "prayed unto Jehovah ... out of the fish's belly ... [and God] brought up [his] life from the pit" (Jon. 2:1,6). After Jonah confessed his sin and trusted God, God "commanded the fish and it vomited out Jonah upon the dry land" (Jon. 2:9-10).

God, in His grace, often gives us a second, third, and even more chances to obey Him. This time, Jonah did not question God but "arose and went unto Nineveh, according to the word of Jehovah" (Jon. 3:3). There he proclaimed his solemn message through the streets of Nineveh; it was heard with all due gravity, and "the men of Nineveh believed God" (Jon. 3:5). What a miracle! So many brought low by one man's preaching!

We are of the most use to God when we are where He wants us to be, doing what He wants us to do. He knows where and when we should serve—be it in office, factory, school, home, or wherever. If it is His will for us that we be there, then that is where we need to be in order to be spiritually useful. God wanted Jonah to be in Nineveh. Where does He want you?

Even when we are in the right place at the right time, we need the guidance of the Spirit constantly as to what we should say or do. We may know this truth, but it is essential that we put it into practice!

W. W. Fereday

The Lord said by vision in the night to Paul, Fear not, but speak and be not silent; because I am with thee, and no one shall set upon thee to injure thee; because I have much people in this city. *(Acts 18:9-10)*

During the course of the apostle Paul's second missionary journey he received a divine call to bring the gospel to Macedonia (Acts 16:9). This work had been attended by the Holy Spirit's blessing, as Paul and his fellow workers labored to make a foothold for the gospel on continental Europe.

Paul now had arrived in the city of Corinth. He had just left Athens, where there appeared to be little fruit for his efforts. The intellectual, philosophical Athenians considered Paul a "babbler," and mocked when hearing of the resurrection, but *some* believed. At Corinth, as Paul began a work there, the Lord spoke to him in a vision. How touching and precious for the troubled apostle! The Lord told him not to fear, nor to be silent, for, "I am with thee." And further, the Lord gave Paul a most surprising and remarkable statement of encouragement as to why he should not fear: **"I have much people in this city."**

Corinth was a wealthy port city, and known for its wickedness. In the Greek world of that day, if a person lived a debauched lifestyle, he was proverbially called, "a Corinthian." Yet, the Lord told Paul, "I have much people in this city." How lovely to see that the Lord chose us and loved us "before the world's foundation" (Eph. 1:4). He knew those who were His before they were saved. This does not cancel the necessity for the gospel—our responsibility is to believe its message. Indeed, the Lord tells Paul to "speak and be not silent." The gospel must be proclaimed. Jaded and empty by sin, the Corinthians were ripe for the gospel (1 Cor. 6:9-10). The proud Athenians had rejected it, but the Lord had "much people in Corinth."

B. Reynolds

[Jesus] comes therefore to Simon Peter ... Peter says to Him, Thou shalt never wash my feet. Jesus answered him, Unless I wash thee, thou hast not part with Me. *(John 13:6,8)*

FEET WASHING (2)

The incident when the Lord Jesus washed His disciples' feet is full of important lessons which the Lord wanted His disciples and us to learn. One lesson is emphasized by the Lord's words to Peter, "Unless I wash thee, **thou hast not part with Me.**" This means you cannot have fellowship with the Lord, if you insist on having dirty feet. The feet refer to our daily walk in this defiled and defiling world. These feet need to be washed if we are to have fellowship with our holy God.

Our fellowship is with the Father and with His Son Jesus Christ. We cannot walk carelessly and enjoy such fellowship; so we need to have our feet cleansed. Peter in his zeal answered: "Lord, not my feet only, but also my hands and my head" (v. 9). The Lord then tells him that he who has been washed all over needs only to have his feet washed. This proves that He is speaking of spiritual washing. The believer has been washed all over when he received Christ as his Savior. This does not need to be repeated every time he gets defiled by sin. But he repeatedly needs to have his feet cleansed—his walk with the Lord restored. This is done by the "water of the Word" (Eph. 5:25-27).

But the Lord also wanted us to have the privilege of washing each other's feet, and to do it the same way He did. He wants us to lay aside our garments, which means to put off pride, and to take a lowly place, so as not to look down on our brethren. We must also be careful not to wash with boiling water, nor with ice cold water, but by wisdom from above, and with tender love towards those whose feet we want to wash. We should do this so that it may be to His glory and the blessing of the saints.

A. M. Behnam

Joseph brought in his father Jacob and set him before Pharaoh; and Jacob blessed Pharaoh. Pharaoh said to Jacob, "How old are you?" And Jacob said to Pharaoh, "The days of the years of my pilgrimage are one hundred and thirty years; few and evil have been the days of the years of my life, and they have not attained to the days of the years of the life of my fathers in the days of their pilgrimage." So Jacob blessed Pharaoh, and went out from before Pharaoh. *(Genesis 47:7-10 NKJV)*

Jacob's 130 years of pilgrimage had come to a conclusion when he left Canaan and traveled to Egypt. His spirit revived at the news of Joseph, when he saw the wagons that his son had sent to bring him there. Then God allowed Jacob to stay in the presence of Joseph for seventeen years (v. 28), the same number of years he had enjoyed his son's company in Canaan (Gen. 37:2).

Speaking to Pharaoh, Jacob said that these years had been *few*. They had been *few* in comparison to his father and grandfather, who had passed away at the age of 180 and 175 years, respectively. Also, his days had been *evil;* some translate this: *unpleasant*. They had been evil because of the evil course of this world, since Jacob as a sojourner had been exposed to the Canaanites' evil influence. His days had been evil, too, because his beloved son Joseph had disappeared in a mysterious manner.

But now, God had brought everything to a happy ending, and the 130-year-old patriarch was standing before the mightiest ruler of those days. Not only that, he was able to bless Pharaoh. This shows the moral height that Jacob had reached, spiritually and morally. This poor shepherd was greater than this mighty king: amazing! Scripture confirms this point, "Now beyond all contradiction the lesser is blessed by the better" (Heb. 7:7). Are we a blessing to those above us in this world?

A. E. Bouter

I do not set aside the grace of God; for if righteousness is by law, then Christ has died for nothing. O senseless Galatians, who has bewitched you; to whom, as before your very eyes, Jesus Christ has been portrayed, crucified among you? *(Galatians 2:21–3:1)*

The Galatians, though saved by grace, were taking up with the law as a standard of conduct. It is little wonder that Paul, as he considers the principles and tremendous issues involved in this, breaks out in words of earnest remonstrance and entreaty. Had it not been portrayed before their very eyes, preached with most diligent insistence, that Jesus Christ had been crucified? Would they again exchange the blessedness and joy of the knowledge of the Son of God, who had willingly given Himself for them, for the hard cold exactions of a law that gave, or could give, nothing? Would they lightly turn away from the sight of His bitter agony on Calvary's cross? Would they ignore the fact that the world's strictest professors of law-keeping had poured contempt, insult, and injury upon the Son of God? Would they be oblivious to His cry of tender compassion from the cross, "Father, forgive them, for they know not what they do," or to that heart-rending cry of pain and anguish, "My God, My God, why hast Thou forsaken Me?"

Indeed, nothing can be so dreadful as turning from Christ. Nowhere else is there a ray of hope: it is choosing darkness rather than light, death rather than life.

Not that it had come to this with the Galatians (nor indeed will God allow it to go to such an extent with any believer), but the least measure of estrangement of heart from Christ is dangerous; and when law was assuming such a place of importance in their eyes, it was taking Christ's place.

L. M. Grant

David was greatly distressed; for the people spoke of stoning him; for the soul of all the people was embittered, every man because of his sons and because of his daughters; but David strengthened himself in Jehovah his God. *(1 Samuel 30:6)*

The distress was very real for David. Lack of faith at a critical time had brought David and his men into an unholy alliance with the Philistines. They were about to join battle with them against Israel, the people of God. This God would not allow. He was using the Philistines as His rod to chastise Saul because of his disobedience and self-will. Providentially, God overruled, preventing David from fighting against his own brethren.

David and his men returned to Ziklag only to find the city burned with fire and their wives, sons, and daughters taken captive by the Amalekites. Some of the men who had followed David in his rejection were now ready to stone him, being grieved at their great loss. David was learning the hard way that his own reasoning had brought him and his men into the very danger he sought to avoid. **But David strengthened himself in the Lord**. He then called for Abiathar the priest and inquired of the Lord, something he had failed to do when he went to the Philistines. The Lord told David to pursue the enemy and assured him of victory. Thereupon he went and recovered all, and in addition gained much spoil. Nothing was lacking of all that had been taken from them.

How often we too contribute to the problems in which we find ourselves. Yet the Lord remains unchanging in His love and care for His people. He uses these trials to wean us from our pride and self-will. When we turn our eyes away from ourselves and fix them upon the Lord, He will guide us with His eye and we will not have to retrace our steps.

J. Redekop

Lord, You have been our dwelling place in all generations ... from everlasting to everlasting, You are God.

(Psalm 90:1-2 NKJV)

The God who is completely outside of time has made Himself known to us within it. Isaiah 57:15 says He inhabits eternity—a remarkable expression! Yet He also dwells with the humble. Psalm 90, a prayer of Moses the man of God, elaborates on this theme in several ways.

The years of humanity are as nothing in comparison to God. If 1000 years pass, to Him they are merely like yesterday or a few hours of the night (vv. 3-6). Our sins are keenly felt in the presence of such a God. "We finish our years like a sigh," Moses writes; and even if we live 70 or 80 years' worth of labor and sorrow, we are soon cut off and fly away (vv. 7-10).

Where had Moses been at age 80? He was tending sheep in the desert. At age 40, as a mighty one among the Egyptians, he had determined to deliver God's people (Acts 7:25). But he had acted in a self-willed, unrestrained manner, not according to God's ways or timing, and thus he became a fugitive among a people not his own. It may well be that, when writing this psalm, Moses had this period of his life in mind—a point when he may even have thought his time was nearly over, with no opportunity to serve the Lord in the grand ways he had anticipated.

But the God who is everlasting, to whom our years are as nothing, nevertheless teaches us to number our days. When we learn the brevity of life, like Moses we can call to God for wisdom, compassion, mercy, and gladness, so that our lives become fragrant with meaning for Him (vv. 12-17). What servant of the Lord would not desire His beauty to be upon us each day, the work of our hands being established by Him? From eternity into time and right down into our days, our God meets us for our blessing.

S. J. Campbell

I call God to witness upon my soul that to spare you I have not come to Corinth. Not that we rule over your faith, but are fellow-workmen of your joy: for by faith ye stand.

(2 Corinthians 1:23-24)

Paul had no wish to come among them only to find himself bound to act in severity by reason of sin and grave disorder still being found in their midst. Hence he had waited until he had news of the effect of the earlier epistle he had written to them. He hoped for better things. It was not that he assumed dominion over their faith, but rather that he was just a "helper," or "fellow-worker," to the end that they might be delivered and rejoice.

The chapter closes with the words, "by faith ye stand." This is a fact that we ought very much to lay to heart. If he had assumed dominion over their faith in any matter, their faith in that respect would have ceased to be. He would have merely ordered them to do certain things (quite right things, doubtless) and they would have done them, not as an exercise of faith, but mechanically. There would have been no faith in their actions, but just mechanical action as an outward shell. And then one day they would have scandalized everyone by collapsing.

There are plenty of Christians today who would much like to live their lives on somebody else's faith. They would like to be told what to do. Let somebody else have the exercise, and solve the problem! They will be good and obedient and do as they are told. But this does not work, save disastrously. It is by faith we stand, not by somebody else's faith. By somebody else's faith we fall. And further, it is not good for the somebody else. Such forceful individuals begin to love having dominion over the faith of their brethren, and so becoming little popes. Consequently it ends disastrously for them.

F. B. Hole

These are the beginning of sorrows. *(Matthew 24:8 KJV)*

Earthquakes, tsunamis, hurricanes, wars, and a seemingly endless series of other disasters continue to fill the headlines and claim our attention. What is going on? Is God involved in the convulsions that we see round about us? All of these things were predicted over 2000 years ago by a Man dressed in the humble garments of a Galilean. As He spoke on the Mount of Olives this great "Prophet" quietly unfolded a vista of future events to His disciples as they viewed the temple (Mt. 24:3; Dt. 18:15).

There have always been wars and earthquakes, but in Christ's discourse He prophesied that they will increase dramatically at the time of the end. He described these troubles as "the beginning of sorrows" (Mt. 24:8)—the word *sorrows* here literally means, *birth pangs*. The metaphor is of a woman going into labor—her pain increasing in rapidity and severity as the time of delivery draws near. The Great Tribulation will follow these things and the judgments will increase exponentially (Mt. 24:21). It will be evident that these calamities come directly from God—yet men will not repent (Rev. 16:9).

People today often explain away these things as natural events: earthquakes are caused by the moving or subduction of the tectonic plates, or the wild weather patterns as a result of global warming. It would be wrong to deny that there are physical explanations, but what is really behind the convergence and increase of these things? Ultimately, there will be no need for scientific explanations, for God will shake the earth in "that day" and it will be recognized by men as "the wrath of the Lamb" (Isa. 24:18-20; Rev. 6:16). But whether it is the current world events, or the coming birth pangs leading to the Great Tribulation—God is working out His purposes. One has said, "God is behind the scenes and is moving the scenes that He is behind."

B. Reynolds

January 20 Lord's Day

This do in remembrance of me ... For as often as ye shall eat this bread, and drink the cup, ye announce the death of the Lord, until He come. *(1 Corinthians 11:24,26)*

He cannot bear to be forgotten by those He loves on earth to the end. Worthless hearts, we may say truly. Yes; but Jesus cares for them: He has died to make them His, and counts on our remembrance of Him—giving us only that which may be the sweet expression of it. If the Supper of the Lord means anything then, as we partake of it, it means this, that we love Him and miss Him in the world that has cast Him out. He invests it with just this character Himself: "For as often as ye eat this bread, and drink this cup, ye do show forth the Lord's death till He come."

It is the garments of the Church's mourning in a scene that has been desolated for her by the death of Christ, and in which she finds no rest for her heart. She is only lingering round the spot where His cross and grave express the heart of the world towards Him. By faith we know Him in the glory, and have rest in communion with Him there. But this only makes the earth's rejection of Him more keenly felt, and the cross that by which the world is crucified to us and we unto the world.

We call our hearts from this blighted scene, and get away in spirit as far as possible from it, only seeking more complete identification with Him in His rejection, as the best and brightest portion He could give us in such a world. This is not the attainment of an advanced Christian, but what Christ looks for from every heart that loves Him. Hear Him say, "This do in remembrance of Me," and again, "Ye show forth the Lord's death till He come." Is it not as though He said, "Do they miss Me?" "Do they long for Me to come again?" Oh, beloved, what answer do our hearts give to the challenges of His love?

J. A. Trench

He is despised … and we esteemed Him not.   *(Isaiah 53:3)*

The word *esteem* is often prefixed by the word *self* to become a major concern in today's world. We are told that lack of self-esteem is among the top ten problems facing teenagers. Among adults, everything from poor job performance to extramarital affairs may be blamed on lack of self-esteem. Christians aren't quite sure how they fit in to all this. Some see it as essential to fruitful living while others view it as promoting that which really needs to be abased—namely self.

The Funk and Wagnalls Dictionary defines self-esteem as "a good opinion of oneself; an overestimate of oneself." It calls this word a synonym of pride. In the Bible, the word translated esteem usually implies the thought of considering, reckoning, or valuing. Let's look at some of the verses that use this word: "He is despised…and we esteemed Him not" (Isa. 53:3). This is the primary problem of the unbeliever. He does not esteem the One whom God esteems.

"Write [mercy and truth] on the tablet of your heart, and so find favor and high esteem in the sight of God and man" (Prov. 3:3-4 NKJV). This verse suggests that esteem is not to be pursued, but rather will result from pursuing other things, namely mercy and truth. "Let each esteem others better than himself " (Phil. 2:3 NKJV). This is one of several verses which direct us, not to self-esteem, but to esteeming others. By faith Moses esteemed "the reproach of the Christ greater riches than the treasures of Egypt" (Heb. 11:23-26). Here's a great example for us to follow—to esteem that which is of faith and which centers on Christ. This will provide the basis for rightly esteeming everything else—including ourselves.

G. W. Steidl

We wonder at Thy lowly mind, / And fain would like Thee be,
And all our rest and pleasure find / In learning, Lord, of Thee.

J. G. Deck

I write to you, little children, because ye have known the Father.
(1 John 2:13)

The essence of Christianity is in the above words. And let me say this to you, Above all things cultivate the knowledge of the Father. If you leave yourself in the hands of the Spirit of God, He will lead you to a very deep and blessed knowledge of the Father. This is what Christianity really is. It is the revelation of the Father through the Son.

Christianity consists of the revelation of the Father by the Son. The Father is made known to all the family by the indwelling of the Spirit of God.

But I find there are very few children of God today that are in the happy enjoyment of the Father, and His love. When John says, "Ye have known the Father," he contemplates them as in the enjoyment of their relationship to the Father. Now in Romans 8:15 I read, "Ye have received a Spirit of adoption, whereby we cry, Abba, Father." That is the blessed term of relationship, and enjoyed relationship and affection too. Again, "Because ye are sons, God has sent out the Spirit of His Son into our hearts, crying, Abba, Father" (Gal. 4:6). This is normal Christian language, and what the Father is seeking to hear.

Many believers today, though they may have received the Spirit of God, enter very little into the enjoyment of the Father, and the knowledge of the Father's love. Therefore, I would say, Oh, seek above all things, to have your souls bathed in the enjoyment of this blessed realization—I am a child of the Father. Your relationship now, is the relationship of Him who, when here, said, "Abba, Father." Of course we must remember that we are before the Father through redemption. That is the ground that enables you and me by grace now to take up and enjoy this relationship before God.

W. T. P. Wolston

The heart is deceitful above all things, and desperately wicked.
(Jeremiah 17:9 KJV)

Many object to the doctrine of total depravity on the ground that all men are capable of some good even if unsaved. All of us recognize the value of decency in behavior, of a kindly spirit, of generosity in caring for the needy, and of similar virtues, which are frequently seen in unconverted and even positively godless men and women.

How then can they be said to be totally depraved? Dr. Joseph Cook, the great Boston lecturer of the latter half of the 19th century, answers this question with the following illustration: He said he had in his home a very beautiful and valuable clock. It had an exceedingly handsome case, a very fine set of works, a nice appearing dial and elegantly finished hands. It was altogether a good clock to look upon but it had one fault. It simply would not, or could not, keep time. It had been gone over by many different clockmakers, but not one had been able to correct this fault. As a timepiece it was totally depraved!

Is not this like man, even at his best, if he has not been born again? There may be much about him that others can admire, but he is positively unable to do the will of the Lord, because his heart is utterly estranged from God, and therefore so far as holiness is concerned, he is totally depraved. Only the new birth—regeneration by the Word and Spirit of God—can enable him to keep in line with the divine will as laid down in the Holy Scriptures. However righteous he may appear in the eyes of his fellows, because of this fatal defect, all his righteousness is as filthy rags in the sight of God.

H. A. Ironside

(To further illustrate the author's words: the doctrine of total depravity does not mean that every man is as bad as he could be, but that every man is not as good as he should be. Ed.)

Ephraim, he mixeth himself with the peoples; Ephraim is a cake not turned. Strangers have devoured his strength, and he knoweth it not; yea, gray hairs are here and there upon him, and he knoweth it not. And the pride of Israel testifieth to his face; and they do not return to Jehovah their God, nor seek Him for all this ... Woe unto them! for they have wandered from Me; destruction unto them! for they have transgressed against Me.

(Hosea 7:8-10,13)

PROPHETS AND THEIR PROPHECIES–HOSEA (5)

God had called Israel out from among the peoples to be a very special people for Himself. But again and again they had mixed themselves with the pagan people round about them, intermarrying with them and bowing down to worship their dead, powerless gods. We Christians today also are called to "come out from the midst of them, and be separated, saith the Lord" (2 Cor. 6:17).

Like Samson of old who "knew not that Jehovah had departed from him," Israel lacked spiritual discernment and balance and was not aware of the danger in which they stood. What a sad refrain we find here: "and he knoweth it not!" We Christians have the mirror of God's Word to reveal to us what we are in God's sight. Do we use this mirror to show us what we are? Is it thus helpful to us? Or do our Bibles sit on shelves, merely collecting dust?

Decline is often gradual, something we are scarcely aware of. We wander away from the Lord rather than deliberately turning against Him. Others usually notice gray hairs popping up on our heads before we see them. We are out of balance spiritually: a cake not turned may burn on one side but is underdone on the other. Pride keeps us from turning to the Lord in our declining condition and need. We try this, we try that, we turn this way and that, but nothing changes. He would gladly help us. Let's not be like Ephraim of old—too proud to ask Him to do so!

E. P. Vedder, Jr.

He answered and said, Whether he be a sinner or no I know not: one thing I know, that, whereas I was blind, now I see.

(John 9:25 KJV)

What a confession! The man who made it had been blind from birth, but the Lord Jesus had brought light into his life. John presents this as an act of sovereign grace (v. 6), but one that demanded obedience from the man before he "came seeing" (v. 7). It is the same with us. The source of our blessing lies in God, and its dispenser is the Son the Father sent to be "the Savior of the world" (1 Jn. 4:14). As He works in our lives and we respond in obedient faith to His words, "Go, wash," we get our spiritual sight. Yes, believing is seeing. The blind man's life had been transformed. This should have been a reason for rejoicing, but there is hardly a note of joy in the chapter. Rather it excited controversy. The man had made it clear that his newfound sight was the result of his encounter with a man "called Jesus," but his neighbors made it a matter of religion. This is but a device of the devil for dishonoring Christ and keeping mankind from blessing. The man, ignorant as he was in some respects, teaches us a lesson by sticking to his confession. Whatever others said about his benefactor, he knew *one thing*: He had transformed His life. No one could take this away from him, whatever they said or did to dismiss it.

Once the man had been blind and the rest seeing. Now in a deeper sense he saw and they were blind. Let us be more like him and speak of the One who makes blind eyes see. We may not be able to explain everything, but we can be sure He will teach us all we need to know, as He did this man. When Jesus revealed Himself as the Son of God, this man said, "Lord, I believe." And he worshipped Him.

S. Attwood

Thy wife shall be as a fruitful vine in the inner part of thy house; thy children like olive-plants round about thy table. Behold, thus shall the man be blessed that feareth Jehovah ... mayest thou ... see thy children's children. *(Psalm 128:3-6)*

Grandparenting is a wonderful experience, but sadly many grandparents fail to have a relationship with their grandchildren. As a result, they miss the opportunity to help them to build their lives in the Lord. Grandparents' obedience to God has a strong effect on their grandchildren (Dt. 6:2).

Titus 2 points out three ways we can influence our grandchildren. First, older men and women can be good *examples* for them, "showing ... a pattern of good works" (Tit. 2:7); second, we can be *teachers*—older women are to be "teachers of good things; that they may teach the young women" (Tit. 2:3-4) and older men are to exhort young men (Tit. 2:1-6); and third, we can be *encouragers*—we are to "speak thou the things which become sound doctrine" (Tit. 2:1)—having profited from our experiences, we can encourage them with the encouragement they need. And First Thessalonians provides us a fourth way—we can "pray without ceasing" for them (1 Th. 5:17 KJV).

There may be a lot of things we can no longer do, but we can still pray for them. When we communicate with them in conversation, by phone, letter, card, or e-mail, we should let them know that we are praying for them and ask for specific prayer requests. There is no more effective way to influence our grandchildren.

Everything we do for our grandchildren is an investment in their future life in eternity. They have us grandparents for only a short time. Let us therefore not miss the opportunity to impact their lives for the Lord. By God's grace we can make our grandparenting grand!

J. Palmer

Who in the days of His flesh, having offered up both supplications and entreaties to Him who was able to save Him out of death ... Though He were Son, He learned obedience from the things which He suffered.

(Hebrews 5:7-8)

Christ, from the onset of His ministry, maintained the place of an obedient servant. He did not enter into public service until called of God, after He had taken the lowest place in John's baptism. Christ ever walked in perfect separation of the inner man, in communion with His Father, and entire dependence upon Him in obedience without a single moment of self-will. He was the most gracious and accessible of men. We observe in His ways a tenderness and a kindness never seen in man, yet we always feel that He was a stranger. Not that He came to be a stranger in His relationship with men; but that which lay deepest in His own heart was entirely foreign to all that influences man.

He abode emphatically alone. It is striking that not once did His disciples understand what He said. The only trace of a heart going with Him was Mary at Bethany; and that had to be told to the whole world (Mt. 26:13). This spirit of self-denial, entire renunciation of His own will and dependence upon His Father, is seen throughout the life of Jesus. After John's baptism He was praying when He received the Holy Spirit. Before calling the apostles He spent the whole night in prayer. After the miracle of feeding the 5000 He went up into a mountain apart to pray.

In Gethsemane, His dread of death is by prayer all laid before His Father; the cup which His Father has given Him, shall He not drink it? The effect is that all is calm before men. He is the Nazarite, separated from men by His entire communion with His Father, and by the obedience of a Son who had no other will than to fulfill the good pleasure of His Father.

J. N. Darby

Jacob said to Joseph: "God Almighty appeared to me at Luz in the land of Canaan and blessed me ... And now your two sons, Ephraim and Manasseh, who were born to you in the land of Egypt before I came to you in Egypt, are mine" ... Joseph said to his father, "They are my sons, whom God has given me in this place." And he said, "Please bring them to me, and I will bless them." *(Genesis 48:3,5,9 NKJV)*

Jacob was greater than the mighty Pharaoh, when he gave his testimony and blessed him (Gen. 47). A father is greater than his son. Genesis 48 shows Jacob greater than his son Joseph who ruled Egypt. This is shown when Jacob, a short time before he died, blessed Joseph's two sons, Manasseh and Ephraim, adopting them as his own sons.

Speaking to Joseph, Jacob referred to God Almighty who had blessed him in the land of Canaan. On several occasions Jacob had learned to submit to this mighty God of Jacob, the Almighty. Abraham had learned to do so before he and Sarah could have their son Isaac. Taught in God's school, Jacob had come to know God's wisdom, and he demonstrated this when blessing his two grandsons, whom he adopted as his own sons.

We read, "Then Israel stretched out his right hand and laid it on Ephraim's head, who was the younger, and his left hand on Manasseh's head, guiding his hands knowingly, for Manasseh was the firstborn" (Gen. 48:14). This verb *to guide knowingly* is a term used in the Psalms for *the wise* (*Maskil*) who will live in the days of Israel's future distress. It is also translated *to prosper* or *deal prudently* (Josh. 1:7; Isa. 52:13). Spiritually speaking, Jacob had become prosperous. So he acted with God-given wisdom when he put Ephraim before Manasseh, even against Joseph's wishes. Jacob the shepherd, had learned from the great Shepherd, before whom he had walked (Gen. 48:15).

A. E. Bouter

O Timotheus, keep the entrusted deposit. *(1 Timothy 6:20)*

I think Timothy is a most encouraging example for young believers today. He was young, not strong in body, and probably knew what it was to be despised. He seems to have been by nature, timid; and at times in much need of encouragement. He knew what tears meant. He knew the temptation to be a coward (2 Tim. 1). But I know of no fellow-servant whom Paul so delights to honor: listen to what he says of him: "Timothy, my dearly beloved son" (2 Tim. 1:2); "Timotheus, who is my beloved son, and faithful in the Lord" (1 Cor. 4:17); "Timotheus … worketh the work of the Lord, as I also do" (1 Cor. 16:10).

Timothy was with Paul in Philippi, Thessalonica, Berea, Corinth, Troas, Miletus, and other places. In his last imprisonment, just before his death, Paul specially longed for Timothy. We do not know if Timothy reached him in time, or not. This young brother was associated with Paul in writing six epistles, and his name is included in the salutation of a seventh. We also have two letters to him written by the apostle. We know he had been in prison for Christ's sake, and had been released (Heb. 13:23).

Paul had a number of companions and helpers, but this young man, weak in body but strong in spirit, seems to have been the dearest to him, and the most trusted. Paul chose this young man to go to the assembly in Philippi, when he himself was unable to go. We never read, as far as I know, of any very great gift that Timothy had though he did unquestionably have special gifts (1 Tim. 4:14; 2 Tim. 1:6); but, as another has said, "It is not great talents, nor great scholarship, nor great preachers that God needs, but men and women great in holiness, great in faith, great in love, great in fidelity, great for God." May you take courage by Timothy's example to seek to be men and women like this!

G. C. Willis

January 30 Wednesday

When Jehovah sent you from Kadesh-barnea, saying, Go up and take possession of the land which I have given you, ye rebelled against the word of Jehovah your God, and ye believed Him not.   *(Deuteronomy 9:23)*

CALEB THE SON OF JEPHUNNEH (1)

The name of Caleb first appears in connection with sending the twelve spies to search out the land of Canaan. From the account Moses gives in Deuteronomy 1, it is clear that this mission was the fruit of the people's unbelief. The Lord met the people in their unbelief, and commanded Moses to send the spies (Num. 13:1-2). He did not approve the desire of the people, but permitted them to carry out their purpose. Knowing all the consequences, He would use these for their chastisement and instruction. The folly of unbelief was never more manifest. How often we have fallen into the same snare!

The spies were chosen at the Lord's command. Among them were Caleb, for the tribe of Judah, and Joshua, the son of Nun, for the tribe of Ephraim. For forty days they searched the Promised Land. In token of its fruitfulness they brought back a cluster of grapes from Eshcol and some pomegranates and figs. All the congregation assembled to hear their report. To begin with they confirmed the word of Jehovah in every particular: "We came to the land to which thou didst send us, and surely it floweth with milk and honey; and this is the fruit of it." So far, well; but no sooner had they stated what they could not deny, than the unbelief lurking in their hearts broke forth. They viewed the obstacles to conquering the land only with the natural eye instead of the eye of faith. Rather than saying, "If God be for us, who can be against us?" they left Jehovah out, and measured the foes by their estimate of their own strength instead of the Lord's.

The Christian's Friend and Instructor

Caleb stilled the people before Moses, and said, Let us go up boldly and possess it, for we are well able to do it. But the men that went up with him said, We are not able to go up against the people. *(Numbers 13:30-31)*

CALEB THE SON OF JEPHUNNEH (2)

The effect of their unbelief was disastrous; for their words produced a dangerous agitation among the congregation. At this juncture Caleb stepped forth, and, dissociating himself from his companions, "stilled the people before Moses." He did not contradict the testimony which had been rendered; but said, "Let us go up at once, and possess it; for *we are well able to overcome it.*" This was the language of faith begotten by confidence in Jehovah. Uttering his confidence in the Lord only intensified the opposition of the natural mind, and the men that went up with him said, *"We are not able to go up against the people; for they are stronger than we."* As boldness in testimony gives increased certainty, so expressing unbelief augments *its* power. Caleb and the eleven spies are striking illustrations of these principles.

The increase of the unbelief of the ten is most marked. They now brought up an evil report of the land. Unbelief, which is always contagious, infected all the congregation, and they "lifted up their voice, and cried; and the people wept that night." They murmured against Moses and Aaron, bitterly complaining that they had not died in the land of Egypt. They reproached Jehovah for all the dangers which existed only in their fears; and, finally, broke out into open rebellion, saying, "Let us make a captain, and let us return into Egypt." On the borders of their inheritance, a land on which the Lord's eyes always rested, they were ready to sacrifice everything in their forgetfulness of their God and Redeemer.

The Christian's Friend and Instructor

If You Are Enjoying

The Lord Is Near
Daily Bible Meditations

- May we suggest you give your friends a copy
  so they too can enjoy and benefit from it?

- You can place your order at either your local
  Christian bookstore or from one of our distributors.

- Lists of distributors in several countries can be
  found at the end of this booklet.

Giving all diligence, add to your faith virtue; and to virtue knowledge; and to knowledge temperance. *(2 Peter 1:5-6 KJV)*

The apostle is not pressing the great fact that we have life, but he is insisting upon the deep importance of living the life we have. Every believer has a new life, but we may well challenge our hearts with the question, Are we content to know that we have that life, or are we seeking to live the life? The fact of having life, blessed as this is, will not in itself enable us to escape the corruptions of this world. If we are to be preserved from lust and lawlessness, we must live the life of practical godliness.

The first great quality of this overcoming life is faith. John can say, "This is the victory that overcometh the world, even our faith." Moreover, faith must have an object: "Who is he that overcometh the world, but he that believeth that Jesus is the Son of God?" (1 Jn. 5:4-5). Faith turns from everything of sight and sense and looks to Jesus, in the realization that He knows all things about me and He alone can keep me (Jn. 21:17).

With our faith we shall need virtue, or spiritual courage, and energy (as the word implies). By this moral energy we shall be enabled to refuse the working of the flesh within and to resist the devil without. To live a practical life of godliness in a world such as this will demand spiritual energy to deny ourselves, refuse the world, and resist Satan. With virtue we shall need knowledge, by which we acquire divine wisdom to guide us in all our practical ways. Apart from the knowledge of God and His mind, as revealed in His Word, our very energy may lead us into paths of self-will. Knowledge may puff up; therefore with knowledge we need temperance, or self-restraint. Without this self-restraint, knowledge may be used to exalt ourselves.

H. Smith

Joshua the son of Nun, and Caleb the son of Jephunneh ... rent their garments. And they spoke to the whole assembly ... saying, The land, which we passed through to search it out, is a very, very good land. If Jehovah delight in us, He will bring us into this land, and give it us.   *(Numbers 14:6-8)*

CALEB THE SON OF JEPHUNNEH (3)

Joshua and Caleb were God's chosen instruments to stem this torrent of unbelief. Expressing their horror at the sin of the people, they rent their clothes, and, raising their voices above the din and confusion, they courageously reiterated their declaration that the land was "an exceeding good land." They thus boldly contradicted the evil report of their fellows, and, in so doing, separated themselves morally from them, and took their stand on the Lord's side. They also stated plainly the conditions of possessing the land. First, "If the LORD delight in us," they said, "then He will bring us into this land." In this they showed that they were in communion with Jehovah's mind. He did delight in His people and all depended upon what He was, and upon His power, and not upon what the people were, or could do. Secondly, they said, "Only rebel not ... fear not ye the people of the land." Israel had only to follow its divine Leader. And, lastly, they declared that the source of all their strength was the Lord's presence with them.

Such were the simple conditions (conditions which are as applicable today as when they were propounded) under which alone the possession of the land could be obtained. Ponder them well, for they unfold the pathway into all spiritual blessing. If they be forgotten or refused, believers now, as well as the Israelites, will either turn back in heart to Egypt, or wander aimlessly in the wilderness, to their own sorrow and loss.

The Christian's Friend and Instructor

Thou, Bethlehem Ephratah, little to be among the thousands of Judah, out of thee shall He come forth unto Me who is to be Ruler in Israel: whose goings forth are from of old, from the days of eternity.

(Micah 5:2)

JESUS IS JEHOVAH (1)

When Herod inquired of the chief priests and scribes where Messiah would be born they quoted this verse. Their quotation of this ancient oracle—Micah's prophecy was uttered 700 years before Christ was born—should have stopped Herod. The coming Ruler in Israel would be born in Bethlehem, but His goings forth were from the days of eternity. He would be a Divine Person.

Of course for Christians, the truth that the Lord Jesus is "God manifest in the flesh" (1 Tim. 3:16) is not only the bedrock of our faith but the joy and rejoicing of our hearts! It is the confession of all believers that He is the Word who was with God and was God (Jn. 1:1); that before Abraham ever lived He was "I am" (Jn. 8:58); that He is the Creator, Sustainer, and Upholder of the universe (Col. 1:16-17; Heb. 1:2-3); and that He is "the true God and eternal life" (1 Jn. 5:20). These and many more verses in the New Testament declare again and again to us the deity of the Lord Jesus.

However, it is a wonderful and remarkable fact that there are also many Old Testament prophecies that reveal that the coming Messiah, who was to be of the seed of David, would also be Jehovah—the Eternal God. Micah's prophecy clearly shows that the Ruler who was to be born in Bethlehem had no beginning—His goings forth could not be measured, for they were from the days of eternity. Obviously Herod had no appreciation for the majesty of the One who was born in Bethlehem, or of the great stoop of Him who came from glory's heights to live in such humble circumstances.

B. Reynolds

It came to pass as He drew near to Bethphage and Bethany at the mountain called the Mount of Olives, He sent two of His disciples, saying, Go into the village over against you, in which ye will find, on entering it, a colt tied up, on which no child of man ever sat at any time: loose it and lead it here. And if anyone ask you, Why do ye loose it? thus shall ye say to him, Because the Lord has need of it. *(Luke 19:29-31)*

We tend to be much occupied with our needs. We love to think of the Lord Jesus who met the needs of crowds and individuals, young and old, and of those from every class of society; and it is good to know Him in this way. But how about His own needs? On several occasions, He was pleased to use others to supply for His own need:

• He used the owner of a colt to supply the means of transport He required.

• He requested the use of Peter's boat to address the multitudes from the lake.

• He asked the woman at Samaria's well for water (mainly to speak to her about the water He could give, but it also says that He was tired).

• The two fishes and five loaves a young boy gave Him (He was pleased to use) with much blessing.

• He accepted the pound of ointment of spikenard which Mary poured out. Some were unhappy about such allocation of resources. But the Lord defended her cause. It was no waste. It had been done for Him. "Let her alone," He said.

• Nicodemus was used to speak a word in favor of His Lord: "Does our law judge any man, before it hear him?"

• Joseph of Arimathea supplied a grave for the Lord's body.

The Lord is no doubt almighty and powerful, and yet, "the Lord has need." He would like to use you. Have you asked Him how you could meet His need today?

M. Hardt

The law has been our tutor up to Christ, that we might be justified on the principle of faith. But, faith having come, we are no longer under a tutor; for ye are all God's sons by faith in Christ Jesus. *(Galatians 3:24-26)*

The teacher and all that he teaches are only a means to an end. He should of course strive with earnest energy to put his pupils on the right track; but he has completely failed as to his proper function if those pupils settle down indefinitely in subjection to him and depend on him for everything. His teaching ought to make them independent of his help.

Such is the true function of the law: it directs toward Christ. And it is a powerful teacher to those who honestly listen to it, for it will teach how inexpressibly urgent is our need of Christ: it will drive the soul to a deep sense of the ruin that sin has caused, and the consequent need of One who is able to cleanse from sin, the Lord Jesus Christ. Not that it brings us to Christ, but as this careful translation renders it, "up to Christ." That is, its goal was Christ: it pointed away from itself to Christ, who, now revealed, is the Object of faith which justifies.

Now that Christ has come, faith has come, faith that is the energy independent of everything but God known in Christ. Why then put legal restraints on one who has learned what it is to walk by individual faith in God? The schoolmaster is no longer needed.

A good and faithful teacher we appreciate,
And to learn his wisdom is our wisdom too:
But when the proper time has come to graduate,
Shall we demand his services our whole life through?
                 L. M. Grant

My servant Caleb, because he hath another spirit in him, and hath followed Me fully, him will I bring into the land whereinto he came; and his seed shall possess it. *(Numbers 14:24)*

CALEB THE SON OF JEPHUNNEH (4)

Our attention may be arrested by the approbation expressed as to Caleb. "My servant Caleb," said Jehovah, "because he hath another spirit in him, and *hath followed Me fully*" (v. 24). This reveals how grateful to the Lord's heart Caleb's faithful testimony had been. He also exemplified the spirit of devoted discipleship in an evil day; he followed fully, and this became his distinguishing characteristic—a characteristic which Caleb himself delighted to accept and recall.

Caleb and Joshua, spared in the judgment that was visited upon the guilty people, crossed the Jordan. They shared in the victories of faith when engaged in conflict with the enemy for the possession of the land. Coming to Joshua 14, Caleb is again brought to our notice. He came to Joshua in Gilgal to apply for the inheritance which the Lord had promised to him. What he said is full of interest. First he recalled the past; then he reminded Joshua (showing how he had treasured it) of the promise Moses made to him; next he testified to the Lord's faithfulness in preserving him alive, and to his strength, through all his long and varied experiences.

Lastly, requesting the possession of his inheritance, he expressed his confidence that, if the Lord should be with him, he would be able to drive out the Anakim, and to take their cities, notwithstanding that they were great and fenced, as the spies had reported. Joshua blessed him, and gave Hebron to him as his inheritance "because that he wholly followed the Lord God of Israel." The man of faith must ever be foremost in the conflict with the enemy; but his victory is ensured.

The Christian's Friend and Instructor

When Israel was a child, then I loved him, and out of Egypt I called My son. As they called them, so they went from them: they sacrificed unto the Baals, and burned incense to graven images. And I it was that taught Ephraim to walk—He took them upon His arms—but they knew not that I healed them. I drew them with bands of a man, with cords of love; and I was to them as they that take off the yoke on their jaws, and I gently caused them to eat. *(Hosea 11:1-4)*

PROPHETS AND THEIR PROPHECIES—HOSEA (6)

Again and again through different prophets God testifies of His love for His earthly people, Israel. More than 150 years after Israel had divided into two kingdoms and the northern kingdom, often referred to as Ephraim, had turned away from God, God uses Hosea to remind them of how tenderly He had loved them.

God goes back to their early history as a nation, referring back to the time when He had called them out of Egypt. He speaks of Israel as His child, His son, and the tender care with which He had treated him in the beginning days of their nationhood. He speaks of taking them on His arms, of teaching them to walk, of healing them, drawing them with cords of love, taking the yoke off their jaws and gently causing them to eat. One can just see a kind father over and over again helping and teaching his little son. Jeremiah later refers to "the day of My taking them by the hand, to lead them out of the land of Egypt" (Jer. 31:32).

And yet, like toddlers often do, that same little son kept going in the opposite direction when his loving father called him. God called through His servants the prophets, but these, the Lord tells us, they beat, they stoned, and they killed. Ephraim was bent on backsliding from God and sacrificed and burned incense to idols. This grieved their loving God! Our lack of response to His kindness and our going our own way deeply grieves Him too.

E. P. Vedder, Jr.

It came to pass, that the beggar died, and was carried by the angels into Abraham's bosom: the rich man also died and was buried; and in [Hades] he lifted up his eyes, being in torments.

(Luke 16:22-23 KJV)

On a certain tombstone are the words, "Pause, stranger, when you pass by, as you are now, so once was I. As I am now, so will you be, so prepare for death and follow me." A passerby read the words and scratched beneath them: "To follow you I am not content, until I know which way you went." These might elicit a little chuckle, yet they convey two solemn and awe-inspiring facts which are confirmed by the above Scriptures, namely, that we have an appointment with death, and secondly, that the course taken in life determines the terminus of the soul.

Death is the great leveler of mankind. Rich and poor, small and great, saint and sinner—all alike die. In the case of the rich man and Lazarus, while in life their lot was vastly different, in death their circumstances were wholly reversed. The Lord draws back the veil and gives us a glimpse into the unseen world of the dead.

Lazarus is in Paradise—the place of comfort and rest, while the rich man is in Hades—the place of torment. Lazarus was not in Paradise because he was poor, and the rich man was not in Hades because he was rich. Their assigned places were the result of the choices they had made in life.

Lazarus had made a conscious decision to trust in Christ for his salvation, while the rich man trusted in his wealth. The rich man tried to make things right in Hades but was too late, for after death our eternal state is fixed forever. Jesus warns us that "wide is the gate, and broad is the way, which leadeth to destruction … and narrow is the way which leadeth unto life" (Mt. 7:13-14). Which road are you on? Which direction are you going?

R. A. Barnett

February 9 Saturday

Thus shall ye eat it: your loins shall be girded, your sandals on your feet, and your staff in your hand; and ye shall eat it in haste; it is Jehovah's Passover. *(Exodus 12:11)*

The Lord's Passover is a type of Christ's death on our behalf. We "have been redeemed ... by precious blood, as of a lamb without blemish and without spot, the blood of Christ" (1 Pet. 1:18-19). If I truly appreciate that Christ loved me and gave Himself for me, it will constrain me to worshipfully meditate on it. Four things should characterize us in relation to feeding on the Lamb:

1. Our loins girded. This refers to a state of alertness, of being sober and ready. One does not go to bed wearing his belt. Our girded loins show that we are ready to do His bidding, to start moving at a moment's notice. The slothful servant who says, "My master delays his coming," does not bother to gird his loins.

2. Our sandals on our feet, because the road may be rough with rocks and thorns, but the believer has heard the call and must go, headed towards a new home. He must leave his former home where he was a slave, where darkness prevailed. In Egypt the Israelite was a slave, but he left Egypt and became a free man. He gave up the food of Egypt, for he was going to the land that flows with milk and honey. Alas, some left Egypt physically but went back to it with their hearts.

3. Our staff in our hand. The picture is that of a pilgrim leaving the old homestead and ready to move on.

4. Eat it in haste. There is no desire to linger, for the heart is now set on another home where the King sits at His table, and the pilgrim delights to sit in His shadow. There the Lord's fruit is sweet to his taste more than the food of Egypt. O that all this may be true of us! Then we can say from the heart: **Amen, come Lord Jesus**.

A. M. Behnam

The voice of one crying in the wilderness: Prepare ye the way of Jehovah, make straight in the desert a highway for our God! Every valley shall be raised up, and every mountain and hill shall be brought low; and the crooked shall be made straight, and the rough places a plain. And the glory of Jehovah shall be revealed, and all flesh shall see it together: for the mouth of Jehovah hath spoken. *(Isaiah 40:3-5)*

JESUS IS JEHOVAH (2)

Isaiah has been called the "Evangelist of the Old Testament" and his 66-chapter book "the Fifth Gospel." In it the sublime prophet sings the song of salvation, and prophetically points to the Messiah who will bring light to the nations.

In chapter 40 Isaiah predicts the coming of the forerunner of the Lord: John the Baptist. We know it applies to the Baptist because it is quoted by all four Gospels of the New Testament in reference to him! John himself quotes this prophecy declaring that he was only a "voice crying in the wilderness," and that he was not the Messiah but rather was preparing the way for Him (Jn. 1:23).

But there is a thrilling truth in this prophecy that somehow seems to get overlooked. Isaiah states clearly that this voice would herald and prepare the way for none other than Jehovah Himself! This voice would cry, "Make straight in the desert a highway for our God!" The Messiah would be Jehovah-God, and at His coming the glory of Jehovah would be revealed! When we turn to the fulfillment of this prophecy in the New Testament we see that it is the Lord Jesus who is heralded by the Baptist! We may well sing with the hymn writer: "There is no other name than Thine, Jehovah-Jesus, name divine." How unfathomable is this mystery of grace! He that came into this world to be "the Man of Sorrows … acquainted with grief" (Isa. 53:3) was Jehovah and is worthy of all our worship and obedience!

B. Reynolds

Gather together and hear, O sons of Jacob; and listen to Israel your father ... and this is what their father said to them when he blessed them. He blessed them, every one with the blessing appropriate to him. *(Genesis 49:2,28 NASB)*

Jacob had learned many lessons from his God, the Almighty, the Shepherd, the Angel who had redeemed him from all evil (Gen. 48:16). The patriarch had shown wisdom when standing before Pharaoh and also when blessing Joseph's two sons. Now the day had come that Jacob could use this wisdom he had acquired to bless his own sons. He showed them God's thoughts, as applied to each one of them. If what Jacob said didn't always seem to be a blessing, as in Reuben's case, yet communicating and applying God's thoughts to every one of them was a blessing.

It still is a blessing for us to be occupied with this wisdom and to try to learn from what Jacob had learned. He had been taught at the feet of his Shepherd, who is our Good, Great, and Chief Shepherd. When Jacob referred to the *Angel* who had *redeemed* him from all evil, he mentioned two other precious names and qualities of his God. Jacob shared with his sons resources he had discovered in his God: what a blessing! In his God-given wisdom, Jacob adapted his words to each one of his sons' needs according to their future place in Israel.

Genesis 49 presents a master-plan of God's ways with Israel. It deals with failures, bringing corrections, restoration, and the fulfillment of His plans: blessings He alone can give.

Jacob spoke about Shiloh: the scepter would not depart from Judah before Shiloh would have come. When the Romans destroyed the temple in A.D.70, Jews climbed onto the walls, crying to God in despair, that Shiloh had not yet come. They didn't realize that He had come but had been rejected by His people. Blessing comes when one accepts God's thoughts, repents, and believes.

A. E. Bouter

When the fullness of the time was come, God sent forth His Son, come of woman, come under law, that He might redeem those under law, that we might receive sonship. But because ye are sons, God has sent out the Spirit of His Son into our hearts, crying, Abba, Father. *(Galatians 4:4-6)*

In the Old Testament believers are looked at as little children, under tutors and governors, preparing for eventual graduation. The fullness of time is when God had decreed that the change was to be made. He sent His own Son to accomplish this great work of bringing souls out from a place of childhood training into that of the liberty and dignity of sonship. This could only be by means of His sufferings and death on the cross of Calvary, by which the Lord Jesus has redeemed those who were once practically slaves, differing nothing from servants. For the tutors and governors had to do with law and its restraining bondage, from which now the great redemption that is in Christ Jesus has set us free.

Redemption therefore has transformed the child into a "son." The child is seen now as having come to maturity by virtue of the redemption that is in Christ Jesus. He is no longer a servant, but a son, no longer under legal restraints, but brought into a place of liberty, dignity, and trust.

This implies, not merely submission as a child to the Father's will, but the understanding of that good and acceptable and perfect will, and wholehearted acquiescence in it. This is the true character of Christianity as contrasted to Judaism. Being in a place of mature understanding therefore, the believer is entrusted with his Father's goods. Precious indeed is this sonship, and precious the grace that has given it!

L. M. Grant

I became dead, and behold, I am living to the ages of ages, and have the keys of death and of hades. *(Revelation 1:18)*
The dead shall be raised incorruptible, and we shall be changed ... But when this corruptible shall have put on incorruptibility, and this mortal shall have put on immortality, then shall come to pass the word written: Death has been swallowed up in victory. Where, O death, is thy sting? Where, O death, thy victory?
(1 Corinthians 15:52,54-55)

Are you at times afraid of the *last enemy*, death (1 Cor. 15:26)? Do you see for yourself a dark shadow ahead over the terminating portals? When you first see the darkening portals, the promptings of nature may produce fear, but He says, "Fear not" (Rev. 1:17). He knows that by His resurrection He has divested the grave of all its terrors. He has the keys of death and He will bear you through the portals of death into His presence. Know that He understands—He Himself has died! And He wants the rest of your pilgrimage here to be peaceful and unclouded.

Death is our last enemy, but He will take away every vestige of weeping—because of Him death no longer has a sting. Through Him the ashes of the sepulchre will spring up into a body of glory like His. At death, the soul will be with Him, but its bliss will not be perfect until it is united with its incorruptible tabernacle. The call shall be, "Awake and sing in triumph, ye that dwell in dust" (Isa. 26:19).

We cannot tell all the joys that await us, but we do know its chief glory—"We shall be like Him" (1 Jn. 3:2). Having this hope in you, are you one who "purifies himself, even as He is pure" (1 Jn. 3:3)? We are not to fear dying, but are to look forward with triumphant hope to that day when all believers are resurrected and with Him in the Father's house.

J. R. MacDuff

O Israel, return unto Jehovah thy God; for thou hast fallen by thine iniquity. Take with you words, and turn to Jehovah; say unto Him, Forgive all iniquity, and receive us graciously; so will we render the calves of our lips. Assyria shall not save us; we will not ride upon horses: neither will we say anymore to the work of our hands, Thou art our God; because in Thee the fatherless findeth mercy. I will heal their backsliding, I will love them freely; for Mine anger is turned away from Him. *(Hosea 14:1-4)*

PROPHETS AND THEIR PROPHECIES – HOSEA (7)

Here in this last chapter of Hosea's prophecy God's final appeal to His people Israel through the prophet awakens a response. For chapter after chapter God has pleaded with His wayward people. Peter later reminds us that while judgment is sure and coming soon, God is still longsuffering, not willing that any should perish, but that all should come to repentance (2 Pet. 3:9). Thank God for such longsuffering! Here in Hosea—and often today as well—God's purpose of love is attained; there is repentance resulting in forgiveness, joy, and eventual fruit for God.

Notice the expression in verse 2: "So will we render the calves of our lips." Hebrews 13:15 picks up on this, when it defines the sacrifice of praise as "the fruit of the lips confessing His name." But for such sacrifices to be offered acceptably to God, dependence upon human might—Assyria; the world's resources—horses; and any idols of one's own making must be totally given up. Nor can we come to God to demand of Him rights we may feel we are entitled to. No, "In Thee the fatherless findeth mercy."

How graciously God replies to those who turn to Him repentantly! He loves them freely; His anger is turned away; He refreshes, revives, beautifies, makes fruitful, and attractive. Indeed, God's ways are right; the wise will understand and walk in them.

E. P. Vedder, Jr.

In temperance endurance, in endurance godliness, in godliness brotherly love, in brotherly love love. *(2 Peter 1:6-7)*

With self-restraint, by which we govern ourselves, we need patience with others. Without this patience, the very temperance by which we restrain ourselves may lead to irritation with others who are less restrained. Our patience is to be exercised with godliness, or the fear of God; otherwise patience may degenerate into compromise with evil.

Godliness supposes a walk in communion with God, living our life under His guidance and direction. Do we take all the changing circumstances of life, prosperous or adverse, that test our piety, from God and to God? With godliness that thinks of what is due to God, we are not to forget brotherly love, or what is due to our brother. Godliness will lead our affections to flow out to those who, being God's children, are our brethren.

With brotherly love we are to have love—divine love—otherwise our love may be limited to our brethren, instead of flowing out in the largeness of the love of God to the world around. Moreover, brotherly love may easily degenerate into partiality and mere human affection. One has said, "If divine love governs me, I love all my brethren; I love them because they belong to Christ; there is no partiality. I shall have greater enjoyment in a spiritual brother; but I shall occupy myself about my weak brother with a love that rises above his weakness and has tender consideration for it." Brotherly love makes our brother the prominent object. "Love" is a deeper thing and has God in view, even as we read: "By this we know that we love the children of God, when we love God, and keep His commandments" (1 Jn. 5:2 KJV).

H. Smith

In peaceful wonder we adore / The thoughts of love divine,
Which in that world forevermore, / Unite our lot with Thine.

J. N. Darby

In the third year of the reign of Jehoiakim king of Judah came Nebuchadnezzar king of Babylon unto Jerusalem, and besieged it. And the Lord gave Jehoiakim … into his hand, and a part of the vessels of the house of God; and he carried them … to the house of his god. *(Daniel 1:1-2)*
I am Jehovah, that is My name; and My glory will I not give to another, neither My praise to graven images. *(Isaiah 42:8)*

Nebuchadnezzar's action in relation to the vessels of the house of God was meant to honor his false gods, and to elevate them above the true and living God, the LORD of hosts. Approximately 450 years before, the Philistines captured the Ark of the Covenant and put it in the house of their god Dagon, only to find Dagon fallen on his face. The ark is a type of Christ, and God did not delay to punish the Philistines. The next day Dagon was not only fallen but shattered (1 Sam. 5:1-5).

In the case of Nebuchadnezzar the punishment was delayed for a while, for God was going to teach Nebuchadnezzar the important lesson recorded for us in Daniel 4, namely that the Most High, the God of the heavens, is the only true God "whose dominion is an everlasting dominion … and He doeth according to His will in the army of the heavens, and among the inhabitants of the earth." Did God then forget about the vessels? No, indeed! Read Daniel 5:17-28 and listen to Daniel's words to the last Babylonian emperor, Belshazzar. Babylon fell and the next empire returned the vessels to God's temple that was being rebuilt.

Now, is this not a lesson for us? We have a fallen nature that is not a bit better than that of Nebuchadnezzar, or Belshazzar, or Herod who was eaten by worms because he did not give glory to God (Acts 12:22-24). This nature wants to take credit for what God bestows by grace (1 Cor. 4:7). His grace should not make us proud but humble. Let us remember the Lord's solemn words: **"My glory will I not give to another."**

A. M. Behnam

I saw the Lord sitting upon a throne, high and lifted up; and His train filled the temple. Seraphim were standing above Him: each had six wings; with twain he covered his face, and with twain he covered his feet, and with twain he flew. And one called to the other and said, Holy, holy, holy is Jehovah of hosts; the whole earth is full of His glory! *(Isaiah 6:1-3)*

JESUS IS JEHOVAH (3)

In the year that King Uzziah died times were dark in Israel. The king indeed had died, but Isaiah saw the throne of God and the glory of the King who sat upon it. It was the perfect antidote for troubled times—as another has said: "When the outlook is bleak, try the uplook." This holy scene had a great impact upon Isaiah! "Woe unto me! For I am undone … for mine eyes have seen the King, Jehovah of hosts" (v. 5).

Jehovah imparted a message to the prophet to give to the people, and it was a message of judgment: "Hearing ye shall hear and shall not understand, and seeing ye shall see and shall not perceive" (v. 9). A season of blindness was to fall upon Israel. This prophecy would be confirmed years later, as the apostle Paul showed (Acts 28:24-28; Rom. 11:25).

The apostle John declares that Israel's blindness was supremely manifested when they rejected the Lord Jesus, for although He had done "many signs before them" yet His people "believed not on Him" (Jn. 12:37). In response to the unbelief of the people, John quotes the prophetic message of Isaiah (Jn. 12:39-40). And then John makes an amazing commentary on Isaiah's prophecy, saying that Isaiah wrote these words **"because he saw His glory and spoke of Him"** (Jn. 12:41). The meaning of this is as striking as it is profound. John says that what Isaiah saw was the glory of Christ. The Lord Jesus is "the King, Jehovah of Hosts," before whom the seraphim cry, "Holy, holy, holy."

B. Reynolds

February   **18**   Monday

Let the peace of Christ preside in your hearts, to which also ye have been called in one body.   *(Colossians 3:15)*

Before leaving this world, the Lord Jesus said to His own, "I leave peace with you. I give My peace to you." (Jn. 14:27); and this is the peace that is to preside in our hearts in the midst of all the evils and trials of the present scene. The same peace that possessed the heart of the Son of God and left Him undismayed amid all the opposition and hatred of evil men is to be ours. This peace, which we can enjoy individually, is to be *ours together*, for we have been called to Christ's peace "in one body." We are to share it as those that have been united to each other by the Spirit of God, and united to Christ in the membership of His body.

Peace should characterize all the gatherings of the saints, for to this God has called us. After the Lord Jesus rose from among the dead, He appeared in the midst of His gathered disciples with the words "Peace unto you" upon His lips. No other circle on earth can know this peace which Christ gives to His own. The Spirit of God taught the saints at Colosse that they had been called to it as having part in the "one body." How necessary it is for us, in these last days, to be reminded afresh of this precious truth.

Very soon the Lord will be here to rapture the Church to heaven, and the day for holding fast His precious truth in testimony will be over. The privilege of having been taught the truth of the Assembly's present function on earth brings with it the responsibility of endeavoring to live in the light of it for the pleasure and glory of God. Let us then at all times seek to walk in the light of the truth of "the Church, which is His body," holding this, and every other precious feature of the truth in relation to Christ, our exalted Head.

W. C. Reid

To Caleb the son of Jephunneh he gave a portion ... And thence
Caleb dispossessed the sons of Anak ... And Caleb said, He that
smites Kirjath-sepher and takes it, to him will I give Achsah my
daughter as wife. And Othniel the son of Kenaz ... took it; and
he gave him Achsah ... and it came to pass as she came, that she
urged him to ask of her father a field.   *(Joshua 15:13-14,16-18)*

CALEB THE SON OF JEPHUNNEH (5)

Once more Caleb is seen in the history of God's people. In Joshua
15 the narrative is given of his expelling from Hebron the three sons
of Anak, and of his giving his daughter Achsah as wife to Othniel,
his nephew, who had smitten and captured Kirjath-sepher. At her
instance, and at the request of her husband, Caleb gave her a field,
"a south land." Emboldened by his grace, when he asked further,
"What wouldest thou?" she said, "Give me a blessing; for thou hast
given me a southern land; give me also springs of water." Caleb
gave her the upper springs and the lower springs (v. 19).

In the land, warring in the power of the Spirit, and victorious over
the enemy in the energy of faith, he walked in the truth of grace,
and could thus be a giver. Springs of water would be, in type, life in
the Holy Spirit's power; consequently, in figure, Caleb's gift would
comprise heavenly and earthly blessings.

The lesson for us is that the one who maintains fidelity to God in
walk and testimony, who rises to the level of his calling, is kept in
spiritual power and becomes God's most faithful representative to
all with whom he comes into contact. Himself indebted to grace for
all that he possesses and enjoys, he will become a model of grace in
his walk and ways. He will live in the energy of the Spirit, whether
for communion or walk. All things, moreover, are possible to him
that believes.

The Christian's Friend and Instructor

February 20 Wednesday

I am persuaded that neither death, nor life, nor angels, nor principalities, nor things present, nor things to come, nor powers, nor height, nor depth, nor any other creature, shall be able to separate us from the love of God, which is in Christ Jesus our Lord. *(Romans 8:38-39)*

SAFETY: THE WAY OF SALVATION

Jesus went to the cross as a Lamb led to the slaughter. There He "suffered for sins, the Just for the unjust, that He might bring us unto God." He "has been delivered for our offenses and has been raised for our justification" (Rom. 4:25). Thus God does not reduce His righteous claims against sin when He justifies the sinner who believes in Jesus, for Jesus fully paid the righteous penalty.

Do you believe on the Son of God? If so, God makes good to you the full value of Jesus' sacrifice. Isn't this wonderful way of salvation worthy of God Himself? His love, His precious Son's glory, and the sinner's salvation are all bound together. What grace and glory that God's Son should do all the work and get all the praise, and you and I, believing on Him, should get all the blessing!

But you ask, "Why don't I have assurance of my salvation? If my feelings let me say one day that I am saved, they may ruin every hope the next. I am like a storm-tossed ship with no place to anchor." There is your mistake! Did you ever hear of trying to anchor a ship by fastening the anchor inside the ship? The anchor must be hooked solidly outside the ship. You may understand that Christ's death alone gives you safety, but you think that what you feel inside gives you certainty. Place your trust on Him and what He has done, and not on yourself and how you feel.

G. Cutting

Ye are saved by grace, through faith; and this not of yourselves; it is God's gift: not on the principle of works, that no one might boast.

(Ephesians 2:8-9)

CERTAINTY: THE KNOWLEDGE OF SALVATION

How can I be sure that I have the right kind of faith? Well, have your confidence in the right Person—in the Son of God. It isn't a question of the amount of your faith, but of **the trustworthiness of the Person in whom you place your confidence.** One man takes hold of Christ with a drowning man's grip, while another only touches the hem of His garment, but both are equally safe. They both confidently rest in the eternal effectiveness of His finished work. That is believing on Him.

Make sure that your confidence is not based on your works, religious observances or feelings, or moral training. You may have the strongest faith in such things and perish eternally. **The feeblest faith in Christ eternally saves,** while the strongest faith in self is of no use.

"I do believe on Him," said a girl to me one day, "but when asked if I'm saved, I don't like to say 'Yes' for fear I might be lying." This girl was a small town butcher's daughter. Her father had not returned from market. So I said, "Now, suppose you ask your father how many sheep he bought today, and he says 'ten.' Later, someone asks you how many sheep your father bought today and you reply, 'I don't want to say because I might be lying.'" With righteous anger, her mother, who was standing with us, replied, "But that would be making her father a liar!"

In like manner, this girl was making Christ a liar by saying, "I believe on Him but I don't like to say I'm saved because I might be lying," when Christ has said, "He who believes on Me **has** everlasting life" (Jn. 6:47).

G. Cutting

If these things be in you, and abound, they make you that ye shall neither be barren nor unfruitful in the knowledge of our Lord Jesus Christ. But he that lacketh these things is blind, and cannot see afar off, and hath forgotten that he was purged from his old sins ... rather, brethren, give diligence to make your calling and election sure. *(2 Peter 1:8-10 KJV)*

In these verses the apostle sets forth the blessed effects of having these qualities and the serious consequences to the one in whose life they are lacking. A life marked by these qualities would be a full and abundant life, according to the Lord's desire that His sheep should not only have life but have it abundantly (Jn. 10:10). So too our knowledge of the Lord Jesus would not be barren and unfruitful. The life of practical godliness is one in which there is fruit for God and usefulness and blessing for man.

The one who lacks these qualities of the life of godliness, even if possessing divine life, will fall into spiritual blindness. Suffering from short-sightedness, he will only see the present things of the world and its lusts. He will not be able to see afar off. A heart occupied with its own will and the gratification of its lusts will no longer see "the King in His beauty" and "the land that is very far off" (Isa. 33:17). Not only will such lose sight of coming glories, but he will forget the mighty work by which he has been purged from his sins. If we fail to live the life of godliness, we shall lose sight of the coming glory; we shall slip back into the world around and fall into the very sins from which we have been cleansed.

With this solemn warning, the apostle exhorts us to give diligence to live this practical life and thus make our calling and election sure. We keep the consciousness of our election fresh in our own souls, while giving no uncertain testimony to the world around.

H. Smith

Behold, what manner of love the Father hath bestowed upon us that we should be called the sons of God.   *(1 John 3:1 KJV)*

Undoubtedly the love of the Father is the most exalted theme in the revelation of Christianity. The love of the Father specially irradiates the family circle of grace. The love of God is for the whole world in its illimitable measure, and is proclaimed to all men for the ears of faith. "God so loved the world, that He gave His Only-begotten Son, that whosoever believeth in Him should not perish, but have everlasting life" (Jn. 3:16). And nothing can separate those who believe from the love of God which is in Christ Jesus our Lord (Rom. 8:39). But the **Father's love!**

What sort of love, then, is it that the Father has given us, and that we are exhorted to behold? Is it a love which was awakened and even caused by our dire need? We are too apt to assume hastily and somewhat selfishly that the Father's love derives its special character from the fact that we, the sinful and unworthy subjects of divine grace, are enabled to stand before Him in the relationship of beloved children. And if this is our only viewpoint of His love, we shall miss its invisible heights altogether, as well as its boundless length and breadth.

No, love receives its prime quality from the lover rather than from the loved one. And our highest joy, therefore, is not that we are the objects of divine love, though we should never forget the love that made us and calls us the children of God. We who know Him that is from the beginning rejoice, not only in the love that is of God, but in the God who is love (1 Jn. 4:7-8), in Him who loves as only the God who is love can love. Moreover, in a deeper intimacy still, we bless the Father, not merely, nor even chiefly, because we are loved of Him, but because the Father Himself loves us, and because He loves us as only the Father who is God can love. The **Father's love!**

W. J. Hocking

February 24 Lord's Day

If a man have committed a sin worthy of death, and he be put to death, and thou have hanged him on a tree, his body shall not remain all night upon the tree, but thou shalt in any wise bury him that day (for he that is hanged is a curse of God).

(Deuteronomy 21:22-23)

I have great grief and uninterrupted pain in my heart, for I have wished, I myself, to be a curse from the Christ for my brethren, my kinsmen, according to flesh; who are Israelites. *(Romans 9:2-4)*

Christ has redeemed us out of the curse of the law, having become a curse for us (for it is written, Cursed is everyone hanged upon a tree). *(Galatians 3:13)*

God's instruction in Deuteronomy 21 follows immediately upon His command as to what was to be done with an unmanageable and rebellious son. The parents of such a son, God said, were to openly testify against their wicked son before the elders of their city. Then all the men of his city were to stone him to death. God went on to say: "And thou shalt put evil away from thy midst; and all Israel shall hear and fear."

In Exodus 32, when Israel had sinned against God by making and worshipping a golden calf, God was ready to consume them and make of Moses a great nation. But Moses pled for his people, going so far as to say, "And now, if Thou wilt forgive their sin … but if not, blot me, I pray Thee, out of Thy book that Thou hast written." But this great leader was a sinner, just like his people, and thus could not take their place. The apostle Paul's heart yearned for His people Israel's salvation, but he, also a sinner, could not take their place under the curse of God.

God testified from heaven several times about our Lord Jesus, "This is My beloved Son, in whom I have found My delight." Yet He, the Holy One, became a curse for us, taking our place under God's wrath when He was nailed to the cross. Wonderful Savior!

E. P. Vedder, Jr.

February 25 Monday

His bow remained in strength, and the arms of his hands were made strong by the hands of the Mighty God of Jacob (from there is the Shepherd, the Stone of Israel), by the God of your father who will help you, and by the Almighty who will bless you with blessings of heaven above, blessings of the deep that lies beneath, blessings of the breasts and of the womb.

(Genesis 49:24-25 NKJV)

Amazing Blesser, amazing blessings! Despite, and even through, many shortcomings and failures, Jacob had learned special lessons from his God. Now the time had come to share God's thoughts with his sons, and bless them accordingly.

Earlier, when blessing Joseph's two sons, Jacob referred to God (Elohim) as "my Shepherd" and the Angel who had redeemed him from all evil (Gen. 48:15 NASB). Now, speaking to Joseph himself, Jacob refers to his Mighty God, a name implying that He is One who makes things come to pass. In verse 25 he refers to the Almighty One, El-Shaddai, a different name of God. The first time it occurs is in relation to Abraham (Gen. 17:1). It occurs five more times in relation to Jacob, today's verse being the last one in Genesis. Through faith Jacob had learned to draw wonderful resources from his God. Thus he could say that the blessings with which he blessed Joseph surpassed those of Jacob's own forefathers (Gen. 49:26).

One of our challenges is to really draw from our God what He has made available to us. This is very practical, also for us. Our position and relationship with God, our Father, is more intimate than what Jacob enjoyed with the God he had come to know so well. Our position gives us more privileges, and therefore also more responsibilities. Jacob had learned to draw from God and God had helped him despite his shortcomings. God is faithful, and wants to help us as well, and bless us even more, because Christ's work has been accomplished.

A. E. Bouter

February   26   Tuesday

Blessed the meek, for they shall inherit the earth. *(Matthew 5:5)*

The Chinese communist leader, Mao Tse-Tung, taught that power grows out of the barrel of a gun. His philosophy is shared by millions who see self-assertion and "fighting fire with fire" as the only way to obtain their rights and inherit their share of the earth. Such people usually confuse meekness with weakness, and see it as the characteristic of the downtrodden, defeated, and desolate masses. They scoff at the words of our Lord. But who are the meek? Who are those mighty myriads that triumph through apparent defeat and rise to heights of glory by going down? Their strength is in harness—like a mighty river that does not dissipate itself and destroy others by overflowing its banks and becoming a turbulent flood; like fire in a hearth that gives warmth and light, rather than destruction in a forest.

There's Moses, leading the throngs of Israel through the "waste howling wilderness," bearing with their rebellion and murmurings, their lack of gratitude, and even the foolish taunts of those closest to him. In meekness he cast himself upon the Lord, looking to Him alone as his shield and defender. Scripture calls him "the meekest of men" (Num. 12:3). Will he inherit the earth? Indeed he will, not through self-assertion, but in company with the Everlasting God who "formed the earth and the world" and in whose sight a thousand years are like yesterday when it is past (Ps. 90:1-4).

But above all, there's the Lord Jesus who referred to Himself as "meek and lowly in heart" and who promises rest to those who take His yoke and learn of Him. His meekness extended all the way to the death of the cross. Soon He will reign over all the earth, sharing His inheritance with those who have meekly suffered for His sake. Indeed, the meek shall inherit the earth!

G. W. Steidl

I will sing unto Jehovah as long as I live; I will sing psalms to my God while I have my being. My meditation of Him shall be pleasant; I will rejoice in Jehovah. *(Psalm 104:33-34 marg.)*

It has pleased the Lord to teach me the truth that the first great and ordinary business to which I ought to attend every day is to have my soul happy in the Lord. If I am not happy in the Lord and not being nourished and strengthened in my inner man day by day, the things I do to serve the Lord might not be done in the right spirit. I have begun therefore to meditate on the Scriptures early each morning, not for the sake of the public ministry of the Word, but for my own soul. I often find, however, that the Lord is pleased to use that which He has communicated to me to minister to other believers at a later time. This occurs even though my meditation was not for the sake of public ministry of the Word, but for the profit of my inner man.

It often now astonishes me that I did not sooner see this point. In no book did I ever read about it. No public ministry ever brought the matter before me. No private discussion with a fellow-believer stirred me up to this matter. And yet, now, since God has taught me this point, it is as plain to me as anything that the first thing the child of God has to do is to obtain food for his inner man.

What is the food for the inner man? Not prayer, but the Word of God. It is not the simple reading of the Word of God, so that it only passes through our minds, just as water runs through a pipe; rather, it is considering what we read, pondering over it, and applying it to our hearts. What a difference it makes in service, decisions, and the trials of life for the soul to be refreshed and happy in the Lord.

G. Muller

Now the Jews' feast of tabernacles was at hand. His brethren therefore said unto Him, Depart hence, and go into Judea ... show Thyself to the world. *(John 7:2-4 KJV)*

The Lord illustrated the expression, ***"in the world, but of the world"***—a form of words which has been derived from what He Himself says in John 17:15: "I pray not that Thou shouldest take them out of the world, but that Thou shouldest keep them from the evil." He illustrates this condition all through His life; for He was ever in the world, active in the midst of its ignorance and misery, but never of it, as one that shared its hopes or projects, or breathed its spirit.

But in John 7 He is eminently seen in this character. It was the Feast of Tabernacles, the crowning joyous time in Israel, a foreshadowing of the coming kingdom, the season of ingathering, when the people had only to *remember* that they had been wanderers in a wilderness in other days. His brethren propose to Him to take advantage of such a moment, when "all the world," was at Jerusalem. They would have Him make Himself important, make Himself "a man of the world." "If Thou do these things," they say, "show Thyself to the world" (v. 4). He refused. His time had not then come to keep the Feast of Tabernacles. He will have His kingdom in the world, and be great to the ends of the earth, when His day comes. He will not go to the feast to be *of the feast,* though He will be *in it*; therefore, when He reaches the city at this time, we see Him in *service* there, not in *honor,* not working miracles as His brethren would have had Him, that He might gain the notice of men; but teaching others, and then hiding Himself.

Very peculiar and characteristic indeed is all of this—the moral glory of the Man, the perfect Man, Jesus, in His relation to the world. He was a conqueror, a sufferer, and a benefactor—**in the world, but not of it**.

J. G. Bellett

Upon the earth distress of nations, with perplexity ... Men's hearts failing them for fear, and for *looking after* those things which are coming on the earth ... And when these things begin to come to pass, then *look up*, and lift up your heads; for your redemption draweth nigh.

(Luke 21:25-26,28 KJV)

The disciples, to whom the Lord spoke these words, are looked at representatively, not only as the Jewish remnant in the last days, but also as the Christian company at the present time. Therefore, the moral teachings are as applicable to us today as they will be to the remnant in the time of Jacob's Trouble.

Already we are seeing great unrest among nations, which is but the birth pangs of the Great Tribulation which is to come upon all the earth. Fear and distress fill the hearts of those who know not God. There is a cry for freedom, peace, and prosperity; a more equal distribution of wealth.

We Christians can easily be caught up in the frenzy of a world hoping for the best, and forget that we have the best hope. The Lord Jesus, mindful of this tendency in them and us to lose sight of our heavenly calling, said, "And when these things begin to come to pass, then look up, and lift up your heads; for your redemption draweth nigh."

We, who have been redeemed by the precious blood of Christ, are not appointed "to wrath, but to obtain salvation through our Lord Jesus Christ" (1 Th. 5:9). We shall be kept "from the hour of temptation, which shall to come upon all the world" (Rev. 3:10).

This blessed hope for which we look, is the only effective antidote against a secular, and even a religious view of things. If the stage is being set for the appearance of the man of sin, how much closer then must be the coming of the Lord for His saints! In which direction you are looking? Are you "looking after" things here or "looking up"?

R. A. Barnett

Behold, the day cometh for Jehovah ... and I will assemble all the nations against Jerusalem to battle ... And Jehovah will go forth and fight with those nations, as He fought in the day of battle. And His feet shall stand in that day upon the **Mount of Olives,** which is before Jerusalem toward the east.   *(Zechariah 14:1-4)*

JESUS IS JEHOVAH (4)

Zechariah describes in vivid language the scene that follows the battle of Armageddon and Christ's return to earth. *Jehovah* will go forth and fight against the nations that have besieged Jerusalem just as He did in time past in Israel's sad history. Correspondingly, we read that *Christ* will defeat the nations, "And I saw heaven opened, and behold, a white horse, and one sitting on it ... and He judges and makes war" and He will **"smite the nations"** (Rev. 19:11,15). In this prophecy Christ is viewed as a warrior King who makes war against the nations. The only conclusion that we can draw from this is that the Jehovah of Zechariah and the Christ of Revelation are the *same Person*.

Zechariah gives another striking detail that confirms our theme: **His feet shall stand upon the Mount of Olives.** Some Bible commentators reject the implications of this prophecy and deny that Jehovah will literally stand upon the Mount of Olives. But their reasonings are to no avail for He who is God manifest in flesh *has already* stood upon the Mount of Olives and will stand there yet again (Acts 1:11).

Zechariah's theme in this chapter is Jehovah's coming and Kingdom. In this regard he also prophesied that when Jehovah comes He will bring His saints with Him, "Jehovah my God shall come, and all the holy ones with Thee" (v. 5). This is exactly what is spoken of Christ: for when He "is manifested ... then shall ye also be manifested with Him in glory" (Col. 3:4; see also Jude 14; Rev. 19:14). This is incontrovertible testimony to the glorious fact that the Lord Jesus is Jehovah.

B. Reynolds

Myrrh and aloes, cassia are all Thy garments; out of ivory palaces stringed instruments have made Thee glad. *(Psalm 45:8)*

THE GRACE THAT MEETS OUR NEED

Of old it was commanded, "Thou shalt love the Lord thy God with all thy heart, and with all thy soul, and with all thy might." Though our Lord's claim upon us is now not one whit less, it is not by command that He secures the love of His Church or of any heart in it. Love cannot be secured in that way, as man's sad history declares. He has another way, a way that cannot fail—He gains our love by disclosing His own; He gains His desire to have us for Himself by showing Himself to us.

His claim to our love has a triple basis: He claims us because He can meet all our needs by His grace; He claims us because of what He is in His own glorious Person; He claims us because of the love that He has for us, love that led Him into the deep suffering of death on our behalf. Psalm 45 declares these three great things, for it is full of Christ. It is Himself—and He showed His disciples things concerning Himself out of the Psalms. The end in view is that the fair daughter might be attracted to the great King, for His joy and glory. Hence He is spoken of to her in glowing words that can apply to none but Christ.

"Grace is poured into His lips"—He speaks in tender tones to the heart. He spoke words in season to the weary: the woman by Sychar's well, she who wept at His feet in Simon's house, the widow who mourned her only son, and a host of others—all of these found Him to be fairer than the children of men, because of the grace that was poured into His lips.

Has our experience been less blessed? We have heard His voice speaking in words of pardon and peace to our once troubled and burdened hearts. Grace has poured out of His lips for us.

J. T. Mawson

The disciples were filled with joy and the Holy Spirit.

(Acts 13:52)

THE JOY OF SALVATION (1)

You are saved by Christ's work and assured by God's Word, but your joy is maintained by the Holy Spirit who indwells you. Christ's work and your salvation stand or fall together; your walk and your enjoyment stand or fall together. Christ's work cannot fail so your salvation cannot fail. However, your walk can fail and when it does, your enjoyment fails with it. Your spiritual joy will be in direct proportion to the spirituality of your walk.

Have you made the mistake of mixing up enjoyment and safety? When through self-indulgence, loss of temper, or worldliness you grieved the Holy Spirit and lost your joy, did you think your safety was lost too? Your safety depends on Christ's work for you; your assurance depends on God's Word to you, and your enjoyment depends on not grieving the Holy Spirit in you. When a child of God grieves the Spirit, his communion with the Father and the Son is stopped. When he judges self and confesses his sin, the joy of communion is restored. Suppose your son has done something wrong. His communion with you is broken because of his disobedience. You have assured him of forgiveness if he confesses his wrong, but pride and self-will keep him from doing so. All his joy is gone because communion has been interrupted.

What has happened to your relationship? Has that gone too? Of course not! Relationship depends on birth; communion on behavior. As soon as your son confesses, you take him in your arms, and his joy is restored because communion is restored. The communion we have with the Lord is the joy we have of salvation.

G. Cutting

Who Himself bore our sins in His body on the tree, in order that, being dead to sins, we may live to righteousness. *(1 Peter 2:24)*

THE JOY OF SALVATION (2)

Don't think that God's judgment of the believer's sins is less than that of the unbeliever's sins. When a believer sins, the question of criminality cannot be raised against him because the judge settled that on the cross; but the question of communion is raised within the believer by the Holy Spirit every time He is grieved.

On a moonlit night, a man, looking at the reflection of the moon in a still pool, remarks how beautiful the moon is. Suddenly someone throws a stone into the pool and the man exclaims, "The moon is broken up, and the pieces are shaking!" His friend replies, "Look up, man. The moon hasn't changed. The pool's condition has changed."

Your heart is the pool. When you don't allow evil in your life, the Holy Spirit reveals the glories of Christ for your comfort and joy. But when sin enters, the Holy Spirit begins to disturb the pool and your happy experiences are broken up. You are restless and disturbed within. But when you confess the sin, the joy of communion is restored.

While your heart is in unrest, has Christ's work changed? No! Then your salvation hasn't changed either. Has God's Word changed? No! Then the certainty of your salvation also hasn't changed. What then has changed? The Holy Spirit's action in you has changed. Instead of filling your heart with Christ's worthiness, He is grieved to have to fill you with the sense of your sin. He takes away your joy until you judge and resist the evil that has grieved Him. When this is done, He restores your communion.

G. Cutting

Though the fig-tree shall not blossom, neither shall fruit be in the vines ... Yet I will rejoice in Jehovah, I will joy in the God of my salvation. Jehovah, the Lord, is my strength, and He maketh my feet like hind's feet, and He will make me to walk upon my high places. *(Habakkuk 3:17-19)*

Wickedness among the people of Israel was the cause of God's judgment upon them in the days of Habakkuk. The faith of the faithful was truly put to the test. "Jehovah, how long shall I cry and Thou wilt not hear? I cry out unto Thee, Violence! And Thou dost not save?" (ch. 1:2) But God strengthened His own and, even if to outward appearance nothing changed, the just lived by their faith (ch. 2:4).

Habakkuk's time resembles ours in many respects. A flood of evil surrounds us, and we, too, may well wonder why God allows unrighteousness to have free course. Habakkuk spoke to God and poured out his heart before Him. The prophet waited until God made the matter clear. God answered him (ch. 2:2). To comfort the faithful, Habakkuk was to write down plainly what God showed him, so that whoever read it might run. Salvation might be far away, but it would certainly come. But before it came, God wished to encourage them to live their life by faith. Habakkuk's vision was powerful: "The earth shall be filled with the knowledge of the glory of Jehovah as the waters cover the sea" (ch. 2:14).

The godless bring judgment upon themselves, but the God-fearing remember the Lord's power and glory, as had been revealed by mighty events in Israel's history. This power is the source of true rest in the day of tribulation. Even if visible blessing was lacking and circumstances were abnormal (ch. 3:17), the Lord was Habakkuk's strength. And God was able to lead him to the heights of blessing. Today, too, the Lord wants us to look to Him and trust in His promises.

The Good Seed

The burden of the word of Jehovah to Israel by Malachi. I have loved you, saith Jehovah; but ye say, Wherein hast Thou loved us? ... Wherein have we despised Thy name? Ye offer polluted bread upon Mine altar; and ye say, Wherein have we polluted Thee? In that ye say, The table of Jehovah is contemptible.

(Malachi 1:1-2,6-7)

PROPHETS AND THEIR PROPHECIES–MALACHI (1)

God's Word gives us no details about the life of Malachi, simply his prophecy, the burden of Jehovah's word which he was inspired to pen. Coming at the very end of the Old Testament, his book constitutes God's final loving appeal to His earthly people.

From its beginning we see the grief of God's heart. He had loved His people, and His appeal to them shows clearly that He still loves them. Repeatedly He expresses His sorrow at their attitude and conduct; repeatedly they talk back, defiantly challenging what He is saying to them and attempting to justify themselves.

The book contains a number of these exchanges. It begins with an unequivocal statement of God's love for Israel. God knows the objection they bring up, the "but ye say" that we hear so often in this book. He immediately responds. What a contrast between His sovereign love to them and His hatred for their brother Esau and his descendants, the wicked people of Edom! Yet they were showing the same defiant attitude God was condemning in Edom.

God rightfully expects His people's honor and respect. Their priests, those set apart to approach Him with sacrifices and to teach the people His law, should have led in this. They despised God's name and had no heart for God's glory. Their service was but a form of godliness, offering God lame, blind, sick animals that they would not have dared bring to their human governors.

And we—are we truly honoring God, or are we merely going through the motions of serving Him while our hearts are far from Him?

E. P. Vedder, Jr.

March **8** Friday

Love not the world, nor the things in the world. If anyone love the world, the love of the Father is not in him. *(1 John 2:15)*

Both the world and worldly Christians offer attractive opportunities to exercise Christian graces, and seek to enlist men and women of success in their benevolent projects. And there are temptations for those full of goodness, compassion, and energy. Movements designed to advance morality, help and elevate the unfortunate, reform those who have fallen, and to correct social and civic evils are especially alluring. They seem to offer opportunity to exercise spiritual gifts and knowledge.

But Christian love is the love that is of the Father. The activity of His love should mark the believer, not the activity of the love that is of the world.

The Christian is to be in the world for the Lord Jesus Christ—who is not of this world. If he does not love the world or the things of the world, he will find the Lord to be his satisfying portion in every way. How great is our loss if we divert our energies, time, and means into channels where the profit is merely present things—not eternal things. The Spirit of God would have us spend our strength seeking the things of Christ. "Seek the things which are above … not the things that are on the earth" (Col. 3:1-2). The world is passing away and the lust thereof.

For the believer to be ensnared in the love of the world, whatever may be gained thereby, in the end it will be a sad experience. The stamp of death is on the present scene, and the world of fallen man is under the judgment of God. It must pass away. It will not abide. But the one who practices the will of the Father will abide forever.

C. Crain

He led Him to Jerusalem, and set Him on the edge of the temple, and said to Him, If Thou be Son of God, cast Thyself down hence; for it is written, He shall give charge to His angels concerning Thee to keep Thee. *(Luke 4:9-10)*

And rising up they cast Him forth out of the city, and led Him up to the brow of the mountain upon which their city was built, so that they might throw Him down the precipice; but He, passing through the midst of them, went His way. *(Luke 4:29-30)*

The devil had no thought of the Lord's death at the bottom of the pinnacle, none whatever. He tempted Him—as he had tempted the woman in the garden—to magnify Himself, to make Himself to be as God. He sought to corrupt the sources of motivation in Christ, as he had corrupted them in Adam, and to get the pride of life in as one of the master-springs. But Jesus kept the form of a servant. He would not cast Himself down, but obediently remembered, "Thou shalt not tempt the Lord thy God" (Lk. 4:12).

So He did at the hill of Nazareth. That hill was not higher than the pinnacle of the temple. Jesus was in no more danger at the one spot than at the other. He would have been as entirely unhurt at the foot of the hill as at the bottom of the pinnacle. But how then should the Scripture be fulfilled, that He came not to honor Himself? He, therefore, "passing through the midst of them, went His way." He retired unnoticed and unknown, fulfilling His form as a servant.

We dare not speak of such things as being done to save His life. The thought is contrary to the glory of His Person, "God manifest in flesh." In the days of His flesh Jesus was again and again refreshed in spirit when faith discovered His glory under the veil. And so now, when the form of a servant is presented to our thoughts afresh, He will joy in saints discovering His glory.

J. G. Bellett

Behold, the days come, saith Jehovah, when I will raise unto David a righteous Branch, who shall reign as king, and act wisely, and shall execute judgment and righteousness in the land. In His days Judah shall be saved, and Israel shall dwell in safety; and this is His name whereby He shall be called, Jehovah our Righteousness.

(Jeremiah 23:5-6)

JESUS IS JEHOVAH (5)

Jeremiah describes the Messiah as one who will come from the line of David. He will arise from very humble beginnings because the nation of Israel and the house of David had been almost destroyed. But a righteous Branch (*Sprout*) would spring out of David's line as a sprout out of a fallen tree.

Next Jeremiah shows the character of Messiah's coming millennial kingdom. He will "execute judgment and righteousness in the land." How different from the corruption and injustice which characterize governments in the world today! Another striking feature of that day is that "Judah shall be saved and Israel shall dwell in safety." This prophecy has not been fulfilled, for it is evident that Israel does not yet "dwell safely." Their enemies still threaten them and would cut them off. But when Messiah comes then "all Israel shall be saved" (Rom. 11:26).

Jeremiah introduces another description of the Messiah by declaring that His name shall be called: **"Jehovah our Righteousness."** One thing the Bible tells us about the Jewish people is that they "have not submitted to the righteousness of God," and are presently seeking to "establish their own righteousness" (Rom. 10:3). However, in a coming day their eyes will be opened to see the salvation that God has provided. But before that day arrives, believers of this dispensation can say that Christ **"has been made to us ... righteousness"** (1 Cor. 1:30). *He is our righteousness.* The lowly sprout from David's line, the Lord Jesus Christ, is "Jehovah our Righteousness"!

B. Reynolds

This you know, that all those in Asia have turned away from me, among whom are Phygellus and Hermogenes. The Lord grant mercy to the household of Onesiphorus, for he often refreshed me, and was not ashamed of my chain; but when he arrived in Rome, he sought me out very zealously and found me. The Lord grant to him that he may find mercy from the Lord in that Day—and you know very well how many ways he ministered to me at Ephesus. *(2 Timothy 1:15-18 NKJV)*

Demas was not the only one who had left Paul. Before that, men of renown had wrongly influenced the believers in Asia—the area around Ephesus in today's Turkey. As a result, believers in that area had turned away from the apostle, except for Onesiphorus, whose name means "profit bringing." Before that defection, this brother had been quite useful to Paul; something Timothy remembered well (v. 18).

Then, in a much more difficult situation, when Paul was not only rejected by believers, but put on death-row by the authorities, Onesiphorus had traveled all the way to Rome. It was almost impossible to find the apostle there, and it was also dangerous to go and try. Yet Onesiphorus succeeded in locating Paul and remained with him to comfort him. Almost nobody cared for Paul, not even in Rome; yet Onesiphorus not only visited him in the dungeon of his prison, but stayed with him to refresh him!

The zeal this brother displayed is a beautiful illustration of "first love" and of being "an overcomer." How sad it would have been for Paul had this brother also joined the defection. Paul's prayer, "The Lord grant mercy to the household of Onesiphorus," may indicate that Onesiphorus had passed away. No word of criticism, or bitterness, came from Paul's pen. Instead, he showed a spirit of grace towards those who had failed: this is another feature of a true overcomer.

A. E. Bouter

Ye have been called to liberty, brethren; only do not turn liberty into an opportunity to the flesh, but by love serve one another. For the whole law is fulfilled in one word, in Thou shalt love thy neighbor as thyself. *(Galatians 5:13-14)*

Liberty and love go together: there is no such thing as true liberty if it does not occasion the spontaneous outflow of love. But liberty is the very sphere into which the Christian is introduced, liberty from the bondage of sin, of law, of self-will; liberty, in fact, to honor God. The exercise of self-will is bondage rather than liberty. The devil seeks to turn such liberty to corruption, to make it rather a license for the indulgence of the flesh. We have no excuse for being deceived by him. The place of liberty is that of utter dependence upon, and subjection to God. This is the liberty of the Spirit. How dishonorable then to use it as an occasion to the flesh! How despicable to take ungodly advantage of the kindness of God! The very essence of Christianity is, "By love serve on another."

How simple and straightforward is the true character of the child of God. There is no great, involved scheme of practice pressed upon him, no legal forms and ceremonies as contained in the Old Testament. In fact, the law itself is actually fulfilled in that one searching expression, "Thou shalt love thy neighbor as thyself." For this goes to the root of the matter. It absolutely cuts off selfishness, which is the unvarying motive of the legalist. The more legal-minded one is, the more thoroughly he is ignoring the claims of the law. But knowing Christ alone gives true liberty of love.

L. M. Grant

> *Oh, to grace how great a debtor*
> *Daily I`m constrained to be!*
> *Let that grace, Lord, like a fetter,*
> *Bind my wandering heart to Thee.*

R. Robinson

Abraham said to his servant ... thou shalt go to my land and to my kindred, and take a wife for my son Isaac. And the servant said to him: Perhaps the woman will not be willing ... Abraham said ... Jehovah ... He will send His angel before thee, that thou mayest take a wife for my son thence. *(Genesis 24:2,4-5,7)*

THE GOOD AND FAITHFUL SERVANT (1)

The story about Abraham sending his servant to get a wife for Isaac, as recorded in Genesis 24, teaches us many valuable lessons about the "good and faithful servant." The first important and practical lesson is this: the good servant must get his instructions from his master. Abraham's servant was well experienced, for he ruled over all that Abraham had.

He was trustworthy and, no doubt, an intelligent man, yet he did not trust in his own experience, nor did Abraham say to him, "Use your own judgment." When he had a question about what to do in case the woman would refuse to go with him, he inquired directly of his master. He did not consult with his fellow servants. He wanted the truth from the source of the truth. We too have access to the truth through the Word of God and the throne of grace. We have the Holy Spirit who guides us into all truth.

The result was wonderful. Abraham told him very clearly what **not to** do, as well as what to do. Not only that, but he promised **help from above** based on what God had done for him thus far, and on God's promises to him. "Jehovah the God of the heavens ... who has sworn to me, saying, Unto thy seed will I give this land—He will send His angel before thee, that thou mayest take a wife for my son thence" (v. 7). No wonder Abraham is called "faithful Abraham." The faithful servant obeyed his faithful master who trusted the faithful God. The lesson for us is very clear: *trust and obey*. And the promise is: "I will instruct thee and teach thee the way in which thou shalt go" (Ps. 32:8).

A. M. Behnam

The priest's lips should keep knowledge, and at his mouth they seek the law; for he is the messenger of Jehovah of hosts.

(Malachi 2:7)

PROPHETS AND THEIR PROPHECIES – MALACHI (2)

Amid the Lord's sad statements in Malachi about the failures of Israel's priests we find this clear indication of one of the most important of their many privileges and responsibilities.

The priest's responsibility was first of all Godward—"that he may serve Me as priest ... when he goeth into the sanctuary before Jehovah." But he was also to come out as God's representative and spokesman to the people (Ex. 28:1,3-4,35). At the end of Leviticus 8 and 9, after Aaron and his sons had been consecrated to their office as priests, we find that "Aaron lifted up his hands toward the people and blessed them." "Moses and Aaron went into the tent of meeting, and came out and blessed the people; and the glory of Jehovah appeared to all the people."

In Deuteronomy God specified that His people were to bring matters too hard or controversial for them to the place which He would choose. The Levitical priests and the judge in that day were to declare God's mind on the matter, and the people were not to "decline from the word which they shall declare unto thee, to the right hand, or the left" (Dt. 17:8-13). God told the priests how to diagnose leprosy, how to know when the leprosy was cured, and what to offer for the leper's cleansing (Lev. 13:14; Dt. 24:8). The written copy of the law was entrusted to the priests to read to the people every seven years also (Dt. 31:9-13).

How sad that God had to castigate Israel's priests for despising Him, departing out of the way, and causing many to stumble at the law! How is it with us who are called both holy priests and kingly priests? Are we setting forth the excellencies of Him who has called us out of darkness to His wonderful light? We should!

E. P. Vedder, Jr.

That thou mayest know how one ought to conduct oneself in God's house, which is the Assembly of the Living God.

(1 Timothy 3:15)

The House of God is to be marked by godliness (l Tim. 3:14-16). This is not sanctimoniousness, nor is it merely an amiable and benevolent life such as it is possible for the natural man to exhibit. The godly life is lived in the fear of God and expresses God. The secret of this life lies in having before our souls the perfect pattern of godliness as set forth in Christ.

What a marvelous expression of God there would have been in the sight of the world if the Church as the House of the Living God had remained true to the principles of God's house. The world would have seen a company of people marked by holiness, dependence on God, subjection to authority, good works, and care for bodies and souls. Unfortunately, it is evident that those who compose the House of God have utterly failed. We have failed to maintain the great principles of God's house and thus have failed to give a true expression of God before the world.

Has God's purpose to dwell among men been thwarted by the failure of man? Surely not! Though all breaks down in the hands of men, whether it be Israel of old or the Church in the present day, yet God remains true to His purpose, and there rises up before us the vision of another House, in a millennial day, and "the latter glory of this House shall be greater than the former" (Hag. 2:9).

Yet even this House will pass away, for the glorious millennial age will end in gloom and judgment. But God will not give up His purpose. There is unrolled before us "a new heaven and a new earth." We hear a great voice out of heaven saying, "Behold, the tabernacle of God is with men, and He will dwell with them" (Rev. 21:1,3 KJV). There we see God's great purpose throughout the ages at last fulfilled, nevermore to be marred again.

H. Smith

The servant took ten camels of the camels of his master ... for all the goods of his master were in his hand ... And he said O, Lord God of my master Abraham, I pray Thee, send me good speed this day, and show kindness unto my master Abraham.

(Genesis 24:10,12 KJV)

THE GOOD AND FAITHFUL SERVANT (2)

Having received clear instructions from his master in verses 1-9, Abraham's servant goes on his journey to fulfill his mission. Let us notice three things in verses 10-12:

First. He goes on his mission with the rich provisions of his master. All the wealth of Abraham was present to meet his needs, whether the camels and servants, or the jewels and precious things. Everything needed for the success of his mission was there at his disposal. He did not need to look for help from other sources. The lesson for us is obvious. The unsearchable riches of Christ are all for us and with us. The servant was conscious of the all-sufficiency of his master's goods. When the Lord Jesus sent His disciples out He promised to be with them to the end (Mt. 28:19-20). This should be our confidence too.

Second. As soon as he arrived in Mesopotamia, before he spoke to anyone else, he spoke to the Lord, remembering Abraham's promise of divine help in verse 7.

Third. His desire for the success of his mission was not motivated by selfish desire. It is an ever present temptation to want to succeed in the service of the Lord so that we may be praised, or thought of as spiritual; hence the need to watch lest we lose our reward. Christ warned us against the desire for the praise of men because He knew our nature. The prayer of Abraham's servant was brief but came from his heart and showed what was in that heart: "O Lord God of my master Abraham, I pray Thee, send me good speed this day, **and show kindness unto my master Abraham.**"

A. M. Behnam

Thou art fairer than the sons of men; grace is poured into Thy lips: therefore God hath blessed Thee forever. Gird Thy sword upon Thy thigh, O Mighty One, in Thy majesty and Thy splendor.

(Psalm 45:2-3)

THE GLORY OF CHRIST'S PERSON (2)

Christ is glorious as well as gracious. He stands out in His glory above every name that is named. He will triumph over all that hate Him, even as He is tender to all who hear and love Him. This also must be declared of Him, that we may know that His grace is not weakness. In His majesty He will ride prosperously because of truth and meekness and righteousness—three great attributes that will be seen when He comes to judge, but were not wanting when He stooped to save us.

He is as **great** as He is **gracious**, for He is God, with an everlasting throne. His claim must be supreme. It stands before all other claims. The claims of father, mother, brother, sister, husband, wife, children, and self also, must recede into the background before His claim. None but God has a right to supersede these relationships which He has ordained. He who would win our undivided hearts is God, whose throne is forever and ever, and to His claim we must yield.

But the final appeal is even more touching. *"Myrrh and aloes, cassia, are all Thy garments; out of ivory palaces, stringed instruments have made Thee glad."* These fragrant spices which clothe our Savior like a garment stir our memories; they carry us back to the time when instead of glory and honor, a life of sorrow was His. The gold speaks of His divine glory; the frankincense of His holy, fragrant humanity; and the myrrh of His suffering even to death.

We look back to it now and it is the fragrance of the myrrh that greets us and attracts us.

J. T. Mawson

Behold, a hand touched me, which set me upon my knees and the palms of my hands. And he said unto me, O Daniel, man greatly beloved, understand the words which I speak unto thee.
(Daniel 10:10-11)

The Spirit of God alone explains Scripture. His power can unfold any part of God's Word. Real entry into God's mind in Scripture supposes that one watches against the old man, desires the glory of God, has full confidence in His Word, and depends upon the Holy Spirit. Understanding Scripture is not a mere intellectual process. The mind is only the vessel—not the power. The power is the Holy Spirit acting upon and through the vessel; but it must be the Spirit that gives one to know the things of God.

The important thing is that understanding the Word of God depends much more upon what is moral than what is of the mind—upon a single eye to the Lord Jesus Christ. The Holy Spirit can never give us anything to save us from the necessity of dependence and waiting upon our Father—but that He does give us.

In humbleness of mind Daniel expresses his unfitness for receiving such communications. First, one like one of the sons of men touches his lips and instructs him to speak to the Lord. He confesses his weakness—that there is no strength left in him. But "one like the appearance of a man ... strengthened me, and said. O man, greatly beloved, fear not: peace be unto thee, be strong, yea, be strong."

Until men are thoroughly established in peace, and their hearts know the real source of strength, they are not able to profit by God's Word. Here Daniel is set upon his feet, his mouth is opened, and his fears hushed before the Lord can open the Word to him. His heart must be in restful peace in the strength of the Lord.

W. Kelly

March **19** Tuesday

The flesh lusts against the Spirit, and the Spirit against the flesh: and these things are opposed one to the other, that ye should not do those things which ye desire; but if ye are led by the Spirit, ye are not under law. *(Galatians 5:17-18)*

The flesh and the Spirit have no point of agreement: the work of the one leaves no room for the other. God will not give His glory to another; and the flesh will not abandon its dishonest selfishness. If God is to be allowed to work, the energy of the flesh must cease. In fact, it is only His voice that can still the soul in order that His work may be seen and rejoiced in. But when flesh is active we will have no spirit of thankfulness, no recognition of God's true glory. It is not impossible for a believer to do what is pleasing to God, but the intrusion of the flesh has the effect of hindering our doing what we desire.

Nor is walking in the Spirit a requirement comparable to the exactions of law, as some souls conceive it. They try then to attain such a state. But there is no such thing as attainment here: it is rather the patience of faith and quiet rest in God's presence that is asked—no labor, no pressing, no forcing, for "If ye are led by the Spirit, ye are not under law." *The Spirit of God never leads a soul to set up legal standards as guides: He Himself guides the soul:* guides into all truth, engages the heart and mind with Christ, a standard infinitely more pure, more full than law. How sweet a place of rest is this, where one, not by constraint but willingly, rejoices to bow his shoulder to the easy yoke of the Lord Jesus.

L. M. Grant

Living for Christ, my members I yield,
Servants to God, forevermore sealed,
"Not under law," I'm now "under grace,"
Sin is dethroned, and Christ takes its place.
Glory be to God.

T. Ryder

March **20** Wednesday

Test all things; hold fast what is good.

(1 Thessalonians 5:21 NKJV)

A short blurb from *Servant* magazine caught my eye. It quoted Jonathan Edwards, a faithful preacher in the American colonies during the eighteenth century, as giving "Five signs that a revival is of God":

1. It raises people's esteem of Jesus as Son of God and Savior.
2. It leads them to turn away from sin and toward holiness.
3. It increases their love for the Bible.
4. It grounds them in the basic truths of the faith.
5. It evokes greater love for and service to God and other people.

These five tests are very helpful in evaluating the rash of revival movements going on in Christendom today. Without such guidelines, we can easily become drawn into either of two harmful extremes in viewing contemporary "revivals."

One extreme would view them all as powerful movements of the Spirit of God and ignore those who urge us to examine them more closely. The other extreme would regard them all as either Satanic delusions at worst or fleshly enthusiasm at best and criticize any who speak well of them. Between these two extremes, Edward's tests steer us into a balanced middle position. We do well to apply them, not only to "revival movements," but also to our own lives and local assemblies. What kind of revival is going on in our own hearts? Is our love and esteem for our Lord Jesus Christ growing?

Are our lives characterized by holiness? How much of our daily lives are we spending in the Bible? Are we being grounded and established in the basic truths of God's Word?

Is our love and service for the Lord and for other people on the increase? True revival always begins with individuals drawing near to God.

G. W. Steidl

Bring the whole tithe into the treasure-house, that there may be food in My house, and prove Me now herewith, saith Jehovah of hosts, if I open not to you the windows of the heavens, and pour you out a blessing, till there be no place for it. And I will rebuke the devourer for your sakes, and he shall not destroy the fruits of your ground ... And all nations shall call you blessed; for ye shall be a delightsome land, saith Jehovah of hosts.

(Malachi 3:10-12)

PROPHETS AND THEIR PROPHECIES–MALACHI (3)

In the previous chapter and earlier in this chapter the Lord had enumerated quite a list of things which His people were doing that displeased Him. There was hypocrisy; unfaithfulness in marriage; divorce; rejection of God's standards; sorcery; adultery; false swearing; oppression of hired servants, widows, fatherless, and strangers. Above all, they did not fear the Lord—and we know from other passages of the Word the importance of the fear of the Lord! To all this, the Lord adds the serious charge that they had been robbing Him in tithes and offerings.

How does the Lord assess our lives? Do we truly fear Him? If so, other things in our lives should fall into line. Are we robbing Him in some way: interest in His Word, time, finances, service, whatever it may be? Is our attitude that of God's people here in Malachi's time? They were saying, "It is vain to serve God; and what profit is it that we keep His charge?" (ch. 3:13-15).

The Lord pleads with His people, wanting to bless them. How He delights to bless when His own honor Him! He even wonderfully provided for His rebellious people for forty long years in the wilderness as they journeyed from Egypt to the Promised Land! He miraculously provided food in abundance at the gate of Samaria for His starving people in 2 Kings 7! How He would love to bless us too, "far exceedingly above all which we ask or think"!

E. P. Vedder, Jr.

In which time Moses was born, and was exceedingly lovely, who was nourished three months in the house of his father.

(Acts 7:20)

THE PARENTS' FAITH

According to Pharaoh's decree, issued shortly before the birth of Moses, the Israelites were to cast every newborn son into the river. What an exercise of soul it must have been for Jochebed during the long months prior to the birth of her child! Would it be a daughter whom she would have the right to keep, or a son?

The child came into the world, and it was a son, but not an ordinary boy. By faith his parents discerned he was exceedingly lovely— beautiful to God. Therefore his parents hid him.

There was no room in the world for this one whom God singled out from birth as special for Himself. Centuries later, there would be no room at Bethlehem for the Child Jesus. King Herod would try to slaughter Him just as Pharaoh tried to destroy Moses. Moses' parents were not afraid of the king's edict. For the first three months the parents did all they could to keep their child hidden. Yet the moment arrived when this was no longer possible. With what care the mother then prepared an ark of reeds, plastered it with resin and pitch, put the child in it, and placed it near the bank of the Nile. There his sister Miriam would watch him from afar.

For a few years the children of Christian parents are under their mother's special influence, protection, and care. Then the moment comes when they must be exposed to the world outside through contact with neighborhood children and in school. Knowing well she cannot keep her treasure with her forever, a Christian mother will carefully take every possible precaution to protect her child from being exposed to harmful influences during this new period. Above all, she will need faith to commit him to the care of the Lord who alone is able to keep him.

G. Andre

Having said these things, Jesus was troubled in spirit, and testified and said, Verily, verily, I say to you, that one of you shall deliver me up. The disciples therefore looked one on another, doubting of whom He spoke. Now there was at table one of His disciples in the bosom of Jesus, whom Jesus loved. Simon Peter makes a sign therefore to Him to ask who it might be of whom He spoke. But he, leaning on the breast of Jesus, says to Him, Lord, who is it? Jesus answers, He it is to whom I, after I have dipped the morsel, give it. And having dipped the morsel, He gives it to Judas son of Simon, Iscariote. *(John 13:21-26)*

The Eleven, stunned, as it seems, by this terrible disclosure, fail to grasp the meaning of the Lord's words. Judas has no such misapprehension. The presence of the Lord has become intolerable to this devil-possessed man. Having received the sop he arises. Since Judas was entrusted with the bag, the disciples judge he is leaving to meet the needs of the feast or to relieve the poor. Without a word Judas passes into the night, only a little later to pass into a deeper night—that horror of great darkness—from whence there is no return.

It has been remarked that in this entire solemn scene there is no denunciation of Judas, no reproach is heaped upon him, no word of expulsion is uttered against him, no demand to depart is given to him. The presence of a false one is revealed; the sin he is about to commit is foretold, the man who will commit it is indicated. Then, amid a silence more terrible than words, he leaves the light that was too searching, the holy Presence that he no longer could endure, and passes into the night for which no morning will ever dawn.

Let us remember that but for the grace of God, and the precious blood of Christ, we should each one be following Judas into the night.

H. Smith

Fear ye not their fear, and be not in dread. Jehovah of hosts, Him shall ye sanctify; and let Him be your fear, and let Him be your dread. And He will be for a sanctuary; and for a stone of stumbling, and for a rock of offense.   *(Isaiah 8:12-14)*

JESUS IS JEHOVAH (6)

The New Testament writers seamlessly and without hesitation connect Old Testament references concerning Jehovah to the Lord Jesus Christ. Sometimes they do this in a most striking manner. The apostle Peter is no different in this regard, as we will find in meditating upon today's verse.

Peter wrote his first epistle to encourage the saints who were suffering greatly because of persecution. The Christians were passing through the fiery crucible of suffering at the hand of Nero, as history has recorded. It was not just martyrdom, but a brutal death—unspeakable in its manner. The apostle calls it the "fiery trial" (1 Pet. 4:12 KJV), and to encourage them he quotes the prophet Isaiah saying that they should not be afraid of "their fear" (1 Pet. 3:14 "threats" NKJV). They should rather, **"sanctify the Lord the Christ in [their] hearts"** (1 Pet. 3:15 JND). How exquisite and remarkable is Peter's quotation of Isaiah! The prophet tells his hearers to sanctify **"Jehovah of hosts,"** and the apostle substitutes Christ for Jehovah!

But this is not all. Isaiah goes on to say that **"[Jehovah] will be … for a stone of stumbling, and for a rock of offense."** Peter again directly applies this to Christ—He was the "stone" which the leaders of Israel, "the builders," rejected. They cast Him away as worthless because He was "a stone of stumbling and rock of offense" (1 Pet. 2:7-8). This is also true for many today who reject Christ—they find the gospel offensive and they stumble because of Him. But for the believers of Peter's day and of the present time, this rejected Stone is precious and is none other than Jehovah of Hosts!

B. Reynolds

Be diligent to present yourself approved to God, a worker who does not need to be ashamed, rightly dividing the word of truth.
(2 Timothy 2:15 NKJV)

Paul was in a difficult situation in prison, yet was able to truly encourage his younger friend and co-worker. The apostle endured much hardship, but as a true overcomer he was concerned for the Lord's interests and, thus, about the next generations, from Timothy and onward. The young disciple worried about Paul's situation. So Paul encouraged Timothy in a number of ways, challenging him and strengthening him in view of carrying on the burden of the Lord's testimony. We find a similar concern with Peter, expressed in different words, that the generation after him might have spiritual zeal and the diligence of true overcomers (2 Pet. 1:5,10; 3:14).

The Lord's interests cannot be mixed with the interests of self-will or of this world. The Lord desires to have the only place in our hearts and lives. God's purpose is that Christ may be all to us and in us (Col. 3:11). "First love" and being an "overcomer" represent our side: a response of loving hearts and committed lives. Such commitment shows itself in a desire to pass God's test, "Present yourself approved to God"—not to gain man's approval, but rather God's.

In his instructions, Paul compares Timothy to a child committed to his father's interests, a soldier to his general, an athlete to his competition, or a farmer to his field. But here it is to a worker, facing great challenges, yet seeking to honor God. To do this, Timothy needed to use the right resources, in the right way, for the right purpose: so it should be with us. If he would become discouraged or wrongly influenced, he would not be approved, but keeping things in balance, rightly dividing God's Word, the Lord could support him.

A. E. Bouter

March   26   Tuesday

Ahab told Jezebel all that Elijah had done, and in detail how he had slain all the prophets with the sword ... And [Elijah] went a day's journey into the wilderness, and came and sat down under a certain broom-bush, and requested for himself that he might die; and said, It is enough: now, Jehovah, take my life; for I am not better than my fathers. *(1 Kings 19:1,4)*

After Elijah had a mighty victory for the Lord at Carmel, Queen Jezebel threatened him with execution and he, discouraged and disheartened, ran away to a desolate place. He sat under the broom-bush and asked God to take his life. We may be surprised that a man of God could have such an illustrious career of service and then suddenly be plunged into such a state of discouragement and soul weariness; but this is what can happen to us if we take our eyes off the Lord and focus instead on the situation around us!

It appears that when Elijah momentarily took his eyes off of God, he first tried to run away from his troubles, then sat down and gave up! This is a sad state for any child of God to be in, and yet how often when trial and challenge come do we find ourselves in just such a place of discouragement and self-pity. We should not be surprised when our adversary, Satan, and his demons, seek to use discouragement to block the gospel and destroy our testimony.

We too, can become weary and ready to give up when we become absorbed with our problems. We may begin to think that God can no longer use us or that He is setting us aside. But God does not cast His obedient servants aside when they fail! We see, in Elijah's case that God sent His angel to provide just what he needed to get ready for the work that still lay ahead of him. This same gracious God, who did not cast Elijah aside, but strengthened him, will strengthen and encourage us too!

S. J. Faulkner

Whatever ye do, do all things to God's glory.

(1 Corinthians 10:31)

As a boy I worked for a Scottish shoemaker named Dan Mackay, a forthright Christian. It was my responsibility to pound leather for shoe soles. A piece of cowhide would be cut to suit, then soaked in water. I had a piece of iron over my knees and, with a flat-headed hammer; I pounded these soles until they were hard and dry. It seemed an endless operation, and I wearied of it many times.

What made my task worse was the fact that, a block away, there was another shop, and in it sat a jolly, godless cobbler who regaled the neighborhood with lewd tales that made him dreaded by respectable parents. Yet, somehow, he seemed to thrive. I noticed that he never pounded the soles at all, but took them from the water and nailed them on, with the water splashing from them as he drove each nail in. One day I ventured inside. Timidly, I said, "I notice you put the soles on while still wet. Are they just as good as if they were pounded?" He gave me a wicked leer as he answered, "They come back all the quicker this way, my boy!"

Feeling I had learned something, I related the instance to my boss. Mr. Mackay stopped his work and opened his Bible to the passage that reads, "Whatever you do, do all to the glory of God." "Harry," he said, "I do not cobble shoes just for the money I get from my customers. I am doing this for the glory of God. I expect to see every shoe I have ever repaired in a big pile at the judgment seat of Christ, and I do not want the Lord to say to me in that day, 'Dan, this was a poor job.' I want Him to be able to say, 'Well done, good and faithful servant.'" He went on to explain that just as some men are called to preach, so he was called to fix shoes, and only as he did this well would his testimony count for God (cf. Col. 3:23-25).

H. A. Ironside

The sun shall no more be thy light by day, neither for brightness shall the moon give light unto thee; but Jehovah shall be thine everlasting light. *(Isaiah 60:19)*

This descriptive prophecy will be fulfilled for Israel during the Millennium and for all saints in eternity. God's thoughts have been *from* everlasting and they are *to* everlasting. In eternity there will be a nobler light—a peerless Sun—to supersede the need of all luminaries. There also, in John's vision was "no need of the sun nor of the moon, that they should shine … for the glory of God has enlightened it, and the lamp thereof is the Lamb" (Rev. 21:23).

Also, God's works and ways, His character and faithfulness, His ever-present fellowship and love, will form a perpetual theme and material for contemplation. The ever-new song of the ransomed will be the old strain of earth: "How precious are Thy thoughts unto me, O God! How great is the sum of them! If I would count them, they are more in number than the sand" (Ps. 139:17-18). Life may now be to you a dreary landscape, but a glorious resurrection-time is at hand, when the gladsome announcement shall be made, "Behold the winter is past … the time of singing is come … Arise, my love, my fair one, and come away!" (Song 2:11-13). Oh, blessed prospect!

In God's light, we shall see light (Ps. 36:9). All the unexplained things of the present will be made luminous for the glory of that unsetting sun. We can be certain of it for He says, "Assuredly as I have thought, so it shall come to pass; and as I have purposed, it shall stand," for "Jehovah of hosts hath purposed and who shall frustrate it? And his hand is stretched out, and who shall turn it back?" (Isa. 14:24,27).

J. R. MacDuff

> *There all's unsullied light,*
> *Our hearts let in its rays;*
> *And heav'nly light makes all things bright,*
> *Seen in that blissful gaze.*

J. N. Darby

March **29** Friday

When the thousand years have been completed, Satan shall be loosed from his prison, and shall go out to deceive the nations which are in the four corners of the earth. *(Revelation 20:7-8)*

In Ezekiel 45:25 we see that the sin offering, burnt offering, and meat offering are to be included in the sacrifices to be offered at the Feast of Tabernacles in millennial days. In Numbers 29 we get some most remarkable instruction concerning the sacrifices of the bullocks during the seven days of the feast. On the first day of the feast, the sacrifice consisted of thirteen young bullocks, two rams, and fourteen lambs of the first year. On the second day, there were but twelve bullocks offered. On the third day, eleven; the fourth day, ten: till on the seventh day we find but seven bullocks were offered unto the Lord. Does this tell us of a decreasing sense of value of the worth of the sacrifice that won for them this glorious kingdom? In the earthly side of the kingdom this would seem to be the case.

As the years pass by, their gratitude to the One to whom they owe all grows less and less. By the time the thousand years are finished, and the devil is loosed from his prison in the bottomless pit, we find nations, the number of which is as the sand of the sea, in the four quarters of the earth. These nations are ready to follow Satan to battle against the King of kings, who has held such just and gracious rule for a thousand years.

This may well be a very solemn lesson to us. Let us watch our love, lest it grow cold, like the Church in Ephesus (Rev. 2:4). Let us watch lest, day by day, our sacrifice of praise grow less. It is only as our eyes and hearts are engaged with that Blessed One who has done all for us, that the last day will find the same sacrifice as on the first day. May it be so with each one of us!

G. C. Willis

The Word became flesh and tabernacled among us (and we beheld His glory, glory as of an only-begotten from beside a father), full of grace and truth. *(John 1:14—W. Kelly Translation)*

Here it is not what the Word was, but what He became. He was God; He became flesh and dwelt among us, full of grace and truth. It was no transient vision, however momentous, as on the holy mount. It was a contemplation of His glory granted to His witnesses, not that of an earthly conqueror, nor Messianic even, but glory as of an only-begotten from beside a father.

No sword girds His thigh, no riding to victory, no terrible things in righteousness: the Incarnate Word dwelt among us, full of grace and truth. Such is He that was in and from the beginning, and thus known. He was the King undoubtedly, but not so portrayed here. He is infinitely more than King, even God, yet God on earth, Man dwelling among men, full of grace and truth. So only could God be displayed, unless in judgment which would have left no hope. But for infinitely different purposes had He come, as this passage itself declares in due season, perfectly knowing and feeling the universal evil of mankind.

He tabernacled among us full of grace and truth—it was not a visit or a theophany, as in the Old Testament. So He here manifested God, who is love. But grace is more; it is love in the midst of evil, rising above it, going down under it, overcoming it with good. And such was Jesus, sojourning on earth, full of truth withal; for grace brings in the truth and enables souls to receive truth and to bear it. He, and He only, was full of grace and truth. To make it known, to make God Himself thus known, He came. For as grace is the activity of divine love in the midst of evil, so truth is the revelation of all things as they really are. It comes from God Himself and brings His ways and counsels down to man, and every thought and feeling as well. So He dwelt among us, full of grace and truth.

W. Kelly

All Thy garments smell of myrrh, and aloes, and cassia, out of the ivory palaces, whereby they have made Thee glad. Kings' daughters were among Thy honorable women: upon Thy right hand did stand the queen in gold of Ophir. *(Psalm 45:8-9 KJV)*

CHRIST'S SUFFERING LOVE (3)

The aloes, the central spice of the three, speaks of the love that lay behind all the suffering. It was more fragrant and prized than all other spices; nothing to be compared with it ever came out of the mysterious East.

The aloes tree had to be cleft to its heart if the fragrance of it was to be disclosed. It was on Calvary's cross, when cleft by the sword of God's judgment against our sin, that Christ's heart disclosed all the greatness of His love. There is nothing in the universe more fragrant than that—the love of Christ, which passes knowledge.

Further, His love is far more precious than gold. If the world could offer all the gold it possesses to us in exchange for the knowledge of Christ's love, would any of us exchange that knowledge for so great an amount? We would not, for that love is more precious than gold. It cannot be purchased, but it has poured out its priceless wealth without reserve for us.

But while our Lord and Savior rightly expects that we should open our hearts to Him, this is not the end that He has in view. Nothing will satisfy Him but the marriage day. He has prepared a home for His bride; His heart is opened wide for her. So there comes the appeal, "Hearken, O daughter, and consider, and incline thine ear; forget also thine own people, and thy father's house; so shall the King greatly desire thy beauty: for He is thy Lord; and worship thou Him."

J. T. Mawson

April 1 Monday

Surely I count also all things to be loss on account of the excellency of the knowledge of Christ Jesus my Lord, on account of whom I have suffered the loss of all, and count them to be filth, that I may gain Christ *(Philippians 3:8)*

Our wishes are descriptive of ourselves. "As he thinketh in his heart so is he," the wisest of men said centuries ago. It is true today. There are times and circumstances so solemn and searching that a wish expressed at such times or in such circumstances unveils our innermost being. Our wish describes what we are in the hidden depth of our soul. It is so when death comes or friends are parting never to meet again. It is so in a great spiritual crisis, or in times of sore trial.

Paul expressed his dearest wish. Circumstances rendered the expression of it as recorded in Philippians 3:8-14, the unveiling of his innermost being. As we read the words we seem to feel the throbbings of his heart and the intensity of his all-consuming desire. He is drawing near the end of His life. It had been a busy, eventful life. It was for him, indeed, a solemn moment. Solemn it is for any of us when but a few grains are left in the hourglass of life, when our eager eyes are looking on a vast eternity, soon to be entered, when labor is to cease, when things appear as they really are, and all past activities are fixed beyond reach of change, be they approved or condemned.

Christ had won his heart. He counted all things loss for the excellency of the knowledge of Christ Jesus his Lord. He held nothing back, and nothing held him back, no matter how rugged the path that led to the goal. No matter how steep the hill, or if the way led through death itself, he would follow it to the very end. A bitter end as far as circumstances went, it doubtless was, but a glorious beginning as he entered eternity.

A. J. Pollock

The LORD looked upon [Gideon], and said, Go in this thy might ... have not I sent thee? *(Judges 6:14 KJV)*

Connect your service with nothing but God—not with any set of persons. You may be comforted by fellowship, and your heart refreshed; but you must work by your own faith and energy, without leaning on anyone else; for if you do, you cannot be a faithful servant. Service must ever be measured by faith and one's *own communion with God.* Saul even may be a prophet when he gets among the prophets; but David was always the same—in the cave or anywhere. A man's service must flow from himself, else there will be weakness.

In every age the blessing has been from individual agency. If it ceases to be this, it declines into worldly patterns. All must come immediately from God. The tendency of association is to make us lean upon one another. When there are great arrangements for carrying on work, there is not the recognition of the inherent blessing, which "tarries not for the sons of men." I don't tarry for man, if I have faith in God. Let a man act as the Lord leads him. The Spirit of God is not to be fettered by man.

All power arises from the direct energy of the Holy Spirit in the *individual.* Paul and Barnabas were sent forth by the Holy Spirit, recommended to the grace of God by the church at Antioch, but they had no communication with it till they returned. But then there was joyful concurring of love in the service that had been performed. He that had talents went and traded with them. Paul says: "Immediately I conferred not with flesh and blood." Where there is a desire to act, accompanied by real energy, a man will rise up and walk. If he cannot do this, the energy is not there, and the attempt to move is only restlessness and weakness.

Meat in Due Season

April 3 Wednesday

I fear lest by any means, as the serpent deceived Eve by his craft, so your thoughts should be corrupted from simplicity as to the Christ. *(2 Corinthians 11:3)*

The tendency to hanker after the elaborate, the obscure, the complicated, the far-fetched is always with us. The intellectual men of the world find the gospel far too simple, and they stumble at it. Believers, whose strong point is their intellect, always have a tendency in the same direction, unless they walk in the spirit of self-judgment as regards intellectualism. If they do not maintain self-judgment, all their elaborations, their deep and obscure thoughts, only eventually result in something that corrupts from simplicity as to the Christ.

The mind is a very important part of man, and Satan's acutest beguilements are aimed at it. It is far from being the whole of a man: his affections and his conscience have a very large place. The trouble is that the intellectual person is very apt to give a much larger place to his mind than Scripture gives to it. He forgets that God reveals His truth to us, not for our intellectual enjoyment, but that it may command our hearts, appeal to our consciences, and govern our lives. Let that be properly realized, and we at once find plenty to occupy our spiritual energies in the profound simplicities of the truth, and any itching desire we ever had for mere complexities and novelties and obscurities forsakes us.

"Simplicity as to the Christ!" That is what we need. To know Him: to love Him, as united in heart to Him: to adore Him: to serve Him: that is it! If our minds are thus stayed upon Him in uncorrupted simplicity, all else will be added unto us, and we shall be maintained in the fervor of "first love." Paul knew well that if Satan succeeded in his beguilings at this point, he would succeed all along the line.

F. B. Hole

Unto you that fear My name shall the Sun of Righteousness arise with healing in His wings; and ye shall go forth and leap like fatted calves. And ye shall tread down the wicked; for they shall be ashes under the soles of your feet in the day that I prepare, saith Jehovah of hosts. Remember the law of Moses My servant, which I commanded unto him in Horeb for all Israel.

(Malachi 4:2-4)

PROPHETS AND THEIR PROPHECIES–MALACHI (4)

We are almost at the end of Malachi's burden, in fact, almost at the end of the Old Testament. What a tremendous contrast between these verses and the end of the New Testament! But we must not forget that the law was given by Moses; grace and truth subsists through Jesus Christ. He, the Word, became flesh and dwelt among us, full of grace and truth, 400 years after Malachi wrote.

Jehovah had keenly felt His people's lack of honor and lack of fear. He had taken note of their insolent back talk. He would deal with this. The day will come, "the great and terrible day of Jehovah," "burning as a furnace; and all the proud and all that work wickedness shall be stubble; and the day ... shall burn them up ... so that it shall leave them neither root nor branch." Such is His righteous judgment with regard to the earth and His earthly people. Those of His earthly people who fear His name shall have a part in treading down the wicked in that day.

Yet, we do not leave the Old Testament simply with the threat of "lest I come and smite the earth with a curse." No, amid all the wickedness there were also those that feared Jehovah and thought upon His name. Their fellowship was with one another, not with the world around them. Jehovah observed and heard them and kept a record of them. They will be His peculiar treasure in that coming day; He will spare them; and to their joy Christ, the Sun of Righteousness, will arise for them with healing in His wings.

E. P. Vedder, Jr.

He that hath an ear let him hear what the Spirit saith unto the churches.
(Revelation 3:22 KJV)

The seven churches take in the whole professing company, and are admonished for their failure to be a faithful testimony to the Lord during His absence. Nevertheless, He singles out a little remnant that cleaves to His name and word, and commends them for it. However, the terms "the rest" in Thyatira; "a few names" in Sardis; "a little strength" in Philadelphia, are a painful reminder that we live in a day of small things. How faithful and patient is our Lord who in the face of such departure, would yet redirect our eyes to Himself as our sole resource.

Do we want security? He is the One that holds the seven stars in His right hand. Is it comfort in tribulation we need? He is the First and the Last, who was dead, and is alive.

Is it doctrine, or reproof, or correction, or instruction in righteousness? He has the sharp sword with two edges. Is it life and liberty that we need? He is the Son of God in whom life is inherent; therefore he that has the Son has life.

Is it spiritual power? He has the seven Spirits of God. Do we need an example for godly living? Contemplate Him that is holy, Him that is true. Is it opportunity to serve Him? He has the key of David; He opens and no man shuts; and shuts and no man opens. He is the great administrator of all things. Do we need reassurance? He is the Amen for "all the promises of God in Him are yea, and in Him, Amen." All of the foregoing is a reminder that He is the All-Sufficient One.

Has your love gone so cold that He is standing at your heart's door, knocking? If you hear His voice and open the door, He will come in, and sup with you and you with Him." Finally, He promises that those who overcome will sit with Him in His throne even as He has overcome and is now seated on His Father's throne.

R. A. Barnett.

We see Jesus. *(Hebrews 2:9)*

In reading the Gospels, it is very instructive to find presented to us, not a system of doctrines, but a living Person, even the Lord Jesus Christ, the Son of God. "The Word became flesh, and dwelt among us (and we have contemplated His glory, a glory as of an only begotten with a father), full of grace and truth" (Jn. 1:14). In the simple but vivid and exquisitely beautiful narratives of the evangelists He lives and moves before us. We hear His words of grace and see His acts of love.

The disciples were drawn to Him, and were occupied with Him. They were ignorant of much truth, but they knew Him who is Truth incarnate, and who was then manifested as the living truth and as grace come down among men. Thus Peter says for himself and the rest, "Lord, to whom shall we go? Thou hast words of life eternal; and we have believed and known that Thou art the holy One of God" (Jn. 6:68-69). Thus it is now. The Lord Jesus has died for our sins, but He has risen again. "For if, being enemies, we have been reconciled to God through the death of His Son, much rather, having been reconciled, we shall be saved in the power of His life" (Rom. 5:10). The eye of faith fixes itself not on a dead Christ, but on a risen, living, glorified Savior.

The constant effort of Satan is to draw away our thoughts and our hearts from Christ. How easy it is to have the mind engaged with ordinances, doctrines, or even our service for Christ, instead of cultivating fellowship with Christ Himself. The casket is thought of more than the jewel; the drapery is observed more than the figure. Yet the true blessing of the soul is ever found in steadily contemplating the glorified Person of the Lord Jesus Christ with the eye of faith.

Meat in Due Season

Jehovah appeared to [Abraham] by the oaks of Mamre. And he sat at the tent-door in the heat of the day ... and saw ... three men standing near him ... he ran to meet them from the tent-door, and bowed himself to the earth, and said ... Let now a little water be fetched, that ye may wash your feet. *(Genesis 18:1-4)*

JESUS IS JEHOVAH (7)

While Abraham sat at the door of his tent next to the oak trees of Mamre, Jehovah appeared to him. This most interesting of scenes is deeply instructive and brings to light in a very touching way, the grace and humility of the Lord Jesus. Jehovah appeared to the patriarch in this way: when Abraham looked up he saw "three men." We read later that two of the men were the angels who went down into Sodom to deliver Lot (Gen. 18:22; 19:1). However, Jehovah remained behind speaking to Abraham about the events that were to unfold.

But what a scene in which we view Jehovah and the two angels as the subjects of Abraham's reverent hospitality! He provides a little water so they could *wash their feet* and rest under the tree. How precious to see Jehovah in these humble conditions washing His own feet under the tree with the water provided by Abraham, the friend of God. This is the *first mention* of footwashing in the Bible and as such is richly suggestive.

The Gospel of John presents to us the "True God and Eternal Life" who was manifested here in this world; this is what is foreshadowed in Genesis 18—a visit by a divine Person. It is in this Gospel, where we read that the Lord Jesus poured water into a basin and "began to wash the feet of the disciples" (Jn. 13:5). Abraham had provided water for his guests but did not wash their feet. But here we see Him, who is Jehovah, in the lowly form of a servant, not only providing the water, but also washing the feet of His disciples! What a rich object lesson of humility and lowly service for our own hearts!

B. Reynolds

Use diligence to come to me quickly.   *(2 Timothy 4:9)*

Second Timothy has often been called Paul's spiritual testament, for Timothy himself, as well as for the generations of believers after him. Paul wrote this letter in a cold Roman prison cell to encourage Timothy to continue and not give up. In it, Paul challenged him—and all that would follow "the narrow path"—to be true overcomers. What does that mean? The apostle desired that Timothy would keep following the Lord Jesus, no matter how difficult the circumstances, obstacles, or attacks.

Paul found himself in a dark and terrible dungeon, yet continued as a real example of what "first love" is all about. Christ everything, for us and in us, is God's norm (Col. 3:11) and Paul lived up to it in very trying circumstances. The Lord Jesus wants to be *all* for every believer, wherever and in whatever circumstances he may be. The reason for this is simple, yet profound: *Christ is all-sufficient*. Realizing this through faith, Paul was *not* discouraged, even in his extremely tough situation. Many believers had forsaken Paul (2 Tim. 1:15), possibly because of his arrest by the authorities who looked at him as a criminal guilty of death. Yet Paul was an excellent overcomer. So also were several other believers mentioned in this letter. They had a spiritual zeal for the Lord, a God-honoring commitment. They were not carnal or selfish, but were focused on the Lord and His interests.

The challenge that Paul left with Timothy, was to be such an example: "Make every effort to come to me soon" (2 Tim. 4:9 NASB) adding, "For Demas has forsaken me, having loved the present age." Demas, one of Paul's close co-workers, had not lost his salvation! Sadly, the Lord was no longer Demas' first and all, and so he had lost interest in staying and working with Paul: *Demas had lost his first love*. What about you and me?

A. E. Bouter

This is the message which we have heard from Him, and declare to you, that God is light, and in Him is no darkness at all. If we say that we have fellowship with Him, and walk in darkness, we lie, and do not practice the truth. But if we walk in the light as He is in the light, we have fellowship with one another, and the blood of Jesus Christ His Son cleanses us from all sin.

(1 John 1:5-7)

"In the light" is the sphere of the believer's walk, and *every* believer walks there. It has been well remarked that this is a matter of *where* we walk, not *how* we walk. Notice that we are not only told that "God is light" in verse 5, but in verse 7, "He is in the light." Though His nature is eternally "light," yet in the Old Testament He dwelt "in the thick darkness," for He had not been revealed in the blessedness of His nature, as He is now in the Person of His Son. But now every believer walks in the light of this marvelous manifestation: it is the only place of blessing for anyone today. Moreover, it links every believer together in fellowship, the fellowship of the same blessed life, for all these are of the same family, having the same nature in common.

Yet, we must consider the fact that this light is absolute truth and righteousness, and those who are in the light cannot deny that they have sinned. How can they then have a place there? The answer is immediately given: "The blood of Jesus Christ His Son cleanses us from all sin." Only in the light does this precious blood have its wondrous application, for the light exposes, and only when exposed is sin rightly judged and put away: the claims of the light are fully met by that precious blood, and all hindrance to fellowship is removed.

L. M. Grant

David went up, and all Israel … to bring up from thence the ark of God, of Jehovah, who sitteth between the cherubim … And they carried the ark of God on a new cart. *(1 Chronicles 13:6-7)*

DAVID'S NEW CART (1)

Would you not have thought with all that desire to have things right, that the King—the leader—would have inquired of God as to whether He had given any instructions as to the transport of His own ark? We should be sure to think that he would have gone to the Scriptures to find out the right way. But it was not so. David thought, like many a person today, that a **new cart** was a very good mode of carrying that ark. The way it had reached the land of Israel would surely do to take it to Jerusalem (1 Sam. 6:7). That the Philistines—God's enemies—should furnish the idea was a small matter in his eyes.

What is the new cart? It is anything that is not according to the pattern of Scripture. I could show you some hundreds of new carts, in Christendom today. What different shapes and sizes, characters and colors these new carts present as you glance over Christendom's systems.

The ark of God was connected with His worship—it was the central item of the tabernacle. The ark spoke of Christ, the Person of Christ. The mercy-seat spoke of Him and His work. Inside the ark there was the golden pot of manna, Israel's food in the wilderness; Aaron's rod that budded, Christ's priestly grace in resurrection; and there were the tables of stone, for the law was hidden in Him. Israel had to carry that ark and its contents through the desert.

We Christians also have to carry the ark. Going back to Israel passing through the wilderness, you find there were priests, Levites, and the people, or warriors. Today every Christian is a priest in worship, a Levite for service and everyday work, and a warrior against the enemy.

W. T. P. Wolston

Zacharias his father was filled with the Holy Spirit, and prophesied, saying, Blessed be the Lord the God of Israel, because He has visited and wrought redemption for His people, and raised up a horn of deliverance for us in the house of David His servant ... And thou, child, shalt be called the prophet of the Highest; for thou shalt go before the face of the Lord to make ready His ways; to give knowledge of deliverance to His people.

(Luke 1:67-69,76-77)

PROPHETS AND THEIR PROPHECIES—ZACHARIAS

Chronologically speaking, Zacharias is the first New Testament prophet. This man, the father of John the Baptist, was a priest. He and his wife Elizabeth had already grown aged when an angel appeared to him as he was offering incense in the temple. The angel told him that his supplications had been heard, and that his barren wife would bear a son who should be named John. John would in time turn many Israelites to the Lord their God.

Zacharias initially was skeptical of the angel's words. The angel then introduced himself as "Gabriel, who stand before God." He told Zacharias that because of his unbelief he would not be able to speak until these things should be fulfilled. Zacharias, now unable to speak, spent the next months at home.

The baby's birth unleashed great rejoicing. Relatives and neighbors all came over to circumcise and name the child. When Zacharias insisted that the baby's name was John, he was once again able to speak. Filled with the Holy Spirit and no longer silent, he blessed God and prophesied. In his joyful words is set before us the true object of all prophecy—Christ, the Horn of Deliverance from the house of David, the Dayspring from on High! He would be the fulfillment of all that the prophets had spoken. Zacharias' little son, he said, would be called the prophet of the Highest and would go before the face of the Lord to make ready His ways.

E. P. Vedder, Jr.

Thus saith Jehovah ... Because ye have obeyed the commandment of Jonadab your father ... therefore ... there shall not fail
to Jonadab the son of Rechab a man to stand before Me, forever. *(Jeremiah 35:18-19)*

The Rechabites stand out in Scripture as a special family. Over 200 years after their forefathers, Rechab and Jonadab, had died, they still maintained the same family distinctives: they were to drink no wine; they were to live in tents as nomads; and they were neither to sow seeds nor plant vineyards.

What can we learn from them? First, they were willing to practice a life of self-denial for the sake of obedience. That sure fits us as Christians. It is not that we should obey ancient ancestors. Many of us can't trace our genealogy back more than a couple of generations, nor do we know if our ancestors were saints or scoundrels. Rather, we should obey God, even if this involves self-denial. Jesus said, "If anyone will come after Me, let him deny himself and take up his cross."

Second, their lives were based on solid values. They would not abandon these on the basis of personal convenience, nor did they judge that these values were no longer valid because they were very old. As Christians, our values rest upon the Word of God, written hundreds of years ago, but still alive and powerful in the lives of those who obey it. We do not hold them because they are old, but because they are true. Personal convenience, a subtle corrupter of the truth of God, did not motivate the Rechabites to change their values. Nor should it motivate us.

Third, God used their lives as an example to the rebellious people of Judah and Jerusalem. Do we catch the force of His argument? The Rechabites performed the commands of their forefathers— mere men—but Judah refused to obey the God of Israel. What kind of example do our lives present to those who are following in our footsteps?

G. W. Steidl

Herein do I exercise myself, to have always a conscience void of offense toward God, and toward men. *(Acts 24:16 KJV)*

When two voices within are opposed to each other, while seeking to do the Lord's will, how am I to determine which is His will for me?

These two voices are:

First, the conscience exercised by the Spirit of God through the Word of God and,

Second, the natural heart (Jer. 17:9) prompted by Satan to oppose the will of God.

The single eye for the Christian is singleness of purpose, having only one object, God's glory, and not being double-minded trying to serve two masters (Jas. 1:8).

As to any work for the Lord, if it is really to the Lord's glory, then it will be in accordance with the Word of God. The next questions are: Has the Lord given me this particular work which my heart desires to do? and, When is the right time to do it?

In Numbers 4 the sons of Levi were charged with the service of the work at the tabernacle. Not all received the same work; some could carry the ark, the golden altar, or the candlestick; others had to carry the heavy pillars and sockets; while still others had only the pins. Yet each one had a part in this work for the Lord's glory, and it was up to each individual to be faithful in his allotted task. Every service is important in its place even when not much outward display and glory, not much being in the limelight, is associated with it. One with a single eye is careful for the Lord's glory and sets himself aside.

We have the Spirit of God and the Word of God, and as children of the Father we need no signs. He will guide us with His eye (Ps. 32:8).

The law having a shadow of good things to come, and not the very image of the things, can never with those sacrifices which they offered year by year continually make the comers thereunto perfect. For then would they not have ceased to be offered? … But in those sacrifices there is a remembrance again made of sins every year.
(Hebrews 10:1-3 KJV)

The experiences of a lifetime may include terribly traumatic pains or devastating losses. Their imprint will often remain throughout a person's life. Still, many have found that over time there may be some sense of ease from even the deepest grief.

However, we can never diminish the guilt of sin. In Old Testament times, the Day of Atonement in particular would bring a renewed remembrance of sins every year. Two goats were brought, and one was sacrificed. Then, upon the living goat the high priest would confess "all the iniquities of the children of Israel, and all their transgressions in all their sins" (Lev. 16:21). Look at the emphasis of "all!" We can just imagine the impact this would have on a devout Jewish man or woman. Any forgotten guilt of the past year would come rushing back on that solemn occasion, a day for all Israel to afflict their souls (Lev. 23:27).

How different it is for believers today! The Lord Jesus has offered Himself once, fulfilling the will of God and perfecting forever those who are sanctified (Heb. 10:5-14). There is still a remembrance for Christians, but it is of an entirely different character. We have the bread and the cup, and the word of the Lord who said, "Do this in remembrance of Me." As often as guilt may accuse us, we can remember the meaning of those symbols and worship Him.

S. J. Campbell

Not all the blood of beasts / On Jewish altars slain
Could give the guilty conscience peace, / Or wash away its stain.

I. Watts

April **15** Monday

The words of Nehemiah ... the Jews that had escaped, who were left of the captivity ... they said to me ... the wall of Jerusalem is in ruins, and its gates are burned with fire. *(Nehemiah 1:1-3)*

Taking a general view of this particular movement of the Spirit of God in these last days, can we not see the revivals are analogous to those of the days of Ezra and Nehemiah? In the revival of the early part of the 19th century, God used men of great spiritual and intellectual endowments, men of great force of character, who in any sphere of life would have been leaders of men. Through these men the great truths concerning the Church were revived. Later there came to the front those who gave an immense impetus to the study of prophetic truth, and by their ministry the blessed hope of the coming of Christ, and all the glories connected therewith, were revived to the Church.

Today the conflict is not so much about the exposition of the truth itself, but about the walls and the gates by which the truth is maintained. If holy separation, of which the walls are the symbol, and the exercise of godly care in discipline and access to the privileges of God's house as set forth by the gates, are not maintained, the truth that has been recovered will soon be lost. And as in Nehemiah's day, so in our day, the attempt to build the walls and set up the gates entails conflict—strenuous opposition from within and from without.

And as then, so now, every possible plea is urged against the maintenance of the walls and the gates. The flesh is ever ready to plead the demands of the Lord's service, the liberty of the servant, the help of saints in human organizations, the preaching of the gospel to sinners—things so right in themselves—in opposition to the walls and the gates. And on the other hand let it be noted: legal flesh is quite capable of misusing the walls and the gates for sectarian ends and party purposes.

H. Smith

See what love the Father has given to us, that we should be called the children of God. For this reason the world knows us not, because it knew Him not. Beloved, now are we children of God, and what we shall be has not yet been manifested; we know that if it is manifested we shall be like Him, for we shall see Him as He is. *(1 John 3:1-2)*

To those redeemed by the precious blood of Christ the Father's heart is free to flow forth in its unutterable fullness. The heart of the recipient in turn glows in delight in contemplation of that love. Precious, living reality! But the attention of the child of God must be drawn to this by the Word of God. The awakening word *See* is intended to kindle the earnest interest of the soul in this marvelous outflow of the Father's heart, so vital to the welfare of all His children. To know that we are loved perfectly, eternally, and with infinite wisdom is a most wonderful answer to all the present exercises of trial and conflict on earth.

But not only is this love emphasized here, but its manner—"what manner of love." Philanthropy may call itself love because it gives lavishly, and perhaps lifts one out of misery and poverty into prosperity and comfort. In a certain sense this may be called love, but it is far short of the Father's love. Here is a manner of love that not only rescues enemies from a state of sin, rebellion, and ruin; clothes, feeds, and enriches them; but is satisfied with nothing less than bringing them into His own house permanently as His own children. True love finds its delight in the nearness of its objects. And He owns such publicly as His children, taking delight in calling them this. Let us meditate well upon the noble dignity and sweetness of this holy established relationship, and walk consistently with it.

L. M. Grant

They carried the ark of God on a new cart ... and Uzza and Ahio drove the cart ... Uzza put forth his hand to hold the ark; for the oxen had stumbled. And the anger of Jehovah was kindled against Uzza, and He smote him.   *(1 Chronicles 13:7,9-10)*

DAVID'S NEW CART (2)

Now the particular work of the Levites, we learn from Numbers 4:15 was to carry the ark. And that is what David found out afterwards. But he had not found it out here. I do not doubt God has recorded this for our instruction; how even an earnest person with a large heart, who had the interests of God very deeply at heart, might go astray while seeking to serve God, if he were not absolutely in subjection to the word of the Lord.

"And Uzza and Ahio drove the cart." And by and by the oxen stumble. Of course they do. Uzza thought he could take care of God's ark. But the fact is, God can take care of His own ark, and if Uzza attempts to support the ark, immediately the hand of the Lord is shown. You may depend upon it, the *new-cart* style of things in relation to Christ's Church or Christ's gospel does not do for God. What do you mean by the new cart? Everything, whether in worship or service, that is not absolutely according to the pattern of Scripture, but after some human pattern, which consequently cannot be divine, and therefore should have no authority over the conscience of an obedient child of God.

Uzza's death woke David up to the error of his ways. At first he judged God—later he judged himself. "And the ark of God remained with the family of Obed-Edom in his house three months. And the Lord blessed the house of Obed-Edom, and all that he had" (v. 14). Those three months brought deep blessing into the house of Obed-edom, and during them David evidently took to studying and following God's instructions, which led to his being greatly blessed, as we shall see.

W. T. P. Wolston

As for me, it is good for me to draw near to God. *(Psalm 73:28)*

There is no living comfortably and there is no living with the peace and joy of the Holy Spirit in the heart, if we wander from the simplicity of our confidence in Christ. There are many believers who wander out of their place. What now is a believer's place? A believer's place is in the bosom of his Lord, or at the right hand of his Master, or sitting at His feet like Mary. Ah! Some of you never woke in the morning without thinking of Him, and all day long a sense of His presence was in your heart. How you grudged the world the hours you had to give to business; and when you locked up your heart at night, you always gave Jesus Christ the key! How sweet His ordinances were to you then, because you could see Christ through them! How delightful were prayer meetings and Bible studies then, because you saw Jesus there and talked with Him!

But what about your present state? Perhaps you have wandered from your place; you are not living near to Christ as you used to do. Hence spiritual things have but very little comfort in them; they are dull and tedious; and services which were once as marrow and fatness to you have now become dry bones. Your prayer-closet, too, is much neglected; your Bible is not studied as it was. You have lost your first love.

I appeal to you, have you not lost also your first comfort? Are you not like a bird that has wandered from her nest? Believe me, there is no solid joy, no seraphic rapture, no hallowed peace this side of heaven, except by living close under the shadow of the cross, and nestling in the arms of Jesus.

Oh! That we should be so foolish! The bird does not forget her nest but we do forget our Lord. We have need to say with the psalmist, "Return unto thy rest, O my soul, for the Lord hath dealt bountifully with thee!"

C. H. Spurgeon

One thing is needful: and Mary hath chosen that good part, which shall not be taken away from her. *(Luke 10:42 KJV)*

We read about Mary of Bethany on three occasions: the first is here, the second when the Lord Jesus raised her brother Lazarus from the dead (Jn. 11), and the last when she anointed Him with precious ointment (Jn. 12). Each time we find her at His feet. This is the place to be if we are to learn His Word, His ways and His worship, as Mary did in that order on these three occasions. No wonder then that He spoke so plainly to Martha when she would have replaced her sister's communion with Him with household duties.

We need not add our criticism to our Lord's words to Martha. She had done well in receiving Him into her home, and household duties have their place. But how often we allow less worthy things than preparing a meal to draw us away from Him. Mary's restful, submissive, and attentive enjoyment of His presence was the bedrock of her spiritual experience; the *one thing* needful if she was to grow spiritually as the second and third occasions of patient waiting and silent worship show she did.

When Mary came to give that most eloquent expression of worship it was literally like the frankincense on the meal offering (Lev. 6:15). The Lord alone appreciated it. She had received from Him, and now He, in the closing days of His life as the Man of Sorrows, received from her. In addition, she seems to have been the only one among His disciples—even the twelve—who realized He would rise again, and so she anointed Him in His life while she could. He said, "She has done what she could. She has come beforehand to anoint My body for burial" (Mk. 14:8 NKJV). What a beautiful blend of heartfelt love and spiritual intelligence characterized this woman who had sat at His feet and heard His word. Oh to be like her!

S. Attwood

There was no passover like to that [held] in Israel from the days of Samuel the prophet; neither did all the kings of Israel hold such a passover as Josiah held ... After all this, when Josiah had arranged the house, Necho king of Egypt came up to fight against Karkemish at the Euphrates; and Josiah went out against him. *(2 Chronicles 35:18,20)*

Three words stand out in our verse today: **"After all this."** Josiah was one of the godliest kings in the history of Israel. He had cleansed Judah of idols, gave the Word of God a central place in the life of the nation, and reinstituted the worship of the LORD in the Passover. Indeed, in all the history of Israel there never had been a Passover like it. But at the close of his life we read the words, **"after all this."** Josiah involved himself in a battle to which the LORD had not called him. He disguised himself but was mortally wounded by the enemy.

There is a solemn but salutary lesson to be found in these three words. Josiah's restoration of the worship of God is a picture of the great revivals and recovery of the truth to Christians. After centuries of error and superstition the Lord's Supper was again celebrated in New Testament simplicity; the priesthood of believers was recognized, and the truth of the *one body* acted upon. The Bible also was opened up with clarity and authority.

Yet, **"after all this"** failure came in. These very Christians were sidetracked by battles to which the Lord had not called them. Just as Josiah had disguised himself, they too, acted out of character and failed to walk up to the truth that the Lord in grace had recovered to them. The bright days of blessing came to an end. However, the Lord has not forsaken His people. The truth that was recovered *then* still challenges us to *walk worthy* of its calling *now* and the Lord's grace is still able to maintain us in a day of declension and departure.

B. Reynolds

Who in the days of His flesh, when He had offered up prayers and supplications with strong crying and tears ... Though He were a Son, yet learned He obedience by the things which He suffered. *(Hebrews 5:7-8 KJV)*

Here we are directed to His earthly path. Suffering was to be distinctively His portion. Our sin and our misery but furnished the opportunity to divine love, and this is only shown and learned in Christ, in Him that suffered infinitely here below—and Christ alone from the mystery of His person was capable of such suffering. Thus has He glorified, and thus reached hearts opened by grace to feel in our measure the wonders of His love.

In the days of His flesh we behold the surface and hear the sound of His sorrows which God alone was able to fathom. For this, as for other reasons essential to the purpose of God and the blessing of man, the Word was made flesh and tabernacled among us, and obeyed unto death, yea, death of the cross. And if ever prayers and supplications, if ever strong crying and tears were realities for the heart before God, His were. For His divine nature did not screen Him from pain, grief, humiliation, or suffering, but rather gave Him competency of person to endure perfectly, while all was accepted in absolute dependence on, and subjection to His Father.

It was no small thing for His love to have hatred, and to be despised and rejected of men; not only not to be honored by the people of God and His people, but to be esteemed stricken, smitten of God, and afflicted. More yet, He was deserted by all His disciples, denied by one, betrayed by another; and, far the most terrible of all and wholly different from all, He was forsaken of God just when He most needed His consolation and support. But so it must have been if sin was to be duly judged in His sacrifice, if our sins were to be completely borne away, and God to be glorified as to evil adequately and forever.

W. Kelly

Do your utmost to come before winter.   *(2 Timothy 4:21 NKJV)*

Earlier in this chapter, Paul had challenged Timothy to make every possible effort to come soon (v. 9). Paul wanted his spiritual child to be a true overcomer, to go against the stream, and to come to him at Rome. But there were hindrances to avoid. Winter is a season with great difficulties, as Paul knew from his experience in Acts 27. He encouraged his spiritual son to count on God and to exert utmost effort. Paul wanted him to be an overcomer, and come *before winter*, when traveling would no longer be possible. Paul needed Timothy's help to survive in the harsh conditions he found himself in, as described in chapter 4.

Furthermore, Paul asked Timothy to give his greetings to Prisca and Aquila, as well as to the household of Onesiphorus (ch. 4:19). This committed couple had worked with Paul over the years and the fact that they are mentioned together with Onesiphorus' household, seems to indicate that this household, or at least most of them, had not gone with the defection. Paul, therefore, prayed for mercy to Onesiphorus' house in view of "that day" (2 Tim. 1:16), when all will be manifested before the judgment seat of Christ (2 Cor. 5:10).

For believers, the judgment seat of Christ is not something to be afraid of, but rather to look forward to. During this session, the Lord will manifest each believer's life, showing how He evaluates every detail. He will do so with all born-again Christians, so that from then on each will have exactly the same thoughts as the Lord about everything in his or her life. This way, there will be perfect harmony between each believer and the Lord, and we will share eternal bliss with Him. After the judgment seat the Lord will come back to this world to be glorified in His saints (2 Th. 1:10).

A. E. Bouter

April   **23**   Tuesday

I know the thoughts that I think toward you, saith the Lord, thoughts of peace, and not of evil, to give you an expected end.
(Jeremiah 29:11 KJV)

The Lord of hosts hath sworn, saying, Surely as I have thought, so shall it come to pass; and as I have purposed, so shall it stand.
(Isaiah 14:24 KJV)

In considering the power and majesty of God we are made to realize that whatever His purpose is, He is able to carry it through, and there is no creature power that can prevent His doing so. It is sheer folly to think one can go against His purpose with any success. So the realization in our souls of God's invincible power should have the wholesome effect upon us of restraining us from any course of self-will. Whenever a child of God sets aside God's will to pursue a course of his own, he does so to his own hurt; for he has, in fact, plunged into the battle against Omnipotence with nothing on his side but creature strength and he is certain to lose in the end.

But on the other hand, what a source of peace and comfort for the believer who has surrendered his will to God. God over all things blessed for evermore (Rom. 9:5) is his Father, and he an object of His special love and solicitude. His thoughts are always thoughts of peace towards His children for them to rest upon in all the circumstances of life, however monotonous or changing they may be.

Ever remind yourself then of this great fact. Your Father's hand is acting for you in every circumstance, guided by His thoughts of peace, as the moving power behind the scene working all things together for your good. You can't remind yourself too often of this blessed peace-giving, soul-steadying fact; for it is the bright rainbow in the clouds and the anchor that holds you fast and keeps you from being driven by the storm.

E. C. Hadley

Behold, Rebekah came out ... And the man stooped, and bowed down before Jehovah, and said, Blessed be Jehovah, God of my master Abraham, who ... has led me to the house of my master's brethren.
(Genesis 24:15,26-27)

THE GOOD AND FAITHFUL SERVANT (3)

Genesis 24 sets before us the characteristics of a good and faithful servant. Every child of God in the right spiritual condition desires to serve the Lord Jesus Christ, and to hear one day from His mouth these wonderful words: "Well done, good and faithful servant!" For this reason it is important that we learn how to be good and faithful in serving our Lord.

Abraham's servant is a good example. After getting clear instructions from his master, he began his journey to the appointed place, and the first thing he did was to pray. He prayed for the success of his mission in order to bring joy to his master's heart. And because he had that as his goal, before he finished praying the answer was on the way. He did not rush to any action, but attentively watched the Lord working in Rebecca until it became certain to him that she was the one chosen by the Lord for Isaac. What a glorious thing to be able to say with certainty: "The Lord has led me." Alas that such words are frequently uttered flippantly! O that the Lord may grant us to be led by Him in serving Him.

As the servant saw God's hand in leading him in such a marvelous way, and saw the Lord's excellent choice of a bride for Isaac, he stooped and bowed down *before Jehovah*. He worshipped. He acknowledged God's wonderful help and blessed the Lord. He did not let the joy of his success make him forget who granted him the success. Two things are very obvious in this story: he was a man of faith, and secondly, his desire was to bring joy to his master.

A. M. Behnam

There was a man sent from God, his name John. He came for witness, that he might witness concerning the Light, that all might believe through him ... he ... acknowledged, I am not the Christ ... They said therefore to him ... What sayest thou of thyself? He said, I am the voice of one crying in the wilderness, Make straight the path of the Lord, as said Esaias the prophet.

(John 1:6-7,20,22-23)

PROPHETS AND THEIR PROPHECIES—
JOHN THE BAPTIST (1)

Luke's Gospel gives us the beautiful story of the birth of John the Baptist. John's Gospel simply introduces us to him as "a man sent from God," and tells us the purpose for which he was sent: to "witness concerning the Light." Isaiah and Malachi had spoken of his mission; the angel Gabriel and his own father Zacharias had foretold what he would do. Here we see him in action.

Again and again in John 1 we see John the Baptist witnessing of Jesus. "This was He of whom I said, He that comes after me is preferred before me, for He was before me" (v. 15). The Jewish religious leaders want to know more about this messenger and ask about his credentials for crying out his message. But he does not want to get into discussion about himself—he has a message to bring about Another. This is what is all-important to him!

The more questions he is asked about himself, the more succinct his answers. "Thou, who art thou?" **"I am not the Christ."** "What then? Art thou Elias?" **"I am not."** "Art thou the prophet?" **"No."**

Finally, when pressed further for an answer, he says he is **"the voice of one crying in the wilderness,"** and again proclaims his message, "Make straight the path of the Lord." He goes on to tell of the One they did not know, "the thong of whose sandal" he was "not worthy to unloose." How self-effacing—merely to be an unseen voice, but a voice to make Christ known! How about us?

E. P. Vedder, Jr.

When Samuel was old ... he made his sons judges over Israel ... And his sons walked not in his ways, but turned aside after lucre, and took bribes, and perverted justice. *(1 Samuel 8:1,3)*

In thinking of Samuel's mistake in thus making his sons his successors, we are led to ask how far it showed his failure to bring up his children rightly. Had he unconsciously imitated the weakness of Eli, whose family failure was of such a glaring character as to be the cause of God's judgments? It would hardly seem likely, for he had warning before his eyes and from the lips of God Himself. He himself in his childhood had been the messenger to unfaithful Eli as to this very matter, and he witnessed the captivity of the ark, and the death of Eli's sons. His own personal faithfulness with the people, and his prayerfulness, forbids the thought that he was careless or indifferent as to his responsibility in his own home.

On the other hand, are we not reminded in Abraham, that he would "command his household after him," and in Joshua's strong words, "As for me and my house we will serve the Lord," that they link the family together with the father? Are we not told in the New Testament that one indispensable requisite for a leader of the people of God is that he should "rule well his own house"?

Samuel was not entirely without blame. We may well believe that his frequent absences from home, and the absorbing interest in the nation at large, closed his eyes to responsibilities at home which no weight of public care could relieve him of. "Mine own vineyard have I not kept" has too often had to be the sorrowful confession of those who have labored in others' vineyards. It is not a thing to excuse, but to remember the danger for us all, if such a man as Samuel could commit a similar wrong. May God's mercy be upon the heads of families, giving grace and dependence and prayerfulness that their households may be examples of submission to His order!

S. Ridout

Jehovah said to Moses, I will do this thing also that thou hast said; for thou hast found grace in Mine eyes, and I know thee by name. And he said, Let me, I pray Thee, see Thy glory.

(Exodus 33:17-18)

Moses, the man of God, had been on the mount with Jehovah 40 days. He received the two tables of stone, the Ten Commandments, written with the finger of God. Moses then descends from the mount with the tables of stone in his hand, only to find the children of Israel dancing around a golden calf, the god that Aaron had made. What God had given for man to live by, spelled death due to their disobedience. The law had been broken and Moses intuitively cast down the tables of stone and broke them, lest the people would be consumed by the holy wrath of God.

At this time Moses stands up to plead for mercy with Jehovah on behalf of the people (Ex. 32:30-32). He wants the assurance that Jehovah Himself would go with them. This act of Moses of standing in the gap is a beautiful reminder of the Lord Jesus, who in going to the cross, stood in the gap and by shedding His blood made atonement for sin. On the basis of His sacrifice, Jehovah could continue on with His failing people.

Jehovah responded, "My presence shall go, and I will give thee rest." When Moses heard the answer he perceived that there was a glory, not yet known, far beyond that of the law—the glory of the grace of God. Therefore he pleads, "Let me, I pray thee, see Thy glory." Moses is then instructed to hew two tables of stone and go up the mountain and stand before Jehovah with the two tables of stone in his hand. Jehovah descends and stands beside Moses proclaiming, "Jehovah—God merciful and gracious, slow to anger, and abundant in goodness and truth, keeping mercy unto thousands, forgiving iniquity and transgression and sin" (Ex. 34:6-7). Upon hearing this, Moses bows his head and worships!

J. Redekop

Consider how great this man was.   *(Hebrews 7:4 KJV)*

While this verse directly refers to Melchizedec, Hebrews is a book of superlatives when it comes to Christ. Its purpose is to show how much greater the Lord Jesus is than all who preceded Him. In this epistle we read much of Christ's greatness in contrast with the old order of things which was but a shadow of Him and of the good things to come (Heb. 10:1).

Each chapter in Hebrews highlights this exquisite theme:

In chapter one—He is greater than the prophets and the angels.

In chapter two—He is greater than Adam (compare with Psalm 8).

In chapter three—He is greater than Moses.

In chapter four—He is greater than Joshua.

In chapter five—He is greater than Aaron.

In chapter six—He is greater than basic principles of religion.

In chapter seven—He is greater than the Levitical priesthood.

In chapter eight—He is greater than the Old Covenant.

In chapter nine—He is greater than the Tabernacle.

In chapter ten—He is greater than the sacrifices and offerings.

In chapter eleven—He is greater than the Old Testament heroes.

In chapter twelve—He is greater than Abel.

In chapter thirteen—He is greater than the sin offering and greater than Jerusalem or any other earthly religious system.

He is *greater* because He is a divine Person and all others, whether human or angelic, are but created beings; because His priesthood abides continually according to the power of an endless life; because His sacrifice does not need to be repeated and is effectual in giving eternal redemption; because even the most renowned heroes of the faith were failing men—but He fails not; because the most venerable religious system in the world is nothing compared to Him; because He is the Great Shepherd; and because His covenant is eternal!

B. Reynolds

There was set meat before him to eat; but he said, I will not eat until I have made known my business ... I am Abraham's servant. And Jehovah has blessed my master greatly, and he is become great; and He has given him sheep and cattle, and silver and gold, and bondmen and bondwomen, and camels and asses.

(Genesis 24:33-35)

THE GOOD AND FAITHFUL SERVANT (4)

We have three important lessons in the above verses: *First,* the good and faithful servant knows the importance and urgency of his mission. It is more important to him than even the essentials of life such as food and drink. Abraham's servant would not eat until he had presented his case. In John 4:32,34 we read of the time the disciples brought food to the Lord Jesus to eat, but He said: "I have food to eat which you do not know ... My food is that I should do the will of Him that has sent Me, and that I should finish His work."

Second, the only credential he presents is in the words "I am Abraham's servant." He could have added, "I am the eldest of his house, who rules over all that he has" (Gen. 24:2). But then he would be drawing attention to his own greatness. What a lesson this is for all who want to serve the Lord. How sad it is when a speaker is introduced with words that magnify man! What are we but earthen vessels which God's grace deigns to use "that the ... power may be of God and not from us" (2 Cor. 4:7).

Third, while he makes no reference or hint to his full title, he speaks freely of the greatness of his master. He refers to many proofs of his master's greatness. He delights to speak of his master's wealth. We too go to a needy world offering the unsearchable riches of Christ. May we never spoil the message by drawing attention to ourselves. The world desperately needs what God is offering. May He find us faithful at all times!

A. M. Behnam

God be gracious unto us, and bless us ... that Thy way may be known upon earth, Thy salvation among all nations ... Let the nations rejoice and sing for joy: for Thou wilt judge the peoples equitably; and the nations upon earth, Thou wilt guide them.

(Psalm 67:1-2,4)

It is blessedly true that all the earth shall be full of the knowledge of Jehovah, as the waters cover the sea (Isa. 11:9). But how is this grand and glorious result to be brought about? Is it the purpose of God to use the Church as His agent? Scripture says no! In the Scripture before us we see that it will occur when God shall be gracious unto Israel—when He shall cause His light to shine upon Zion—then, and not until then, will His way be known upon the earth, His salvation among all nations. It is through Israel, and not the Church, that God will yet bless the nations.

The *us* of the foregoing Psalm refers to Israel. Indeed, as we all know, the great burden of the Psalms, the prophets, and the entire Old Testament, is Israel. In it there is not a syllable about the Church, only types and shadows in which, now that we have the light of the New Testament, we can see the Church prefigured. But the doctrine of the Church remained a mystery until the apostle Paul, to whom it was committed fully, unfolded this great mystery which had been hid in God.

God had promised Abraham, "I will multiply thy seed as the stars of heaven ... and in thy seed shall all the nations of the earth be blessed" (Gen. 26:4 marg.). It is God's eternal purpose that the seed of Abraham, His friend, shall yet be prominent in the earth and that the nations shall be blessed in and through them. The blessing of the nations, their conversion, is through Israel, and not the Church.

C. H. Mackintosh

Our commonwealth has its existence in the heavens, from which also we await the Lord Jesus Christ as Savior, who shall transform our body of humiliation into conformity to His body of glory. *(Philippians 3:20-21)*

The Christian's hope or expectation is that the Lord Jesus is coming to change his body of humiliation, and make it glorious, like His own. Whether he is called to die before this event, or otherwise, it will not alter the fact. The change must be; and the hope is certain. If he die before the coming of the Lord, his corruption shall put on incorruption; and if he be alive and remaining upon the earth at that time, his mortal shall put on immortality. The authority for the hope we have is not only in the Word (1 Cor. 15:51-53), but in the finished work of Christ.

The Christian has reason to believe that not only his soul, but also his body is *redeemed* by the precious blood of Christ. If, by the grace of God, salvation has reached his soul, he may be confident it will reach his body also.

The apostle Paul was taught to expect this glorious consummation for himself and for all believers. We limit the salvation of God when we confine its blessing to the soul, and make the change of the body depend upon anything else but redemption.

Some would tell us that the believer's change depends upon his sanctification—others, that it depends on his looking for the Lord's appearing; whereas the apostle tells us that whom God justified, them He also glorified (Rom. 8:30).

Again, He tells us that all who sleep in Jesus, God will bring with Him; and those believers who are alive and remain unto the coming of the Lord shall be caught up together with the dead (who are to rise first) to meet the Lord; and so they shall ever be with Him (1 Th. 4:14-18). The Christian's full salvation will not be completed until the Lord comes.

Meat in Due Season

The king appointed them a daily provision of the king's meat, and of the wine which he drank … But Daniel purposed in his heart that he would not defile himself with the portion of the king's meat, nor with the wine which he drank. *(Daniel 1:5,8 KJV)*

The best that this world has to offer, the king's meat and wine, is nothing in comparison with the blessings that God has bestowed upon us as Christians.

This Babylonian king sought not only to change the diet of Daniel and his companions, but he also changed their names. The moral significance of this is unmistakable, for it was to wipe away the very memory of Jehovah, and thus to deprive them of everything that was godly. Daniel requested pulse and water for himself and his companions. Pulse is crushed grain, and speaks of Christ as the bread of God—the food for the Christian's soul. The water also speaks of Christ who could say, "He that believeth on Me shall never thirst" (Jn. 6:35). After ten days of pulse and water, the difference was so noticeable that the steward took away the appointed food and gave them pulse!

What a contemporary book this is! For this is exactly what is taking place in our culture today. Prayer is banned in schools, evolution is taught instead of divine creation, and there are no absolutes anymore. Evil is called good and good evil. Is it any wonder that those who are the advocates of such a satanic aim are producing a generation that has no hope, no reason for living, and who tragically see suicide as the only way out of a meaningless existence? The more we feed on Christ, and the more we are in communion with Him, the more others will take notice. So it was with Peter and John, for the Jewish rulers "took notice of them, that they had been with Jesus" (Acts 4:13).

May the Lord help us to be resolute in these last days, to be lights in the midst of the increasing darkness around us.

R. A. Barnett

How beautiful are the feet of them that preach the gospel of peace, and bring glad tidings of good things!

(Romans 10:15 KJV)

We must understand what evangelistic work is, lest we are deceived by what is spurious and not of God. That is not evangelistic work which, adopting sensational methods, works upon the feelings of the hysterical, and produces converts which last a day or a week or until the special excitement is over; that is the work of the devil, whatever else it pretends to be. It often results in suspicion of gospel work in general on the part of thoughtful men, or a callous indifference on the part of those who have come under its influence.

Nor is evangelistic work the mere holding of gospel services because the regular time for such has come, and so they *must* be held. In such services there is often a frigid formality that terribly hardens those who attend them regularly. This is often seen in the young who are children of Christian parents. May not this sad condition of "gospel-hardening" be largely due to these dead and powerless services? We thankfully admit that regular Sunday evening services are often means of great blessing to many. This is where those who hold them hold them in dependence upon God and communion with the Master, and where their evangelistic spirit is evidenced in gathering in the unconverted.

Evangelistic activity of the genuine sort springs from the divine love that God implants in the heart of a man who is himself saved, and this love makes him desire the blessing of others. The most fervent desire that ever flamed in the heart of a Christian for the souls of men is as nothing to the desires of the heart of God; nevertheless these desires are the same in nature, for divine love cannot act differently in the Christian from the way it acts in the Christian's God.

J. T. Mawson

May   **4**   Saturday

Jehovah Elohim took Man, and put him into the garden of Eden, to till it and to guard it. *(Genesis 2:15)*

When Adam was placed in the Garden of Eden his task was to till it and guard it. Some translations of this verse render the word "guard" as "keep" and although capturing a part of what the Hebrew word implies, "keep" does not give the full idea. Adam was to "till" or "work" it but he was also to **"guard"** it. This is striking. In fact it is the same word as is used in Genesis 3:24 where the Cherubim and the flaming sword were **"to guard the way to the tree of life"** after the fall of man—this gives the sense of the word. Why was Adam to "guard" paradise? Danger was lurking. As we know, the serpent was not far off. Adam failed in this, and the serpent had access to Eve—the rest is history.

This is instructive in that no matter how perfect or ideal the conditions, we must always guard our own hearts. As Solomon exhorted, "[Guard] thy heart more than anything that is guarded; for out of it are the issues of life" (Prov. 4:23). The battle begins here, and so we must guard our hearts from the snares of the world, the flesh and the devil. It is from our heart that hangs all the "issues of life." Even if all seems well it is just then that we are in most danger. We are very privileged in that we have ideal conditions for spiritual prosperity; we have copies of the Scriptures, loving support and fellowship of our brethren, an "open heaven" and a faithful, sympathetic Great High Priest. Yet, danger lurks.

A striking example of this will be seen during the Millennium. At the end of the 1000 years Satan will be let out of his prison and will lead a rebellion of the nations against the Lord Jesus. One would assume that men would not listen to his voice after experiencing all the millennial blessings. Not so! May our hearts be a "garden enclosed" (Song 4:12) as we pass through this present evil world.

B. Reynolds

To this have ye been called; for Christ also has suffered for you ... who Himself bore our sins in His body on the tree, in order that, being dead to sins, we may live to righteousness: by whose stripes ye have been healed. *(1 Peter 2:21,24)*

Christ was an example for us, for we are called to His path, and to follow His steps. The consideration of Christ in all the glory of His perfection cannot fail to have its effect on us, conforming our thoughts and ways to His. Yet even so, we are not as He was, for we have sins and He had none. We needed, therefore, the atoning sacrifice of which verse 24 speaks. He who did no sin "bore our sins in His own body on the tree." This is something altogether beyond us. We cannot follow in His steps here.

Every part of this wonderful verse deserves our most careful attention. *His own self* became the Sin-bearer, and no other. He *bore our sins.* Isaiah 53 had said He should bear our griefs and carry our sorrows, but it also predicted that He should be "wounded for our transgressions" and "bruised for our iniquities," and be stricken for "the transgression of My people," and His soul be made "an offering for sin." These sins were *ours,* for the verse definitely speaks of the work of Christ, not in its Godward aspect as propitiating Him, but in its believer-ward aspect as bearing his sins—*his* sins, and not the sins of everybody.

He bore our sins *in His own body* as our Substitute. We had sinned in our bodies. He, having become a true Man, apart from sin, bore our sins in His holy body as a sacrifice for sin *on the tree,* for it was exclusively in His death that atonement was effected. He did not bear our sins during His life, but in His death, and we are healed by His stripes. He bore our sins and delivered us from the stripes our sins deserved, in order that we should now live unto practical righteousness.

F. B. Hole

Jonah rose up to flee unto Tarshish from the presence of Jehovah; and he went down.
(Jonah 1:3)

The path of disobedience is always morally downward. Moving in opposition to God's word, Jonah took at least four steps downward. First, he went "down to Joppa." Nothing wrong with Joppa except that it was in the opposite direction of the city of Nineveh to which God had called him. Whenever we move away from the direction that God reveals in His precious Word, we also go down.

Secondly, Jonah went down into a ship at Joppa. For a moment circumstances seemed to favor his downward course as this ship was going to Tarshish—exactly where he wanted to go. But don't miss the significance of that little expression "He paid the fare." Disobedience always carries a price tag—a very expensive one.

Thirdly, Jonah went down into the lower part of the ship. Then, as God stirred up a tempestuous sea, his heathen shipmates cried out to their worthless gods. And what was Jonah doing? Sleeping like a baby! That is, until the desperate sea captain woke him rudely and besieged him with questions that implied a suspicious link between Jonah and the angry sea.

This drew a true confession out of Jonah, but it was not the confession of a clean instrument. Although God used the entire situation to draw the heathen sailors to Himself, Jonah's useful part in this was in spite of himself.

Finally, Jonah went down into the belly of a great fish. There his downward course bottomed out in a condition so horrible that he described it as "the belly of Sheol." With weeds wrapped around his head, he cried out to the God of salvation. And God gave deliverance, but the cost of disobedience had been heavy, as it always is. How much better to choose the upward way of willing and joyful obedience!

G. W. Steidl

Hereby we have known love, because He has laid down His life for us; and we ought for the brethren to lay down our lives. But whoso may have the world's substance, and see his brother having need, and shut up his bowels from him, how abides the love of God in him? *(1 John 3:16-17)*

Let us closely observe here that the sacrificial death of the Lord Jesus is considered as being on behalf of those who have been redeemed by it, for only those have experienced its blessed results. It is true enough that His life on earth was lived in humble service to His saints; but this did not cease until that life was laid down in utmost sacrifice in His death on Calvary. This is of incalculable blessing to every child of God.

This was no mere sacrifice for the sake of helping mankind generally to a greater degree of freedom and self-determination. Today some men will dare to speak of it, as though His death could be compared to those of men who have championed some humanitarian cause, civil rights, or whatever else, and have died in the attempt to make a better world. The Lord Jesus attempted no such thing. He came for the purpose of offering Himself in sacrifice for the remission of our sins.

Yet the fact of His laying down His life for us is also an example for us; so that "we ought to lay down our lives for the brethren." If this should end in death, so be it, but our lives ought to be lived in humble service for the sake of the saints of God. This involves living for them, not only dying for them if occasion requires.

L. M. Grant

With all men we would share the graces
Thy favor has to us made known:
We to all men Thy love commend
For Thou wouldst every one befriend.

When Abraham's servant heard their words, he worshipped the LORD, bowing himself to the earth. And the servant brought forth jewels of silver, and jewels of gold, and raiment, and gave them to Rebekah: he gave also to her brother and to her mother precious things ... And he said unto them, Hinder me not, seeing the LORD hath prospered my way; send me away that I may go to my master.   *(Genesis 24:52-53,56 KJV)*

THE GOOD AND FAITHFUL SERVANT (5)

Let us notice three things in the above verses.

First, when the servant heard Laban and Bethuel say: "Behold Rebekah is before thee, take her and go and let her be thy master's son's wife" (v. 51), and was thus assured of the success of his mission, the first thing he did was worship the LORD who had led him on the way and had prospered his mission. Success did not elate him or fill him with pride, but on the contrary, it humbled him and filled him with gratitude to the Lord. This is a wholesome lesson for anyone serving the Lord.

Second, having spoken of Abraham's greatness and the fact that whatever Abraham had was given to Isaac, the servant now gives definite proof of that. He brought forth jewels of silver and jewels of gold and raiment and gave them to Rebekah. He gave also to her brother and to her mother precious things—practical proof of Isaac's greatness. When we present Christ to others, let us remember that we are speaking to them of the King of kings and Lord of lords, the Creator and the only Savior.

Third, Once his mission was completed, he desired to return to his master. "Hinder me not ... send me away that I may go to my master." He came from his master and returns to his master's presence, reminding us of the words of our Master: "Where I am there shall also My servant be" (Jn.12:26). A blessed place to be and a practical lesson for all who want to serve the Lord.

A. M. Behnam

In the high priesthood of Annas and Caiaphas, the word of God came upon John, the son of Zacharias, in the wilderness. And he came into all the district round the Jordan, preaching the baptism of repentance for the remission of sins ... He said therefore to the crowds which went out to be baptized by him, Offspring of vipers, who has forewarned you to flee from the coming wrath? Produce therefore fruits worthy of repentance. *(Luke 3:2-3, 7-8)*

PROPHETS AND THEIR PROPHECIES–
JOHN THE BAPTIST (2)

Israel was in grave disorder. The rulers of the fourth Gentile empire of Daniel 2 and 7 were in power. Israel's God-given high priesthood was in confusion, two men holding that office at the same time. God had not directly addressed His people for over 400 years since the days of Malachi. God's prophet, like an Elijah of old, "was in the deserts until the day of his showing to Israel" (Lk. 1:80). Then God's word came upon him and he boldly stepped forward, preaching the baptism of repentance for the remission of sins. His text was taken from Isaiah 40.

Great crowds, a very mixed company, flocked out to hear this voice in the wilderness. Some were self-satisfied sensation seekers, for after all, they were descendants of Abraham! How insulted they must have felt when he called them offspring of vipers and warned them to flee from the coming wrath! Others were sincere, and acted on his preaching, repenting of their sins, submitting to baptism to symbolize this, and then asking for directions how they should now live a changed life.

For each one He had an answer. People wondered, "Is this the One we've been waiting for? John seized the opportunity to tell them about the One coming, mightier than himself, who would baptize with the Holy Spirit and fire. So too every true servant of God should divert attention away from self and focus it on Christ!

E. P. Vedder, Jr.

As the eagle stirreth up its nest, hovereth over its young, spreadeth out its wings, taketh them, beareth them on its feathers, so Jehovah alone did lead him, and no strange god was with him.

(Deuteronomy 32:11-12)

Trials teach us faith. Trial is the fruitful soil of trust. Difficulties are the divine incentives which demand and develop our confidence in the divine faithfulness and love. The eagle can only teach her young to fly by tearing up her nest and hurling them out in mid-air, where, thrown upon their own resources, they must either fly or fall. Then it is that they must learn the undeveloped power in their little pinions, and as they strike out upon the air in desperate struggles, they find the secret of a new life and gradually learn to beat their way through the pathless firmament, and upon the wings of the wind and in the face of the sun.

So God teaches His children to use their wings of faith by stirring up their nests, taking away their props, and often flinging them out into an abyss of helplessness, where they must either sink or learn to trust and throw themselves upon the seeming void, to find that God is there beneath them like the supporting wing which the eagle stretches forth beneath her faint and struggling brood.

It is so easy for us to lean upon things we can see, and feel that it is an entirely new experience for us to stand alone and walk with the unseen God as Peter walked upon the sea. But it is the lesson we must learn if our souls are ever to dwell in God's eternal calm where faith must be our only sense, and God our all in all. Often therefore, the crowning lesson of the spiritual life is learned in the school of suffering.

Meat in Due Season

All things subsist together by Him.   *(Colossians 1:17)*

The believers at Colosse were in danger of losing sight of the greatness and glory of the Lord Jesus Christ. They still viewed Him as their Savior, but they were not holding fast to Him as the Head (Col. 2:19), and through the subtle influence of false teachers, they were in jeopardy of falling into serious error. Satan is always active in his effort to rob Christians of their understanding and appreciation of the glory of Christ.

As an antidote to this, the apostle Paul presents to these dear saints (and to us as well), that Christ is the "image of the invisible God" (v. 15)—He is the Creator of all things. All things that exist, both "the visible and the invisible" (v. 16), have been created by Him and for Him. But they have not only been created by Him, they also **"subsist together"** by Him.

The "Deists" of the 17th and 18th centuries taught that a "Supreme Being" created the universe but is not presently maintaining it. They describe creation as a man winding up a clock and then walking away to let it run down by itself. Deism however, is opposed to what is presented to us in Scripture, where we see that all things "subsist together" by Christ. "Subsist" is a very interesting word; it literally means "to stand together" or "to hold together." Scientists have been working for many years to find the "unifying principle" that will explain how the universe is held together. The world of quantum mechanics with its atoms, electrons, protons, and neutrons appears as if held together by some force. This is true of the innumerable galaxies of outer space. Some theorists have talked of a "unifying theory of everything" and speculated about a "string theory" that will explain the link between the galaxies, gravitation, and the sub-atomic world. What holds all these things together? The Bible reveals unequivocally *who it is* and that He is "upholding all things by the word of His power" (Heb. 1:3).

B. Reynolds

Where two or three are gathered together unto My name, there am I in the midst of them. *(Matthew 18:20)*

Those wholehearted for Christ desire to be in His company. They instinctively wend their way to where He is known to be. Is this possible? Yes, "Where two or three are gathered together unto My name." No one who is truly conscious of the greatness and excellency of His Person, and the blessedness of communion with Him, would be willingly absent there.

A neglected Lord's Table, and prayer meeting, speak aloud of the Laodicean state of the heart. Of old "they continued steadfastly in the apostles' doctrine and fellowship, and in breaking of bread, and in prayers" (Acts 2:42). Alas, that there should be such a lack of continuing steadfastly now!

Does the Lord say to the Father, "In the midst of the Church will I sing praise unto Thee" (Heb. 2:12), and can we suppose that He fails to notice whether we are there or not, to join in the song He leads? In the coming day of review before the judgment seat of Christ (2 Cor. 5:10), how shall we take the disclosure, that self-indulgence, a little unfavorable weather, or a tiff with a brother or sister in Christ, has outweighed with us all the motives for a loving response to His wish, "This do in remembrance of Me"? (Lk. 22:19).

It is deeply humbling to think that any who have tasted the Lord's love can take advantage of not having to work on the Lord's Day, to spend its morning hours in bed, and that others can excuse their absence on the ground of visiting, or receiving visits from friends. Priceless opportunities of gratifying the heart of the Lord, and of showing attachment to Him in the scene of His rejection are thus lost.

It is mere mockery to repeat "Come, Lord Jesus," when we betray our indifference to His presence here.

Meat in Due Season

Now may the God of peace Himself sanctify you completely; and may your whole spirit, soul, and body be preserved blameless at the coming of our Lord Jesus Christ.

(1 Thessalonians 5:23 NKJV)

What a prayer! We were at war with God, until we turned to Him away from idols. It was to serve the true and living God—the God of peace—while waiting for His Son to come (ch. 1:9). Without God's help we cannot do anything pleasing to Him and this is one reason for Paul's prayer. We have been sanctified through the accomplished work of Christ and are now perfect in Him. Paul did not have to pray for this wonderful and blessed fact. However, we need God's help to work out this position (Phil. 2:12).

Paul prays to the God of peace who desires that we may enjoy the peaceful relationship of our position, even though we live in a world at war with God. Our sanctification, for which Paul prayed, is not a position: it is a work in progress, continuing until the Rapture. Then we will have reached our ultimate sanctification and *will be*, in actual practice, what *we are*, positionally. Paul's prayer is that *spirit, soul, and body* may be preserved. Is the spirit "superior" and the body "inferior"? No, that is Greek or pagan philosophy, which has penetrated into the Church over the centuries. Our spirit, soul, and body are different and have different functions, yet they belong together in one indivisible unit prepared by Him.

This is the way God has created us: after His likeness to be like Him morally, to visibly represent Him who is invisible. Here is where the resurrection comes in and Paul's prayer refers to a work of God, not only to preserve us now, but also to keep us in that relationship even beyond the power of death. What a magnificent and preserving power! To display this victory, God will bring us back to this scene, demonstrating His glory, when the Lord Jesus will appear with us at His manifestation.

A. E. Bouter

It came to pass after the death of Moses the servant of Jehovah, that Jehovah spoke to Joshua the son of Nun, Moses' attendant, saying, Moses My servant is dead; and now, rise up, go over this Jordan, thou and all this people, into the land which I give unto them, to the children of Israel. *(Joshua 1:1-2)*
For the law was given by Moses: grace and truth subsists through Jesus Christ. *(John 1:17)*

The "weakness and unprofitableness" (Heb. 7:18) of the principles of the law are apparent when the power of God in grace is before us. The law says in effect, "This do, and thou shalt live" (Lk. 10:28)—it requires human obedience as a condition to obtaining life—but the gospel of God brings in life through divine righteousness already magnified by what has been done by the Savior, who died for us.

The law appeals to man, as man in relationship with God truly, but nonetheless to man, as responsible in himself to do good. Grace, on the other hand, flows from God in His mercy to man as he is in his sinfulness (Rom. 5:8). The law commands man to do that which, while in his helpless state, he can never do. The grace of God bestows on man, when helpless, a new life in Christ Jesus. The law commands man to reach up to blessing; grace brings blessing down to man where he is. Spiritual blessings, indeed, are all of grace.

Hence the force of these words, "Moses My servant (a type of the law) is dead" must be kept before the heart if we would rise and follow our Joshua (typifying Jesus, the Lord risen from the dead), and thus lay hold of our heavenly blessings.

H. F. Witherby

Through coming ages Thou wilt trace
(In multiples unknown)
Exceeding riches of Thy grace
In kindness to Thine own.

Eva Coffman

He made him houses in the city of David, and prepared a place for the ark of God, and spread a tent for it. Then David said, None ought to carry the ark of God but the Levites, for them has Jehovah chosen to carry the ark of God, and to serve Him forever. *(1 Chronicles 15:1-2).*

DAVID'S NEW CART (3)

Here we see proof that David had studied his Bible. He said this as though he had made a great discovery, and so indeed it was. But 400 years before, it had been plainly written (Dt. 10:8). The Spirit of God doubtless turned David's attention to this and related scriptures, and he at once prepared to obey the Word of God. I think I hear him saying then, "What a foolish man I was to imitate the Philistines."

This to me is the picture of many a Christian today who has been seeking to worship God, or work for Him according to his own mind. He has allowed his religious life to be molded by what he learned as a child, or saw as a man all round about him, without ever going to God's Word to see whether God had given any plain directions on these points, or not. We may all well learn from David. He got light as to the carrying of the ark and acted on it. And if God has given me light He expects me to respond to it. I cannot help my brethren otherwise.

There is a religion today that suits the world, and suits man in the flesh, and the great effort of Christendom today is to make the things of God acceptable to man in the flesh. I do not believe God has called us to that. And if He has given us heavenly light, let us take care lest we dim it. Further, that light is given to help others. I think sometimes we are little aware how we may affect others. We have to remember that no man lives to himself. Our walk and ways are very far-reaching and telling upon others.

W. T. P. Wolston

He sees Jesus coming to him, and says, Behold the Lamb of God, who takes away the sin of the world ... I beheld the Spirit descending as a dove from heaven, and it abode upon Him. And I knew Him not; but He who sent me to baptize with water, He said to me, Upon whom thou shalt see the Spirit descending and abiding on Him, He it is who baptizes with the Holy Spirit. And I have seen and borne witness that this is the Son of God. *(John 1:29,32-34)*

PROPHETS AND THEIR PROPHECIES–
JOHN THE BAPTIST (3)

These verses are part of John the Baptist's declaration of how he learned the greatness of the Lord Jesus, who He is and what He would do. On the one hand, John had been filled with the Holy Spirit from his mother's womb and had leaped for joy in her womb when the Virgin Mary, just barely pregnant with Jesus, had arrived at his parents' home and greeted his mother, Elizabeth.

But John was now some 30 years old, a man fully occupied in the service to which God had called him: preparing the way of the Lord. To this humble prophet God gave the unique honor of having personal contact with the Object of his prophesying: Jesus. Matthew, Mark, and Luke tell us how John had preached, "Repent," and "Prepare the way of the Lord." They describe the wonderful scene of how John baptized Jesus when Jesus came to him. But here we have John's account of what he had learned on that day.

God had told Samuel in advance about the one God wanted him to anoint (1 Sam. 9:15-17). Likewise God had told John who would be coming to him. At Jesus' baptism God had attested who Jesus is. John had witnessed this. Now he proclaimed Jesus to be far more than what the Jews were looking for. He was the Lamb of God who would take away the sin of the world, the One coming after John, yet before him, the One on whom the Spirit would descend and abide, who would baptize with the Holy Spirit: the Son of God!

E. P. Vedder, Jr.

Thou wilt keep in perfect peace the mind stayed on Thee, for he confideth in Thee. *(Isaiah 26:3)*

Four things are necessary to have peace and rest of soul in time of trial.

First, keep the mind stayed on the Lord, trusting in Him.

Second, keep in touch with God by prayer: "Be careful [anxious] for nothing; but in everything by prayer and supplication with thanksgiving let your requests be made known unto God. And the peace of God, which passes all understanding, shall keep your hearts and minds through Christ Jesus" (Phil. 4:6-7 KJV).

Third, meditate upon the Word: "These things I have spoken unto you, that in Me ye might have peace. In the world ye shall have tribulation: but be of good cheer; I have overcome the world" (Jn. 16:33).

Fourth, yield your will to God and work in concert with Him in trial. "Now no chastening for the present seemeth to be joyous, but grievous: nevertheless afterward it yieldeth the peaceable fruit of righteousness unto them which are exercised thereby" (Heb. 12:11). Chastening here means more than correction; it includes all that goes into the training of a child as the Greek word implies. And note the great end of it all is to make us more like God in righteousness and holiness. This is done by yielding up the will to God and coming to Him in a teachable attitude so that He may show us the reason for the trials.

And last, but not least, let us not forget that even though the thorns may not be removed, and He allows them to go on pricking us for some good end that He knows is best for us, yet "His grace is sufficient for us." He will sustain the soul that submits to Him and leaves all in His hands.

E. C. Hadley

The weight of gold that came to Solomon in one year was six hundred and sixty-six talents of gold. *(1 Kings 10:14)*
Solomon had horses brought out of Egypt. *(1 Kings 10:28 KJV)*
King Solomon loved many foreign women. *(1 Kings 11:1)*

In the event, foreseen by God, of Israel's having a king, he was forbidden to multiply his wives or his riches, and to go down into Egypt to multiply horses (Dt. 17:16-17). Now with whatever blessings we may be surrounded, we can never forsake the law of God with impunity. God had bestowed abundance of riches and honor on Solomon, who had only asked for wisdom; but the study of the law, which was prescribed to the king (Dt. 17:19-20), should have prevented his using the means he did in acquiring his riches. These chapters in 1 Kings teach us that he did precisely that which the law forbade him to do. He multiplied silver and gold, he multiplied the number of his wives, and had a great number of horses brought from Egypt.

God's promise was fulfilled. Solomon was rich and glorious above all the kings of his day; but the means he used to enrich himself showed a heart at a distance from God, and led to his ruin according to the just judgment and sure word of God. Without sending for horses from Egypt, and gold from Ophir, Solomon would have been rich and glorious, for God had promised it. By doing this he enriched himself, but he departed from God and from His Word. Having given himself up to his desires after riches and glory, he had multiplied the number of his wives also, and in his old age they turned away his heart.

The slippery path of sin is always trodden with accelerated steps, because the first sin tends to weaken in the soul the authority and power of the Word of God which alone can prevent our committing still greater sins. It also tends to weaken the consciousness of His presence, which imparts to the Word all its practical power over us.

J. N. Darby

He that loves not has not known God; for God is love. Herein as to us has been manifested the love of God, that God has sent His only begotten Son into the world, that we might live through Him. Herein is love, not that we loved God, but that He loved us, and sent His Son a propitiation for our sins. *(1 John 4:8-10)*

How sadly false is that view of God's love that would speak of the holy and beautiful life of the Lord Jesus in self-sacrificing service to mankind, while ignoring His death on Calvary as the great propitiatory sacrifice necessary for the purging away of sins. Love is not found in man's heart toward God, but in God's heart toward man: this is its living fountain. And the sending of His Son to bear the dreadful burden of our guilt—the guilt of rebels—in His anguish and death on Calvary is proof of love infinitely higher than anything that man naturally calls "love."

In contemplating these two great facts, the incarnation of the Lord Jesus, and His sacrificial death, our thoughts of love will be properly formed. Propitiation is that which completely satisfies God in reference to the putting away of sins. Thereby the love of His heart, expressed already in propitiation itself, is free to flow out in unhindered complacency towards His children. Love has found a way to overcome every great barrier of its abundant outflow. And its pure, unselfish reality is that which awakens within our hearts a responsive affection that is also unforced, spontaneous, and real. "We love because He first loved us."

L. M. Grant

I love Thee because Thou hast first loved me,
And purchased my pardon on Calvary's tree;
I love Thee for wearing the thorns on Thy brow:
'Tis Thou who art worthy, Lord Jesus, 'tis Thou.

W. R. Featherstone

The word of Jehovah came unto Jonah ... saying, Arise, go to Nineveh ... But Jonah rose up to flee unto Tarshish from the presence of Jehovah. *(Jonah 1:1-3)*

Who was Jonah? To some he's merely "That man who got swallowed by a whale." (The Bible actually calls it a great fish.) To those of us who accept the Bible as the Word of God he is far more. In fact, his life provides valuable lessons on such current issues as extreme nationalism and survival in the Middle East.

But above all, Jonah was a prophet of God. Called to preach to Nineveh, he chose rather to disobey. The Bible records that he "rose up to flee ... from the presence of the Lord." The results of this sad choice are recorded in the first chapter of the book which bears his name. They provide some powerful warnings to us: "He paid the fare." This is the cost of disobedience. It always carries a price tag, although we ignore it at the time of our bad choices. The payment comes due however, as we begin to reap what we have sown.

"He went down." This is the course of disobedience. It's always downward, never upward. Like the "muckraker" in Bunyan's Pilgrim's Progress, a person moving downward finally reaches the point where he has neither the desire nor the ability to look up. Thankfully, Jonah never reached that point.

"From the presence of the Lord." This is the curse of disobedience. It is emptiness in time and hell for eternity to be without the presence of the Lord. Those like Jonah who truly belong to God will never suffer the second, but can surely experience a lot of the first through disobedience. How much finer it is to walk as children of obedience, having purified our souls by obedience to the truth. This not only glorifies God, but spares us so much trouble.

G. W. Steidl

Ye are saved by grace, through faith; and this not of yourselves; it is God's gift: not on the principle of works, that no one might boast. *(Ephesians 2:8-9)*

Where are we? Where does our faith apprehend we stand as viewed by our Father? No man can have faith for another; therefore the question is a searching one. Scripture says, "Made us sit down together in heavenly places in Christ Jesus" (Eph. 2:6). We should seek for grace to see ourselves by faith as new creations, as our Father actually sees us in His Son. He does not see His people in the flesh, nor as under the law (Rom. 8:9; 6:14), but in the Lord Jesus Christ at His own right hand.

How am I to get the blessing? is the question often raised by God's people. Get into God's truth about the blessing. When, through grace, a man believes God's Word about the death of the Lord Jesus for sinners, he is secure from the judgment of this world and delivered from the wrath to come. He is secure from the enemy, Satan, in Christ risen from the dead. He is seated in heavenly places in Christ, and is graced by the Father in all the beauty of His Beloved One.

We are speaking of the truths themselves, not of making them real in our experience. Thus we realize what we believe. Realization is not a stepping-stone to faith, but faith is the foundation of practical realization. Our acquaintance with the truth is not the truth itself, thank God! And the truth of God, not our realization of it, is our confidence and rest. Therefore, as our souls, by the ministry of the indwelling Spirit, enter into the truths respecting our blessing, we begin to enjoy the blessing we seek. We obtain blessing by faith, rather than faith by blessing.

H. F. Witherby

My son, despise not the chastening of the Lord, nor faint when reproved by Him ... no chastening at the time seems to be matter of joy, but of grief; but afterwards yields the peaceful fruit of righteousness to those exercised by it. *(Hebrews 12:5,11)*

These verses teach the importance of God's chastening His children. The word *chastening* refers to child training and education. God's chastening is not an angry revenge; it is an evidence of His fatherly love and care. From these verses we learn that there are three possible responses to chastening:

1. A person may *despise* it, give it no importance and assume what happened was just by chance. He does not benefit from it. It is like paying a large sum of money for something and neglecting to possess it. How sad, how foolish!

2. On the other hand, a person may get *discouraged;* instead of seeing the benefit of God's dealing with him he begins to doubt God's love and listens to the enemy of our souls. God does not let us go through a discipline above what we can tolerate, for He always gives grace if we would just listen to His voice. If wise earthly fathers know how to discipline their children, how much more does our heavenly Father. He is "the Father of compassions, and God of all encouragement" (2 Cor. 1:3).

3. The right response to God's chastening is not to ignore it nor to be discouraged, but to be *exercised* by it. That is how we can benefit from it. To be exercised by it means to examine our ways to see where we have failed and why. We ought to search our souls and say with David: "Search me, O God, and know my heart; prove me and know my thoughts; and see if there be any grievous way in me; and lead me in the way everlasting" (Ps. 139:23-24). This way we will experience that God's chastening yields the peaceful fruit of righteousness to those exercised by it.

A. M. Behnam

May   **23**   Thursday

Consider your calling, brethren, that there are not many wise according to flesh, not many powerful, not many high-born. But God has chosen the foolish things … the weak things … and the ignoble things of the world, and the despised, has God chosen … so that no flesh should boast before God. *(1 Corinthians 1:26-29)*

Both the world and worldly Christians offer attractive opportunities for the exercise of Christian graces, and seek to enlist in their benevolent projects those on whom they look as men and women of success. These are opportunities for such as are full of goodness, compassion, and energy: movements designed to advance morality, to help and elevate the unfortunate, to reform those who have fallen into evil ways, to correct social and civic evils, are especially alluring.

These needs seem to offer opportunity for the exercise of spiritual gifts and knowledge. To many Christians, such challenges are very attractive. They say, Here is a chance to do good; and therefore, joining such movements is justified. They argue: Isn't it right to help men to be better? Isn't it serving Christ to help such actions designed for the betterment of society? Ought we not to do all in our power to aid especially "Christian" plans aimed at morally uplifting the unfortunate, the degraded, and the fallen?

From the world's standpoint such efforts are undoubtedly justifiable; but not from the Christian standpoint. That they benefit the world will not be denied; that they promote the Lord's interests is more than doubtful. The world, not the Lord, is their object. The world seeks its own, not the things of Christ. The glory of the world is sought, not the glory of the Lord Jesus Christ.

C. Crain

Upon God alone, O my soul, rest peacefully; for my expectation is from Him. (Psalm 62:5)

(Psalm 62:5)

Believers are oft-times disappointed with themselves. Desiring to do some great work for the Lord, they find they are left to do some quiet work in a hidden corner, and are disappointed. Again they may get sadly disappointed with the local company of saints with whom they walk. They had hoped that God would convert great numbers and bring their little company into prominence as a centre of blessing with the Lord's public approval and instead they find weakness and failure, and are disappointed. Again we may be disappointed with the people of God generally. We perhaps had visions of getting the scattered fragments of God's people together to walk in unity and love, and behold we find only discord and further disintegration and we grow disappointed.

Again the people of God may entertain great hopes from the mission field. With thousands of missionaries working in all parts of the world they had hoped that the strongholds of heathenism would be broken down before the light of Christianity, and yet they find it is hardly touched, and they are disappointed. Others again have entertained the thought that after nineteen centuries of the light of Christianity the world would be morally better and instead they have to admit that never was lawlessness so prevalent and they are disappointed.

If, however, we abandon our own thoughts and rise up to God's thoughts we shall not be disappointed. Our expectations are oftentimes too limited, our outlook too circumscribed. We think of the present moment and look only at things seen. Let us, however, "look beyond the long dark night and hail the coming day." Let us see to what great end God is working, so that, out of the wreck and ruin of this world, He shall secure a Bride that will be suited for the love of Christ.

C. H. Mackintosh.

When I was day by day with you in the temple ye did not stretch out your hands against Me; but this is your hour and the power of darkness. *(Luke 22:53)*

The solemn scene in the Garden of Gethsemane movingly traces the agony of the Lord Jesus and His betrayal into the hands of wicked men. But in this account we also get an indictment of the spiritual state of the world coming from the lips of the Lord. When the chief priests, temple officials, and elders come to arrest Him, the Lord Jesus reminds them that He had been "day by day" with them, teaching in the temple. Yet now they were coming with swords and sticks to arrest Him in the night. Then He makes a remarkable statement, a ringing condemnation of the world and a revelation concerning the dark forces that control it: "But this is your hour and the power of darkness."

It is the "hour" in which man does as he pleases in direct opposition to the revealed will of God. But what is even more solemn is that the Lord Jesus reveals that the rulers of this world are under Satan's power—the "power of darkness." The word for *power* here can mean *authority* in the sense of governmental rule (the same word is translated *jurisdiction* in Luke 23:7). Indeed, a possible paraphrase of this verse is that it is the hour **"when darkness reigns."** Satan was able to marshal the political and religious rulers of the world against the Lord Jesus (albeit in the sovereign purpose of God, cf. Jn. 19:11; Acts 2:23). This speaks volumes as to the dark state of man's heart under the power of the "god of this world" (2 Cor. 4:4).

In blessed contrast with this we read the prophetic, Holy-Spirit-inspired words of King David, "Thy people shall be willing in the day of Thy power" (Ps. 110:3). A day is coming that will be the day of *His power*; a day which will be characterized by the rule of righteousness and binding of all evil powers. Today, however, is still the time when "darkness reigns."

B. Reynolds

He that has the Son has life. *(1 John 5:12)*
Jesus spoke to them, saying, I am the light of the world ... If therefore the Son shall set you free, ye shall be really free.

(John 8:12,36)

There are three things bestowed on every soul who, through grace, believes in Jesus. These are *Life, Light, and Liberty*. In comparison with these all earthly riches are but as the small dust in the balance. In place of Life, Light, and Liberty they are in the shadow of death in darkness and bondage.

Our Lord says, "I give unto My sheep eternal life" (Jn. 10). Someone may say, "I see that, but my difficulty is to know that I am a sheep of Christ." That is putting feelings before Christ and His word. I must have something independent of myself, that is, God's own revelation to rest upon. The eternal truth of God alone forms a real basis of peace which all the power of men and devils cannot disturb. Everyone who hears His word and believes in the One who sent Him is the happy possessor of eternal life.

A believer should know what he possesses. As we get *life* so we get *light* in Christ. God would not give us life and leave us in the dark. The proper sphere for the *life* we possess is the *light* in which we have the privilege to walk. The darkness is passed; the dim twilight has given place to the full-orbed *light of life*, streaming into our souls and upon our path, enabling us to judge ourselves and our surroundings according to the true light.

Of necessity as we get *life* and *light,* so we get *liberty* in Christ. He quickens, enlightens, emancipates! He would not give us life and leave us in bondage. He sets us free from guilt and condemnation, from dread of judgment to come, from fear of death, from the present power of sin, as from its future consequences! May we all lay hold of these things in simple faith and join in fervent praise to the Giver of these three precious gifts!

H. Smith

How can a young man keep his way pure? By keeping it according to Thy Word. *(Psalm 119:9 NASB)*

The expression "according to Thy word" occurs six times in this
marvelous psalm. The Word of God is the prominent theme of the
119th Psalm, describing and exalting the wonderful resources we
have in it. God Himself is the great Speaker as well as the great
Writer: let us take heed to all that He says and writes.

The psalmist continues with a statement and a prayer: "My soul
cleaves to the dust; revive me *according to Thy word*" (v. 25). In
his statement, he acknowledges his utter weakness and nothingness,
but his prayer introduces God who can change all that. It implies his
trust in the tremendous power of God's Word, not only as displayed
in His creation but also in His care of weak creatures. How we need
this divine reviving! "My soul weeps because of grief; strengthen
me according to Thy word" (v. 28). When all around fails and we
find utter weakness in ourselves, we may look up to God and take
courage in Him who strengthens us according to His Word's rich
resources.

"Thou hast dealt well with Thy servant, O LORD, according to Thy
word" (v. 65). God does not have any favorites; there is no party-
spirit with Him. He deals with us according to His Word, and the
psalmist realizes this, obviously with thankfulness. "I am exceedingly afflicted; revive me, O LORD, according to Thy word" (v. 107).
"Let my cry come before Thee, O LORD; give me understanding according to Thy word" (v. 169).

Surely, we can rely on Him and His Word! "According to Thy
word" is one word in Hebrew, and it occurs eight more times in
the Hebrew Bible, related to different persons and circumstances.
Including the six times it occurs in Psalm 119, "according to Thy
word" is found fourteen (2x7) times in total: another marvel of the
perfection of God's Word.

A. E. Bouter

May   **28**   Tuesday

Jonah had gone down into the lower part of the ship; and he lay, and was fast asleep. *(Jonah 1:5)*

It's awful to be in the wrong place at the wrong time, doing the wrong thing. Jonah found himself in this unenviable position as he boarded a ship for Tarshish in disobedience to God's will. Although for a time things seemed to be going so smoothly that Jonah even fell asleep, his slumber didn't last long. The Lord sent along a terrific storm, and as the sea became rough, so did the terrified sailors. They began firing questions at him—questions which are still being fired at those of us who claim to be servants of God: Why are you sleeping when you should be praying? Poor Jonah evidently had no answer and no excuse. Do we? If we really believe what we say about God and the Bible, we'll wake up in a hurry and begin "praying at all seasons, with all prayer and supplication in the Spirit."

Their next question was, "Why are we in this trouble?"

(In those days people still believed that effects had causes.)

Rapidly there came further queries: "What do you do? What is your origin? To whom do you belong? What is your country?"

Then Jonah came out with the whole story, confessing his guilt, and directing them to throw him overboard as the solution to their problem. The sailors tried strenuously to avoid this by rowing to shore, but in vain—the Lord would not allow it.

As the sailors then cast him into the sea, it ceased from its raging. Then, "The men feared Jehovah exceedingly, and offered a sacrifice unto Jehovah, and made vows." God can turn even the disobedience of His servants into an occasion for the display of His glory that men might fear Him! Although He delights in our obedience, He is not thwarted by our disobedience. Surely His ways are perfect.

G. W. Steidl

Bring up the ark of Jehovah the God of Israel to the place that I have prepared for it. For because ye did it not at the first, Jehovah our God made a breach upon us, for that we sought Him not after the due order. *(1 Chronicles 15:12-13)*

DAVID'S NEW CART (4)

There is a great deep underlying principle here for our souls today. God has a **"due order"** as to everything down here for His Church, and *if* we step out of this divine order, there is pretty sure to be a catastrophe. The New Testament contains what David called "due order," very full instructions for God's Assembly. Our Lord intimated what would be its rallying center when He said, "Where two or three are gathered together unto My name, there am I in the midst of them" (Mt. 18:20). His Spirit would gather, His Name and His Name only be the center of unity, and His presence was pledged to all so gathered, even though it might be but two or three. The many have departed from the "due order" in this respect, and are gathered round special points of doctrine, or ecclesiastical organization as to form and mode of worship. All such would do well to ask themselves, Is this really the "due order" of God's Word?

Nowhere in the New Testament can you find the pattern from which many churches are formulated. The idea of *an* assembly *over* which a solitary servant is placed—no matter how gifted he might be—is utterly foreign to God's Word. When the Assembly was formed, Christ, the Head of the Body, gave suited gifts to meet its need. But not one, in any single instance that can be pointed out in Scripture, was appointed as "the minister" of "a church."

Depend upon it, King David's **new cart**, suggested by the Philistines, has its complete counterpart today in Christendom. Who will deny it? If what we see all around us is to be found in God's Word, it would easily be indicated, but it is not there!

W. T. P. Wolston

Rabbi, He who was with thee beyond the Jordan, to whom thou barest witness, behold, He baptizes, and all come to Him. John answered … He that has the bride is the bridegroom; but the friend of the bridegroom, who stands and hears him, rejoices in heart because of the voice of the bridegroom: this my joy then is fulfilled. He must increase, but I must decrease. *(John 3:26-27,29-30)*

PROPHETS AND THEIR PROPHECIES–
JOHN THE BAPTIST (4)

John the Baptist with two of his disciples standing by once more had borne witness to Jesus in John 1:35-37. Looking at Jesus as He walked, he had exclaimed, "Behold the Lamb of God!" Hearing him speaking, the two disciples had followed Jesus, had found where He was staying, and had stayed with Him that day. We never again find them returning to John the Baptist, but this humble servant of God showed no disappointment or resentment at this.

This episode was evidently the beginning of many other similar ones. While John quietly continued his ministry, it soon became clear that Jesus was now drawing more followers than he. Some people brought this to John's attention. Were they perhaps trying to incite him to jealousy? If so, they did not succeed. John plainly told them that a man receives nothing except what is given him from heaven. He was not the Christ, but had been given the honored task of being Christ's forerunner.

The bridegroom was central, the one honored, at weddings then. So it shall be at the Marriage Supper of the Lamb, too, in a day soon to come. Seeing Christ honored, John, as friend of the bridegroom, would rejoice, not resent it. Christ must increase; he must decrease. His own service was coming to an end.

What an example! When Christ is magnified may we rejoice! If our service can contribute to His glory, let's not be anxious about getting credit for it now! He is just. Our reward will be sure.

E. P. Vedder, Jr.

The glory which Thou gavest Me I have given them; that they may be one, even as We are one: I in them, and Thou in Me, that they may be made perfect in one; and that the world may know that Thou hast sent Me, and hast loved them, as Thou hast loved Me. *(John 17:22-23 KJV)*

Of none but the Church could it be said, "At that day ye shall know [here upon earth] that I am in My Father, and ye in Me, and I in you" (Jn. 14:20).

What marks the difference between the Church and Israel, and indeed between the Church and the entire population of the millennial earth, is that the Church is blessed *in the Lord Jesus Christ and with Him*: Israel and the millennial nations will be blessed *by Him* and will be *under His reign.*

There are many things in which those who compose the Church differ not from saints of other dispensations, whether past or future. True believers between the day of Pentecost and the descent of the Lord Jesus into the air at the Rapture, constitute "the Church"; and these, in common with the Old Testament saints and millennial saints, are chosen of God the Father, redeemed by the blood of the Savior, quickened and regenerated by the Holy Spirit, and they are all preserved by almighty grace. In these things the Church differs not from other saints.

That which distinguishes the Church is her oneness with the Lord Jesus Christ. The Church is Christ's body and His bride. It participates in His exaltation to be head over all things both in heaven and on earth. As the body partakes with the head of all the vital energies by which the whole is actuated, so the Church even now partakes with the Lord Jesus of His risen life, and receives from Him the anointing of the Holy Spirit. And as the bride participates in all that is possessed by her husband, so is the Church, the Bride, the Lamb's wife, to participate in His inheritance of all things. Her oneness with Him is the great distinction of the Church.

W. Trotter

June

1

Saturday

I have seen all the works that are done under the sun, and behold, all is vanity and pursuit of the wind. *(Ecclesiastes 1:14)*

Happiness, to be real and lasting, must be built upon a solid foundation. While one is occupied with it, there may be a certain amount of elation in building an air castle. The same is true in reading a novel or in being occupied with sports, parties, and the like. There is also a certain thrill in adventure or in making what the world calls a success in life, but every tick of the clock is bringing you nearer the time when you must leave it all behind. And what will you have then to fall back upon or to look forward to? These things were only momentarily an escape from the sterner realities of life and the certainty of death that is to follow. Such things can give no true and lasting satisfaction.

To try to seek true happiness in such things is to make Solomon's experiment all over again. Solomon had health, riches, fame, and everything that this world could give, and he definitely decided to see what pleasure could be obtained under the sun. He spared himself no pains. He tried everything this world could offer. He then summed up the net returns of it all as to the happiness it afforded him.

Joy to be real and lasting must be based on a solid foundation that cannot be shaken by the storms of life. One could wish that life's journey were always over peaceful waters, but it is not so. The waves are often rough and the going hard. In fact, God has ordered that it should be so, that man might turn to Him for the only source of true satisfaction. True and lasting joy can only be had in God Himself revealed in Christ. You cannot have it in any other way. To seek it in any other way is only a "pursuit of the wind."

E. C. Hadley

The blood shall be to you for a token upon the houses where ye are: and when I see the blood, I will pass over you.

(Exodus 12:13 KJV)

Show me proof that I am saved. Oh! for evidence that I am among God's people! "The blood shall be to you for a token." There is none other granted. Look not for a sign within your breast; see it in the blood of Christ; look not at your feelings, but at His sufferings; not at your joy, but His pain. It would not have been faith but disobedience in Israel to have spent their night in inquiring and looking if the blood marks were upon their house doors. "None of you shall go out at the door of his house until the morning," God had said. And they sat within and waited for the daybreak.

Are they, whose doors are shut, and who assemble in fear and trembling around their paschal lamb, less safe than their neighbors who calmly wait for liberty's coming morn as they keep the feast? It is the blood without the door, not the feelings of them within the house, wherein the safety lies. Faith obeyed God, took the blood and sprinkled it, and in the redeeming blood was the security.

But give me evidence that God is satisfied respecting my sins.

Heed His words: "When I see the blood I will pass over you." His sword of justice has been plunged into the adorable Substitute. His justice asks for no second judgment, no double dying for sin. The very sword which slew the lamb now shelters those for whom the blood was shed. We once bent over a poor dying man and said, "Friend, you are leaving this world. You will very soon appear before God. How is it about your soul? Where are your sins?" He was too weak to lift a finger, but looked up calmly and whispered, "My sins are under the blood." He rested in this—that God looks upon the sacrifice of His Son, and not upon the sins of those who put their trust in Him.

H. F. Witherby

Jesus said to him, Then are the sons free. But that we may not be an offense to them, go to the sea and cast a hook, and take the first fish that comes up, and when thou hast opened its mouth thou wilt find a stater, take that and give it to them for Me and thee.

(Matthew 17:26-27)

The tribute here spoken of is not tribute to the civil power, but the didrachma (a stater equaled two didrachmas) which every grown-up Jew paid for the temple service, and which they had voluntarily imposed upon themselves in Ezra's time—a tribute to Jehovah. The question which the collectors put to Peter was really whether his Master was a good Jew. Peter, with the zeal so often there, yet in ignorance, at once answers, "Yes!"

The Lord then shows divine knowledge of what had occurred by anticipating Peter, to introduce in touching grace the new place He was giving to Peter and those with him. "Of whom," says the Lord, "do the kings of the earth take custom or tribute, of their own children, or of strangers?" Peter replies, "Of strangers." "Then," says the Lord, "are the sons free." We are the children, you and I, of the great king of the temple, and as such, free from the tribute. "Nevertheless that we offend not," the Lord says, bringing in Peter. His next words show His divine power over creation, making the fish bring just what was wanted. And then again He *puts Peter with Himself* in the place of sonship by the overwhelming, but unspeakably gracious words, **"Give to them for Me and thee."**

Do our hearts echo these words, moved to their foundations? If Christ said **"Me and thee"** to us, how should we feel about it? Yet He does say it. Oh, for the Son of God to say to such a one as me, "Me and thee"! I know it is the effect of redemption, but of a redemption He has accomplished, a blessing which only His heart—which answers to the Father's counsels—could have thought of for us.

J. N. Darby

Come, and let us return unto the LORD: for He hath torn, and He will heal us; He hath smitten, and He will bind us up. After two days will He revive us: in the third day He will raise us up, and we shall live in His sight. *(Hosea 6:1-2 KJV)*

Israel and the nations in millennial times by seeing the Church in the same glory as the Lord Jesus, will know that she is the object of the same love of the Father with which the Lord Jesus Himself is loved. Israel and the nations will be happy, Israel preeminently so, under the reign of the King and His glorified saints: but no distinction can be more marked than that which exists between the Bride of the Lamb and the nations over which she, with her Lord and Bridegroom, is to reign.

Israel's distinctive calling is to earthly blessings. Had they been obedient, wealth, power, fame, and prosperity would have been the tokens of God's approval of their ways. By their disobedience, their idolatry, and especially their rejection of the Savior, they have come under the inflictions of God's wrath, and that wrath has been manifested against them in all the heavy temporal judgments which have overtaken them. We refer now to God's dealings with them nationally, in His providential government of the earth. As individuals they are, of course, in common with all men, open to eternal judgment; and, if not saved by grace through faith, that judgment will result in eternal ruin.

Scripture leaves no room for doubt that, in this world, the wrath of God against Israel has been, is, and will yet be, manifested by the infliction of temporal calamities.

Prophecy, on the other hand, proves that God's approbation of Israel, when nationally restored and saved, will be manifested in abundance of temporal prosperity and blessing. Israel's is an earthly calling: and with Israel, consequently, adversity on earth is a token of God's displeasure—prosperity a sign of His favor and His smile.

W. Trotter

Jonah prayed unto Jehovah his God out of the fish's belly.

(Jonah 2:1)

His brief and poignant prayer inside the fish vividly portrays the physical and psychological horrors which he endured there:

"Out of the belly of Sheol cried I ... the waters encompassed me, to the soul: the deep was round about me, the weeds were wrapped about my head ... the bars of the earth closed upon me forever." Why such an experience? What purpose did it serve? For Jonah, it caused him to repent and turn to God in his distress. He prayed earnestly. He remembered the Lord. He even gave thanks and by faith cried out, "Salvation is of Jehovah!" In that horrible place Jonah was restored to the Lord and fitted for the great work which He had for him to do.

For us who hope never to be swallowed by great fishes, it provides a very effective object lesson on the disadvantages of disobedience. The Lord sometimes uses extreme measures to get the attention of His straying servants. As Sovereign, He is not limited to those means which might appeal to human logic and sensibilities. Most significantly, it provides a foreshadow of the death that our Lord Jesus Christ would die hundreds of years after Jonah. He Himself spoke of this shortly before His death, "For even as Jonas was in the belly of the great fish three days and three nights, thus shall the Son of man be in the heart of the earth three days and three nights."

As Jonah burst forth from the mouth of the great fish, so our Lord arose triumphant over the grave. But while Jonah's deliverance was only for himself, the resurrection of our triumphant Savior is for us. Jesus our Lord "was delivered for our offenses, and was raised for our justification" (Rom. 4:25).

G. W. Steidl

June   **6**   Thursday

Ye shall receive power, after that the Holy Ghost is come upon you: and ye shall be witnesses unto Me both in Jerusalem, and in all Judea, and in Samaria, and unto the uttermost part of the earth.   *(Acts 1:8 KJV)*

That Christians should be witnesses unto the Lord Jesus Christ is a fact that is made very clear in the Word of God. That many Christians have failed to be witnesses for our Lord is also a fact, and a very lamentable one. To be satisfied with the fact that one is saved and feels no responsibility beyond that is a sad situation, and may cast doubt about the reality of one's faith. This should lead one to examine himself to make certain that his faith is not the kind described in James 2:26, "For as the body without the spirit is dead, so faith without works is dead also." It is not that every believer is expected to be an evangelist, but every believer should seek to do the work of an evangelist, though it may be on a very small scale.

A believer cannot be totally silent about his faith, and especially where there is freedom of religion. "It is not merely that we are saved from hell," wrote C. H. Mackintosh, "that is true; it is not merely that we are pardoned, justified, and accepted; all this is true, but we are called to the high and holy work of bearing through this world the name, the testimony, the glory, of our Lord Jesus Christ."

The apostle Paul quotes from Psalm 116 in 2 Corinthians 4:13, saying, "*We* having the same spirit of faith, according as it is written, I believed, and therefore have I spoken; we also believe and therefore speak." The apostles Peter and John were not standing before friendly interrogators when they said, "Whether it be right in the sight of God to hearken unto you more than unto God, judge ye. For **we cannot but speak** the things which we have seen and heard" (Acts 4:19-20).

A. M. Behnam

Asher did not dispossess the inhabitants of Accho, nor the inhabitants of Zidon ... and the Asherites dwelt among the Canaanites, the inhabitants of the land; for they did not dispossess them.
(Judges 1:31-32)

These are the nations that Jehovah left, to prove Israel by them ... all the Canaanites, and the Sidonians. *(Judges 3:1,3)*

Jesus, going forth from thence, went away into the parts of Tyre and Sidon; and lo, a Canaanitish woman, coming out from those borders, cried to Him. *(Matthew 15:21-22)*

THE WOMAN OF CANAAN (1)

The story of the encounter of a woman of Canaan with the Lord Jesus has often perplexed expositors and readers, but in reality is full of heart-touching instruction. Before turning to the Gospel account it would be well first to look at this woman's intriguing ancestral background and history.

She was a Canaanite from the region of towns around Tyre and Sidon (Zidon) in what is now the country of Lebanon and was part of ancient Phoenicia. We read in Joshua that this area was included in the allotments given to Israel and in particular given to the tribe of Asher for them to possess (Josh. 13:1-6). The tribe of Asher failed to drive the Canaanites out of Zidon (Judg. 3:1-3). On the human side, Israel failed to dispossess many of the Canaanites, yet on the divine side the Canaanites were left in the land for a purpose. God used them to prove and to scourge Israel (Judg. 2:3; 3:1-3).

The Canaanites were the descendents of Ham and thus were under a curse from God (Gen. 9:25). They were given over to idolatry of the most defiling kind and its resulting demonism. It was for this reason Jehovah had purposed destruction for them (Gen. 15:16; Lev. 18:24). Yet, there would be a daughter of Canaan whose faith could not be denied, and who would receive a blessing in an appointment with the Son of the Living God.

B. Reynolds

Jesus, going forth from thence, went away into the parts of Tyre and Sidon; and lo, a Canaanitish woman ... cried to Him saying, Have pity on me, Lord, Son of David; my daughter is miserably possessed by a demon. But He did not answer her a word ... But she came and did Him homage, saying, Lord, help me. But He answering said, It is not well to take the bread of the children and cast it to the dogs. *(Matthew 15:21-23,25-26)*

THE WOMAN OF CANAAN (2)

Have you ever wondered why the Lord Jesus answered this woman with what appears to be indifference? In looking closely at this passage it will be discovered that it was not indifference on the Lord's part. Rather, the story of the Canaanitish woman is a striking example of how He appreciates and answers genuine faith; a faith that will not be denied and that perseveres.

She had called Him, **"Son of David,"** but she could not really approach Him this way, for she was a Canaanite. The Lord states that He had been sent to save the lost sheep of Israel (v. 24). *As the Son of David* His mission was to Israel only and not to the Gentiles (Mt. 10:5-6). In contrast to this, the attitude of the disciples was dismissive: "Send her away; for she crieth after us" (v. 23 KJV). Their dealing with her was much different from that of the Lord Jesus—to them she was just a nuisance! But the Lord knew her heart; His purpose was to give her a blessing!

She then drops the title, "Son of David," and simply cries, "Lord, help me!" The Lord now explains His initial silence to her, "It is not well to take the bread of the children and cast it to the dogs." The children (the people of Israel) were the heirs of the promises but the dogs (the Gentiles) were "aliens" and "afar off" from the "covenants of promise" (Eph. 2:11-13). Her answer of faith was: **"Even the dogs eat of the crumbs"** which fall from their master's table! Her great faith was answered and her daughter was healed **that hour** (v. 28)!

B. Reynolds

Mary therefore, having taken a pound of ointment of pure nard of great price, anointed the feet of Jesus, and wiped his feet with her hair, and the house was filled with the odor of the ointment.

(John 12:3)

Bethany may mean "house of affliction" or "house of response," but both were true of the house that was a home to the Lord Jesus there. Death had afflicted it, but now, following His gracious and powerful intervention in raising Lazarus, there was response: free-hearted service from Martha, fellowship out of death with Lazarus, and worship—perhaps the most beautiful example of it in Scripture—by Mary.

What she brought to the Lord Jesus had substance and was good: a pound of ointment. It was pure as becomes Him, and a sacrifice because of its great cost to her. She honored Him by anointing Him with it, but not in a formal or routine way. She was "in" what she did. She poured all of it on Him and wiped *His* feet with *her* hair. There was extravagance for Him and self-abeyance for her. It was at once intimate and reverential. She did not speak a word—entirely becoming for a woman in that setting—but the whole house was filled with the odor, the beautiful effect, of what she had offered.

This is probably as much as our minds can take in of worship in picture-form but no doubt the Holy Spirit indites it to help us in our worship, whether audible or silent. Being in the house means it has particular application to the Assembly, but if our worship is like Mary's—scriptural, genuine, treasured up, submissive, from-the-heart; it will have a spiritual effect wherever we are, for the Lord will take pleasure in it. But let us remember that it will be but the fruit in us of what He accomplished on that cross: everything for God and for us; nothing at all for Himself. "Christ loved us, and delivered Himself up for us, an offering and sacrifice to God for a sweet-smelling savor" (Eph. 5:2).

S. Attwood

Command the children of Israel that they put out of the camp every leper, everyone who has a discharge, and whoever becomes defiled by a corpse. You shall put out both male and female; you shall put them outside the camp, that they may not defile their camps in the midst of which I dwell. And the children of Israel did so, and put them outside the camp. *(Numbers 5:2-4 NKJV)*

THE SACRIFICES IN THE BOOK OF NUMBERS (1)

God's people traveling through the wilderness! Redeemed from bondage under Pharaoh, Israel was on the way to the Promised Land. The only nation in the world that truly belonged to God, she was led by Him, and needed to be in tune with His holiness. God therefore gave rules for the whole nation to be organized as a beautiful camp, pitched around the tabernacle, or traveling with God's dwelling-place among them. An impressive view, a beautiful testimony of God's thoughts to the world! Yet, in a sense, everything was temporary, for they were on a journey. Stationary and waiting, or traveling, God Himself was among them and His holiness needed to be respected. There was no room for sin, self-will, or contamination: any form of what was wrong had to be removed from His camp and testimony.

1. Leprosy depicts unrestrained self-will, the power of sin in one of God's people, when one refuses to judge himself.

2. The issue or flux flowing from a person depicts a lack, or even absence, of self-control.

3. Any contact with or "touch of" death implied exposure to—or influence by—something marked by death. Thus, a religious or man-made system, even if originally given by God, is "dead" and without real life. Nicodemus, a chief rabbi and teacher, still had to be born again.

God's people need to be separate and stay away from all such influences. These forms of evil—if not judged—have the potential of thoroughly affecting others: the whole camp would become defiled and God's testimony spoiled!

A. E. Bouter

Whosoever shall confess that Jesus is the Son of God, God abides in him, and he in God. And we have known and have believed the love which God has to us. God is love, and he that abides in love abides in God, and God in him. *(1 John 4:15-16)*

There are no vague uncertainties here, but a living knowledge of the love of God. This is true Christianity. "We have known and believed." Observe too that this is no mere dealing with love as a subjective thing, something that has become a snare to too many. To know and to enjoy love rightly, it must be objective. Feelings are no basis of reasoning at all. It is not a question of whether I feel that I am loved; but of *knowing* and *believing* it on the basis of the fact being true. It is altogether apart from my feelings: therefore I ought to commit myself wholeheartedly to believe it. This is only reasonable and right. The proofs of that love, in the incarnation of the Lord Jesus and in His matchless sacrifice for our sakes, are so strong and unquestionable that only stubborn rebellion would dare to doubt it. God is love. It is His very nature: therefore He loves.

It is not the ardor of my response that determines whether or not He loves me. He does so because it is His nature, apart from anything in me that draws out such love. Therefore I believe it, for it is true. And believing it, I dwell in love, I dwell in God, and God in me. It is a permanent abiding because the love of the eternal God is a permanent love. This provides the only stable basis for the responsive flowing out of love from our own hearts toward God and toward others. And this latter is precious, too, but only when the first is its source.

L. M. Grant

Yes, Thou art love: a truth like this
Can every gloomy thought remove,
And turn our tears and woes to bliss;
Our God is love.

J. Bowring

The priests blew with the trumpets before the ark of God; and Obed-Edom and Jehijah were doorkeepers for the ark. And David, and the elders of Israel ... went to bring up the ark of the covenant of Jehovah ... with joy.   *(1 Chronicles 15:24-25)*

DAVID'S NEW CART (5)

Let us now see the happy effect of the "due order" being adhered to in David's case. If you want to know where to find the due order, read Exodus 25:13-15. The ark was only to be carried after that manner. God had written it plainly enough. But David had read his Bible carelessly. When David's new cart was in use we find that stumbling, death, displeasure, and disappointment were manifested, and joy, gladness, and worship conspicuous by their absence. All this is reversed when the "due order" is observed: "Lifting up the voice with joy" (v. 16) was heard.

Only the priests could blow the trumpets. It takes a priest to give the signal that gathers the assembly together (Num. 10). And who were the doorkeepers? They took the greatest possible care of the ark.

And surely in connection with the order of the assembly when gathered for worship, the testimony of the gospel, the ministry of the Word of God, and the admission to His assembly today, it is of great importance to have the spirit of the doorkeepers here. We are to be very careful with regard to everything relating to Christ and His interests.

That is the sure result of obedience. "God *helped* the Levites that bore the ark of the covenant of Jehovah" (v. 26). Observe God's notice of the Levites when things are thus according to His mind— they are *helped,* and then typically in the sacrifices you see worship flowing up to God. If you and I set ourselves to really obey the Word of the Lord, no matter what it costs, we too shall find that God will help us, and there will be joy in our souls and worship, and fruitful service Godward.

W. T. P. Wolston

Herod had ... bound [John] in prison on account of Herodias, the wife of Philip his brother, because he had married her. For John said to Herod, It is not lawful for thee to have the wife of thy brother. But Herodias kept it in her mind against him, and wished to kill him, and could not: for Herod feared John knowing that he was a just and holy man, and kept him safe; and having heard him, did many things, and heard him gladly. *(Mark 6:17-20)*

PROPHETS AND THEIR PROPHECIES— JOHN THE BAPTIST (5)

John the Baptist's preaching was not restricted to the common people who came to him in the wilderness and on the bank of the Jordan River. He unflinchingly reproved the tetrarch Herod's wickedness in marrying his brother Philip's wife Herodias. As we read the various passages where this is mentioned, it is evident that John was not preaching sermons about Herod's wickedness to the people, but boldly confronted him to his face.

To tell the ruler of the land "It is not lawful for thee" shows clearly that God's Word is more important than any human king's. God's Word is the ultimate authority for all of mankind from the highest down to the lowest. Repeatedly in Scripture we see God's prophets reproving kings when their conduct was openly contrary to God's commands. But many of those who served God thus had to endure suffering, and even death, as John the Baptist ultimately did, in consequence of the stand they took. God's servants today may still face martyrdom as a possible outcome of faithfulness.

Moral purity seems to have become more and more rare in the world today, especially among those in high places. Wicked men do their own thing. Things God calls reprehensible man legalizes and considers his rights! Yet it is interesting to note that Herod both feared John the Baptist and heard him gladly. May our testimony too be respected by all with whom we have contact!

E. P. Vedder, Jr.

He that testifies these things says, Yea, I come quickly. Amen; come, Lord Jesus. *(Revelation 22:20)*

Israel's calling and that of the Church being so different, it follows of necessity that their hopes also differ. The Lord Jesus is the hope both of the one and the other. He is the hope of the Church as the One who will descend into the air, and receive her to Himself, and to the full consummation of her blessedness with Himself in heaven. He is "the hope of Israel," as the One who will further descend to the earth, delivering them from the yoke of the Gentiles. He will execute judgment on all who have opposed them, and set up on the earth His glorious kingdom, of which Jerusalem is to be the center, and in which Israel, forgiven and purified, is to enjoy the most conspicuous, distinguished place.

Such are the hopes held out to Israel by the Word of God. "The day of vengeance" on God's adversaries is to be the day of Israel's deliverance, and the immediate prelude to Israel's exaltation and full blessing under Messiah's reign. It is impossible, therefore, for an Israelite, as such, to desire or invoke Jehovah's intervention, or Messiah's coming, for the fulfillment of Israel's national hopes, without invoking or desiring judgment on the wicked.

The hopes of the Church, on the contrary, are quite unconnected with the thought of judgment on the wicked. She is aware indeed that judgment on the ungodly will ensue on her own removal from the earth: still, that for which she waits is not a state of earthly blessedness which judgment on the wicked is to introduce, but her own translation from amid the scene of evil to meet her Lord in the air, and to be "forever with the Lord." This is the hope which the Church, or the saint, can both cherish and express without a thought of the wicked, or of the judgments to be executed upon them. The descent of the Lord Jesus into the air is the Church's blessed hope.

W. Trotter

June   **15**   Saturday

**Samson said to them, Let me now propound a riddle to you …
And they said to him, Propound thy riddle, that we may hear it.
And he said to them, Out of the eater came forth food, and out
of the strong came forth sweetness. And they could not in three
days explain the riddle.** *(Judges 14:12-14)*

The hand that smote the lion held the honey, and Samson shared it,
the remarkable fruit of his victory, with his parents as they walked
in company with him. The great antitype of this should yield abundant joy to us. All blessing is held in the mighty hand that smote
the power of death, and it is the delight of our Lord Jesus Christ to
dispense to us of that which He holds so securely.

Some would have us believe that salvation, and indeed every
blessing, has been deposited in the Church for us, and that we can
neither know nor realize these things apart from it. Alas for us if
this were so; for the Church in its responsibility has utterly failed,
for it has joined hands with the world. But Christ can never fail: He
has risen up victoriously above all the ruin and wreck which sin and
death have made, and all the promises of God are yea and amen in
Him. As we cleave to Him we shall have our hearts nourished and
made glad by the sweet fruits of His death.

The Philistines who came to the wedding feast, and were only
nominally attached to Samson, did not taste the honey from the
lion's carcase. They represent professors without possession, who
have accepted the form of Christianity without the power. To all
such the truth of God is but so many doctrines to be discussed and
riddles to be solved. There is nothing in the death of Christ that appeals to such; they cannot understand blessing coming out of death;
they cannot see how meat can come forth from the eater, or sweetness from the strong one.

J. T. Mawson

As often as ye shall eat this bread, and drink the cup, ye announce the death of the Lord, until He come.

(1 Corinthians 11:26)

The institution of the Lord's Supper must be regarded, by every spiritual man, as a peculiarly touching proof of the Lord's gracious care and considerate love for His Church. From the time of its appointment until the present hour, it has been a steady, though silent, witness to a truth which the enemy has sought to corrupt and set aside: that redemption is an accomplished fact to be enjoyed by the weakest believer in Jesus. Centuries have rolled away since the Lord Jesus appointed "the bread and the cup." Notwithstanding all the heresy, all the schism, all the controversy and strife, this most expressive institution has been observed by the saints of God in every age.

True, the enemy has succeeded, throughout a vast section of the professing Church, in wrapping it up in a shroud of dark superstition. Yet it still speaks to every spiritual mind, the same deep and precious truth, it "shows the Lord's death till He come." The body has been broken, the blood has been shed *once*, no more to be repeated: and the breaking of bread is but the memorial of this emancipating truth.

With what profound interest and thankfulness should the believer contemplate "the bread and the cup." There is the setting forth of truths most precious and glorious: grace reigning; redemption finished; sin put away; everlasting righteousness brought in; the sting of death gone; eternal glory secured; "grace and glory" revealed as the free gift of God; and the unity of the "one body." What a feast! It carries the soul back and shows us the Master Himself, "in the same night in which He was betrayed," sitting at the supper table, and there instituting a feast which from that memorable night, until the dawn of the morning, should lead every believing heart, at once, backward to the cross, and forward to the glory.

C. H. Mackintosh

God saw their works, that they turned from their evil way; and God repented of the evil that He had said He would do unto them, and He did it not. And it displeased Jonah exceedingly, and he was angry. *(Jonah 3:10–4:1)*

The story of Jonah has no happy ending—at least as far as Jonah was concerned. This remarkable man had so much going for him: tremendous experiences of God's faithfulness and power; direct revelation from God; great success as a preacher. Joy should have filled his heart as Nineveh repented at his preaching, and was spared from the judgment of God. But it didn't! Instead he was filled with anger, self-pity, and deep depression. Why?

First, because God acted contrary to what Jonah thought he should do. Forgiveness for Nineveh was God's idea, not Jonah's. He wanted to see the city burn. After all, it was an inveterate enemy and oppressor of Israel and deserved to be judged.

Second, because Jonah felt the outcome of the matter had tarnished his reputation as a prophet. Nineveh wasn't overthrown in forty days as he said it would be. What would happen to his credibility? Before writing Jonah off, let's consider his actions and attitudes in relation to our own: Do we turn off when the Lord doesn't do what we think He should? Are we concerned with saving face—preserving our pride at the expense of love and forgiveness towards others and repentance towards God?

God's long-suffering patience towards Jonah (and us) is amazing. He reasoned with him, gave him object lessons, and unveiled His own great heart of compassion. "Should not I have pity on Nineveh, the great city, wherein are more than 120,000 persons that cannot discern between their right hand and their left hand; and also much cattle?" (Jon. 4:11).

G. W. Steidl

Herein has love been perfected with us that we may have boldness in the day of judgment, that even as He is, we also are in this world. There is no fear in love, but perfect love casts out fear; for fear has torment, and he that fears has not been made perfect in love.   (*1 John 4:17-18*)

Certainly God desires us to be made perfect in love. But how is this done? It is by knowing and believing the love that God has to us, that is, the plain recognition of the fact that God's love to us is itself perfection.

The knowledge of this unqualified, unchangeable love gives boldness even in view of the day of judgment. In pure love He has given His Son to bear my judgment, fully, absolutely. Then the day of judgment is no occasion of fear whatever: God's love is too great to allow me to entertain for a moment the thought that judgment might possibly overtake me. His love has so wrought as to be the same toward me as toward His own Son: "As He is, we also are in this world." Amazing statement of simple, easy words!

Is Christ not completely immune from judgment now? He has in grace borne this at Calvary, the full, unmitigated penalty against sin being laid upon Him, the willing Sacrifice. The work now finished, He is crowned with glory and honor, eternally exalted, having abolished death, triumphing over it. And so far as judgment is concerned, the believer even now "in this world" is "as He *is*," past all possibility of judgment, accepted in righteousness and joy before the Father's face—a present, permanent place of unmingled blessing.

A child's certainty of his parents' unfeigned, unchanging love gives him confidence. There is no element of terror in that filial relationship. How much more does God's perfect love cast out fear. This realization is being made perfect in love.

L. M. Grant

He leadeth me beside still waters.   *(Psalm 23:2)*

The still waters speak of quietness of heart, not necessarily because circumstances are quiet, but peace and quietness of heart no matter what the circumstances may be. Do you remember that wonderful passage, "Thou wilt keep him in perfect peace whose mind is stayed on Thee, because he trusteth in Thee"? It is not: "Thou wilt place him in the midst of a peaceful environment." It means that we may be in perfect peace in the midst of circumstances that seem all against us.

We have an example of it in the Lord Jesus Himself. Recall that incident on the Lake of Galilee, when a great storm arose. The winds blew and the waves dashed in their fury against the tiny boat in which He sailed, and it seemed as though it would be broken and wrecked by the angry tempest. All in that boat, seasoned mariners though they were, were in a panic of fear, save One.

Why did not the disciples stretch themselves by His side, and share the peace that filled His blessed heart? They awoke Him from His sleep, and with one word He brought those tempestuous billows in quietness to His feet as a man might bring his dog to his heel. But those disciples were just as safe in the storm as they were when a great calm laid itself upon the sea, and there was no reason why they should not have shared His peace. The Lord can give His peace to our hearts, but we shall need a pillow to put our heads upon or we shall not enjoy it. What pillow was it that Jesus put His head upon? The pillow of His Father's changeless love! He knew that His hand held the reins, and in the knowledge of His Father's changeless love, He could rest, and He gives us that same love to rest upon. "We know that all things work together for good to them that love God." But we only enjoy the fact as long as He leads us. If we wander from His side, we are distraught and restless.

J. T. Mawson

John, having heard in the prison the works of the Christ, sent by his disciples, and said to Him, Art Thou the Coming One? Or are we to wait for another? And Jesus answering said to them, Go, report to John what ye hear and see. Blind men see ... and blessed is whosoever shall not be offended in Me. But as they went away, Jesus began to say to the crowds concerning John, What went ye out into the wilderness to see? ... a prophet? Yea, I say to you, and more than a prophet. *(Matthew 11:2-9)*

PROPHETS AND THEIR PROPHECIES– JOHN THE BAPTIST (6)

John the Baptist who had been sought out by crowds of repentant Israelites found prison a hard place to be. Herod had imprisoned him for denouncing his marriage to his brother's wife, Herodias, but kept him imprisoned to keep him safe from her; meanwhile he heard him gladly (Mk. 6:19-20). As day followed day; nothing was changing for John. His thoughts plagued him: Jesus did miracles. Why was He doing nothing to help him? Had he erred in pointing to Him as God's Lamb who would take away the sin of the world?

He sent two of his disciples to pose the question directly to Jesus. "In that hour He healed many of diseases and plagues and evil spirits, and to many blind He granted sight" (Lk. 7:21). Then He sent back the messengers to tell John what they had seen and heard. His power was undiminished. "Blessed is whosoever is not offended in Me." We usually do not understand His ways. His ways and thoughts are higher than ours as the heavens are higher than the earth. But our part is to walk by faith, not by sight!

How vigorously the Lord defends His prophet before the crowd who had heard the doubt he had expressed! John was no reed shaken by the wind. He was in the king's prison, not in his palace! He was a prophet who had been the object of prophecy, and if they would receive it, he was that Elias who was to come. Wonderful Lord!

E. P. Vedder, Jr.

June 21 Friday

Melchizedek king of Salem brought forth bread and wine ... And the king of Sodom said unto Abram, Give me the persons, and take the goods to thyself. *(Genesis 14:18,21 KJV)*

We witness here a deeply interesting scene. Abram himself is about to meet a temptation, repulsed indeed by the power of God in him, but nevertheless, a temptation. The king of Sodom was about to come forth to display his treasures before the eye of Abram. The enemy was about to display his gilded bait before the eye of the man of God, and therefore is Melchizedek at hand to display in his view the divine realities of the kingdom. He was about to feed and strengthen his soul with the "bread and wine," of the kingdom, in order that he might mount above the influence of all the allurements of the world.

Upon what are you now feeding? What constitutes your habitual food? Is it "the bread and wine" which the Lord provides, or "the goods" of Sodom? Are your ears open to the pernicious suggestions of the *King of Sodom*, or to the heavenly communications of the *King of Salem?* The Lord grant that our hearts may ever choose that in which He delights.

But to proceed, Melchizedek leads Abram's soul into present communion with **the Most High God, the Possessor of Heaven and Earth** (vv. 19,22). Thus he completes the wondrous contrast between the King of Sodom and the Most High God, Possessor of heaven and earth; the goods of Sodom and the extensive possessions of heaven and earth. Blessed contrast, which faith ever draws! It is needless to say that Abram at once rejects the offer of the King of Sodom. The bread and wine, and the benediction of the priest of the Most High God, had raised Abram to such a height that he could, in one comprehensive glance, take in the vast possessions of heaven and earth, and further, look down from thence upon the despicable proposal of the King of Sodom and reject it.

C. H. Mackintosh

June 22 Saturday

Woe, woe, the great city ... for in one hour she has been made desolate. *(Revelation 18:19)*

Disaster and desolation in **one hour**! Can it be possible that the great religious and financial systems of the world that man has built through his energy and ingenuity will fall in literally one hour? Many people deny this could actually happen in "one hour." They say Revelation is highly symbolic and therefore is not to be understood literally. However, prophetic symbols are portraying literal events which will actually occur. Most time-related events in Revelation should be understood literally, for example: the half hour of silence in heaven (ch. 8:1), the 42-month reign of the "beast" (ch. 13:5), and the 1000-year millennial reign of Christ (ch. 20:4-6), are all literal periods of time.

Recent events in our world may serve as instructive forerunners of what is possible and indeed, of what will come. On September 11th 2001, New York and Washington were attacked by 19 terrorists. They came very close to achieving their goal, but how quickly it all transpired! Again, more recently, the financial crisis of 2008-2009 is another example. The western governments, especially the United States, came very close to a total financial meltdown. But again, how quickly it all unfolded! Only robust intervention by the governments averted total disaster. Catastrophic events can arise suddenly.

On the authority of the Word of God we can confidently say that the greatest religious and commercial system the world has ever seen, **Great Babylon,** will come crashing down in the space of "one hour." We read, "And a strong angel took up a stone, as a great millstone, and cast it into the sea, saying, Thus with violence shall Babylon the great city be cast down" (ch. 18:21). Seeing that these things are coming upon Christendom, we should walk in separation from all that is dishonoring to Christ while we wait for Him.

B. Reynolds

I am not ashamed of the glad tidings; for it is God's power to salvation, to everyone that believes, both to Jew first and to Greek. *(Romans 1:16)*

Dr. Berry, a preacher famed throughout the English-speaking world, was a liberal theologian when the following incident took place.

"One night there came to me," he says, "a Lancashire girl with her shawl over her head and clogs on her feet.

"'I want you to come and get my mother in,' she said. 'She is dying, and I want you to get her into salvation.'

"I did all I could to get out of it, but it was of no use. I found the house, and upstairs I found the poor woman dying. I sat down and talked about Jesus as the beautiful Example, and extolled *Him* as a Leader and Teacher. She looked at me out of the eyes of death and said: 'Mister, that's no good for the likes of me. I don't want an example. I'm a sinner.'

"There I was face to face with a poor soul dying, and had nothing to tell her. I had no gospel; but I thought of what my mother had taught me, and I told her the old story of God's love in Christ's dying for sinful men, whether I believed it or not.

"'Now you are getting at it,' said the woman. 'That's the story for me.'

"And so I got her in, and I got myself in. From that night" added Dr. Berry, "I have always had a full gospel of salvation for lost sinners."

What a testimony to the old-fashioned gospel preached by Paul, Wycliffe, Luther, Wesley, Whitefield, Spurgeon, and multitudes of sainted men of God—the old, old story for which Huss, Ridley, Latimer, Cranmer, and thousands besides have died, rather than surrender its blessing.

It is still doing its happy work in spite of the flood of evil cast out by the dragon's mouth. It is still winning its peaceful conquests. Nothing can stop it.

A. J. Pollock

The man shall bring his wife to the priest. He shall bring the offering required for her, one-tenth of an ephah of barley meal; he shall pour no oil on it and put no frankincense on it, because it is a grain offering of jealousy, an offering for remembering, for bringing iniquity to remembrance ... But if the woman has not defiled herself, and is clean, then she shall be free and may conceive children ...: the man shall be free from iniquity, but that woman shall bear her guilt. *(Numbers 5:15,28,31 NKJV)*

THE SACRIFICES IN THE BOOK OF NUMBERS (2)

The sacrifices in Leviticus are linked to God's sanctuary. The offerings in Numbers, however, are typically related to Israel's wilderness journey, its challenges and their failures. That journey, described in Numbers, demonstrates the people's unfaithfulness but also God's faithfulness.

A wife suspected of unfaithfulness illustrates Israel's situation. The husband depicts the LORD to whom Israel was married since the giving of the Law. The meal offering was of barley; usually it would have oil and frankincense added to it, but in this case that was forbidden. In Leviticus, the meal offering represents Christ in His perfect humanity, life, and faithfulness, whereas here it is linked with (suspected) unfaithfulness. No oil (the Holy Spirit's activities) or frankincense (Christ's personal perfections) could be added. Yet, this sacrifice was needed as a sin-offering.

These things also apply to the professing Church with its many failures, as well as to individual believers. Here, the jealous husband represents the exalted Christ who desires our true devotion. He expresses Himself through the apostle Paul: "For I am jealous for you with a godly jealousy; for I betrothed you to one husband, that to Christ I might present you as a pure virgin" (2 Cor. 11:2 NASB).

A. E. Bouter

Our commonwealth has its existence in the heavens, from which also we await the Lord Jesus Christ.   *(Philippians 3:20)*

Everybody says that a citizen of the country, a Christian, should be interested in the government of the country to which he belongs, and ought to vote, so as to help to put good men in power. God says differently; in many places and ways He tells me that, as His child, I am not a citizen of any country, or a member of any society; my citizenship is in heaven, and I have henceforth to do with heavenly things; the cross of Christ has crucified me to the world, and the world to me; if I give my mind and heart to these earthly things I shall be the enemy of the cross of Christ.

What then shall we do with governments? Why, *submit to them,* since God orders them; and when they impose tax, pay; and make supplication to God for kings and all in authority. All that a Christian has to do with politics is to be subject to the powers set over him. It is true that in Christ he is heir of all things, including the earth in which the world-system now has its operation, yet (like Abraham in Canaan) God gives him not so much as to set his foot on for *a present* inheritance.

If, then, the true child of God refuses to vote, it is not so much that he thinks voting in itself wrong, as that he has given his vote and interest to the Man in heaven, whom God has exalted as King of kings, and Lord of lords. He has lost his interest in these things by virtue of something he has found which is far more attractive. He sees that the world in essence is ungodly, that its boasted reforms and improvement are all tending to shut out God from the heart of man. He desires to stand as a witness for the truth and for God, and of the coming judgment, at the appearing of Christ when men are congratulating themselves on peace and safety. He desires that others may escape the snare by which Satan is entrapping mankind.

J. N. Darby

It came to pass as the ark of the covenant of Jehovah came to the city of David, that Michal the daughter of Saul looked through a window, and saw king David dancing and playing; and she despised him in her heart.   *(1 Chronicles 15:29)*

DAVID'S NEW CART (6)

Perhaps you will find somebody will despise you, as here we find Michal despising David. Never mind that; I would rather be an obedient David than a despising Michal. God has given to you and me an opportunity, in the absence of the Lord Jesus Christ, to be faithful to His truth. We have the knowledge that the Holy Spirit is still in the Assembly on the earth, and some of us have by God's grace learned the truth as to His Assembly, and what it is to be gathered to the name of the Lord Jesus Christ. Well, if we have that truth, let us be true to it, and let us walk in the liberty of the truth.

There were those who would not have Paul's heavenly line of things, and turned away from him. I think it is a great privilege, a great favor from God, if He has given us to see and seek to act on recovered truth and light. I believe we have it by God's grace. Should it puff us up? God forbid! It was grace that called us as sinners, and if God has given us the light and truth of the Assembly, and what ministry really is, and what it is to be gathered to the Lord's name, it is an immense favor.

God give us grace to be true to what the Lord has taught us. Because depend upon it, "Whosoever hath, to him shall be given; and whosoever hath not, from him shall be taken even that which he seemeth to have" (Lk. 8:18 KJV). If people do not cherish the truth God has given them, by and by their vision becomes dull, and in time they become the most determined opponents of the truth they once prized. That is an awful thing. The Lord help us to be true to Himself for His name's sake!

W. T. P. Wolston

Let it be allowed to speak with freedom to you concerning the patriarch David, that he has both died and been buried, and his monument is amongst us unto this day. Being therefore a prophet, and knowing that God had sworn to him with an oath, of the fruit of his loins to set upon his throne; he, seeing it before, spoke concerning the resurrection of the Christ, that neither has He been left in Hades nor his flesh seen corruption. *(Acts 2:29-31)*

PROPHETS AND THEIR PROPHECIES—DAVID

If we are asked who David was, we may well answer, the shepherd boy who killed Goliath, or a king, or the writer of many psalms. We do not generally think of Him as a prophet, but the apostle Peter, preaching in the power of the Holy Spirit, here calls him that. He refers to one of his prophecies, quoting Psalm 16:8-11, and applying the passage to the resurrection of the Lord Jesus.

When Peter and John in Acts 4 were forbidden by the Jewish high council to speak or teach in the name of Jesus, their Christian brethren broke out in prayer. In their prayer they quoted the first two verses of Psalm 2, ascribing this psalm to David, something not mentioned in the Old Testament. They point out the prophetic significance of this psalm, applying it to the enmity of Herod, Pilate, the nations, and the people of Israel against God's holy Servant Jesus, which resulted in His crucifixion.

David wrote about half of the psalms. It was not only Israel's hymnbook, but it is a prophetic book. We classify many psalms as messianic, for they describe graphically Christ's sufferings and refer to the glories that should follow. In these psalms we find the intense holy feelings of our Lord, especially while enduring the agonies of the cross. The psalms also present a prophetic picture of the feelings of the future Jewish remnant during the Tribulation after the Church has been caught up to glory. And who of us has not personally enjoyed many psalms devotionally?

E. P. Vedder, Jr.

To you it is commanded, O peoples, nations, and languages, that at what time ye hear the sound of the cornet, pipe, lute … and all kinds of music, ye fall down and worship the golden image that Nebuchadnezzar the king hath set up. *(Daniel 3:4-5)*

The special place given to the orchestra in Daniel 3 is very noticeable, as much so as in large worldly religious gatherings at the present time. It excites the emotions, and, thus working upon the feelings, gives people a sense of devotion, which after all may be very unreal. In the Old Testament musical instruments were used in the ornate temple services; but there is certainly no warrant for it in the New Testament. People may call it worship to sit and listen to a trained choir and orchestra rendering sweet strains; but the music simply acts upon the sensuous part of our natures, and has nothing to do with the adoration of the Father and the Son, which must be in spirit and in truth. Those who plead for its use, because of its place in Old Testament times, should remember that it was a "typical" dispensation. The instruments then used typified the melody now made in the heart of God's redeemed ones.

A minister once remarked to me that many people attended his church to *worship God in music*; so he ought to have the best performers and the finest music that it was possible to obtain, as otherwise the people would not attend. In reality they are only gratifying their own taste for melody and harmony, a taste God-given and proper enough in its place, but not to be confounded with true worship. A heart filled with Christ gives forth the sweetest music that ever reaches the ear of God.

Let us remember, then, that in the New Testament dispensation it is "singing and chanting with your hearts to the Lord" (Eph. 5:19) to which the Christian is exhorted. That is where the music is to be—a heart full of praises to the God of all grace. May we know more of it!

H. A. Ironside

Let no corrupt communication proceed out of your mouth, but that which is good to the use of edifying, that it may minister grace unto the hearers. *(Ephesians 4:29 KJV)*
Let your speech be always with grace, seasoned with salt, that ye may know how ye ought to answer every man. *(Colossians. 4:6 KJV)*

The word of God has much to say about our speech. In the book of Proverbs there are several instructions concerning the right and wrong use of the tongue. Here are a few examples: 1. Warning against being talkative, "When there are many words, transgression is unavoidable. But he who restrains his lips is wise" (Prov. 10:19 NASB). 2. Concerning harsh words, "A gentle answer turns away wrath, but a harsh word stirs up anger" (Prov. 15:1 NASB). 3. The power of our words, "Death and life are in the power of the tongue" (Prov. 18:21 NASB).

The seriousness of this subject is expounded upon by the Holy Spirit in James 3, a chapter that has warnings needed for all of us. Many homes were ruined by misuse of the tongue, and many local assemblies of believers lost their testimony because of careless speech. No wonder David, who indited many beautiful psalms, asks the Lord for help: "Let the words of my **mouth,** and the meditation of my **heart,** be acceptable in Thy sight" (Ps. 19:14 KJV). Notice the relation between the mouth and the heart: "For out of the abundance of the heart the mouth speaketh" (Mt. 12:34).

The more we sit in His presence and hear His words, the less likely we will speak carelessly. Of Him it is written that grace was poured into His lips (Ps. 45:2 JND), this is why "all were speaking well of Him, and wondering at the gracious words which were falling from His lips" (Lk. 4:22 NASB). Seeing the seriousness of this subject may each of us take this matter to the Lord and say with David: **"Set a guard, O LORD, over my mouth; keep watch over the door of my lips"** (Ps. 141:3 NASB).

A. M. Behnam

Men of Galilee, why do ye stand looking into heaven? This Jesus who has been taken up from you into heaven shall thus come in the manner in which ye have beheld Him going into heaven.

(Acts 1:11)

If there be no personal coming in glory of Jesus, specifically in person as the Son of God, all is lost, though that cannot of course be. If there is no personal coming of Jesus in glory, His Person ceases to be the great question of glory, which it is with the Father.

His first coming was in witness; His second coming is in Person, when every eye shall see Him, and the glory of Him who was hidden shall be known. The knowledge of the Son all rests in His glorious appearing. Till that appearing, the Church is merely a witness of the truth of Him who shall then be manifested; and they, believing the truth, shall appear with Him in glory.

Let the Church deny this, and it ceases to be a Church. It is gone and it must be cut off in its form. God may bear with ignorance and slowness of heart as He does daily with all of us; but let the Church deny His coming in glory and the ground of its existence has ceased. The Spirit has no office either, for its office is to testify of Jesus, the glory of Jesus as having all things that the Father has. Let the Church deny that He is to have it, and what is she suffering for? Nothing! She is joined to the world. She has ceased in her existence.

Our understanding of His coming in glory may be all mixed up. Our unbelief may quench it. As unscriptural men, we may mistake also other things for it; but if it ceases, the Church ceases—it has no purpose. But His personal coming in glory has not ceased to exist in the Church. God has not left Himself without witness. Let everything be judged, but let not God be denied.

J. N. Darby

They angered him also at the waters of strife, so that it went ill with Moses for their sakes: because they provoked his spirit, so that he spake unadvisedly with his lips. *(Psalm 106:32-33 KJV)*

Perhaps there is no greater hindrance to the Holy Spirit being poured out abundantly than a wrong spirit about wrong things.

These verses sum up Numbers 20:1-13. The people were thirsty and uttered rebellious words against God and against Moses. God came in and wrought deliverance, but the spirit of Moses and Aaron was provoked. Scripture comments: "It went ill with Moses." Who was Moses? Few men had such privileges. See this aged servant of God, who was faithful in all God's house; yet in this fortieth year of the wilderness journey this great disaster came on that man.

Are we not liable to disaster from the same cause? It went ill with Moses, and the crowning honor of his life was withheld. But the people were wicked? Yes, atrociously wrong; "they provoked his spirit." But Moses was wrong, and who can tell the loss it brought into his own life?

Children of God often talk of "righteous indignation"; they feel wrong things so keenly, and the devil takes advantage to provoke the spirit, and the child of God does not see that this is a hateful thing to God, the greatest hindrance in communion and service.

Turning to the narrative in Exodus 17, of the smitten Rock, we have the record of an event which took place forty years before. The people were thirsty and wanted water; there was a wicked, murmuring spirit, much wrongdoing; they were exasperating and ungrateful to the last degree. But the wrong did not get into the spirit of Moses. He put the case into God's hands, and God came in and worked salvation. An unprovoked spirit always calls God to the scene. The provoked spirit shuts God out. This is why the devil works to get us provoked.

Meat in Due Season

Surely I count also all things to be loss on account of the excellency of the knowledge of Christ Jesus my Lord, on account of whom I have suffered the loss of all and count them to be filth, that I may gain Christ.   *(Philippians 3:8)*

With these few words the apostle Paul sweeps the entire old creation into the discard, with no regrets, no looking back. In the knowledge of Christ there is supreme excellency, infinitely above everything that the most exalted experience on earth could afford. Nothing henceforth can turn his eye from Him whom he calls *"Christ Jesus my Lord."* For Him he had suffered the loss of all things. It was not merely that he gave up certain advantages out of appreciation for what Christ had done for him; but the blessed Person of Christ, as now glorified at God's right hand, had so captivated his heart that he would deliberately and fully count everything as "refuse" that he might win Christ.

This is manifestly not the subject of having Christ as the vital *Principle of Life* in his soul, as in chapter 1 of this book; nor having Christ as his *Example,* as in chapter 2 where the humiliation of the Lord is so dwelt upon; but rather having Christ as the *Object* and *Prize* before him—the ultimate end to which he aspires with longing heart. This aspiration is, of course, never to be realized on earth, but only in the glory, where the Object of such hope is seated at God's right hand. His eyes look on to the end of his course, as a racer intent upon the goal: nothing less than arriving where Christ is can ever satisfy his heart.

"Let us also therefore … run with endurance the race that lies before us, looking steadfastly on Jesus the leader and completer of faith: who, in view of the joy lying before Him, endured the cross, having despised the shame, and is set down at the right hand of the throne of God" (Heb. 12:1-2).

L. M. Grant

The righteous shall shoot forth like a palm-tree. *(Psalm 92:12)*

Several interesting facts about the date palm give encouragement and comfort in applying this verse to our lives as Christians:

1. It never grows wild, but must be planted and carefully tended when young. Like ugly weeds, the natural man will grow wild and flourish without being planted or tended. But only God can produce "fruitful trees" by redeeming sinners to Himself and then fashioning them into objects of beauty and fruitfulness.

2. It grows from within. Its bark is only the support and protection of its inner life from whence its fruitfulness comes. The real inner life of a Christian is renewed day by day as he walks with the Lord. It is this inward man that produces fruit for God.

3. It has well over 200 uses, including food and floor mats. Sometimes we foolishly object to some uses God has for us (such as to be a floor mat), but true fruitfulness results from submitting to Him in all things.

4. Its foliage is always green, because of deep roots getting hidden moisture. It thrives even in dry and sandy soil. "Palm tree Christians" do not require a favorable environment to survive; in fact, they often bear the choicest fruit in hostile circumstances.

5. It bears its best fruit in old age. Those Christians who mature and mellow with age become a delight to God, and also serve as a beautiful example to younger saints. They become a source of wonder even to unbelievers. While Satan ruthlessly discards his faithful servants when they become old and feeble, God chooses to give His own a special glow at eventide—a glow that reflects His own glory.

G. W. Steidl

> *To Him I look, while still I run,*
> *My never-failing Friend:*
> *Finish He will the work begun,*
> *And grace in glory end.*

T. Haweis

When He is come, the Spirit of truth, He shall guide you into all the truth: for He shall not speak from Himself ... He shall glorify Me, for He shall receive of Mine and shall announce it to you. *(John 16:13-14)*

The Holy Spirit glorifies Jesus by unfolding to His people Jesus' Person, character, and work. The Spirit is the great ministering agent between the Church on earth and its glorified Head in heaven. He carries up as the Intercessor the ever-recurring needs, trials, perplexities, and sins of believers (Rom. 8:26-27). Then He receives out of Christ's inexhaustible treasury of love, and returns to the people of the Church comfort for their sorrows, strength for their tears, and fullness for their emptiness.

The one sublime object of the Spirit's work, Christ says, is to "glorify Me." The Spirit tells us of Christ's love and delights in magnifying Him in our affections. How faithful He has been in His great office as the "Glorifier of Jesus"! On the day of Pentecost, Peter preached to the Jews with a demonstration of the Spirit and power that Jesus has been exalted "as leader and Savior, to give repentance to Israel and remission of sins" (Acts 5:3). It is still the same peerless truth which the Spirit delights to unfold to the stricken sinner: the glorious beauties of Christ's work.

Do you realize that any understanding you have had of the Savior's glory and excellency is of the Spirit's imparting? And in some hour of sorrow have you experienced the consolation of the thought of the Redeemer's sympathy and sustaining power? This too is the work of the Holy Spirit, taking the things of Christ and showing them to you. As you live your Christian life, seek to bear in mind that the Spirit alone is qualified to impart to you "the excellency of the knowledge of Christ" (Phil. 3:8).

J. R. MacDuff

Let the peace of Christ preside in your hearts, to which also ye have been called in one body, and be thankful ... And everything, whatever ye may do in word or in deed, do all things in the name of the Lord Jesus. *(Colossians 3:15,17)*

In Christ we see the new order of man set forth in perfection. He came down from heaven, and could speak of Himself as "the Son of Man who is in heaven" (Jn. 3:13). He walked amid earth's unrest, but lived in heaven's calm. We pass through a world where there is no peace. Politically, it is a world of wars. Socially, commercially, and religiously, all is unrest and upheaval. The privilege of the Christian is to pass through it, even as Christ, with the peace and calm of heaven in his heart. Whatever the circumstances through which he may be called to pass, with his mind set on things above, he will be kept in the peace which Christ enjoyed.

Furthermore the peace is not only to preside in our hearts, but to be enjoyed in the Christian company; for to this we have been "called in one body." Oneness of the body requires peace between the members if it is to grow with the increase of God. Further, if there is peace in the heart, there will be thankfulness to God. Thus, if marked by grace, love, and peace, the beautiful character of Christ will be reproduced in His people. In the midst of all circumstances we are to give thanks. The Lord, when rejected by Israel, could say, "I praise Thee, Father, Lord of the heaven and of the earth," and Paul could sing in the inner prison, with his feet fast in the stocks (Mt. 11:25; Acts 16:24-25). "Whatsoever we do in word or deed," is to be done in the name of the Lord Jesus. What a simple but searching rule of life. How many questions would at once be solved by this simple test, "Can I do, or say this in the name of the Lord Jesus?" We learn from these exhortations how the character of Christ in the saints, and the practical life they lead, are linked together.

H. Smith

The angel of Jehovah called to him from the heavens, and said, Abraham, Abraham!
(Genesis 22:11)

THE SEVEN DOUBLE CALLS OF PEOPLE (1)—ABRAHAM

There are seven people in the Bible who experienced a unique "double call" of their name at a critical point in their life. This striking fact surely has significance, for our God never does what is random or without meaning. In the lives of Abraham, Jacob, Moses, Samuel, Simon Peter, Martha, and Saul of Tarsus can be traced the sovereign purpose of God in graciously dealing with each of these as an "elect vessel" dear to His heart.

In Abraham we trace a life of faith which pleases God. He answers the call of God to live a life separated from all natural support, leaning entirely on the promise of God. He believed that God would give him an heir, the "promised seed," and this faith was "reckoned to him as righteousness" (Gen. 15:6). Abraham's example of faith was used by the apostle Paul to depict the doctrine of "justification by faith" (Rom. 4:9).

Abraham's faith shines most powerfully in the test of his willingness to offer up his son Isaac. His obedience to God in delivering up the promised heir was a work of faith (Jas. 2:21). He fully believed that God was able to raise Isaac from the dead, for we hear the words of Abraham to the young men that "I and the lad will go yonder ... **and come again to you**" (Gen. 22:5; Heb. 11:19). He knew that Isaac would return with him from the mount! Thus the truth of resurrection shines out in one of the most remarkable "types" found in Scripture! Both Abraham and Isaac ascend the mount "together" (v. 6). The beloved son of the father willingly submits to be sacrificed on the altar. But a divine intervention occurs; a voice "from the heavens" stays his hand with the words, **"Abraham, Abraham!"** A substitute is provided—a blessed picture of the God who "spared not His Son"! Then we see the son "in a figure" raised from the dead!

B. Reynolds

This is My beloved Son, in whom I have found My delight.

(Matthew 3:17)

The Father has given us the very object He delights in for the object of our affection. The Father could not be silent when Christ was here. The perfection of the object is the reason for the imperfectness of our apprehension of it; but that is the way God brings our affections into tune with Himself. He could say at the beginning, because of Christ's intrinsic perfectness, and at the end because of His developed and displayed perfectness, *"This is My beloved Son."* Then what do we say? In weakness and poverty, yet surely each can say with unhesitating heart, I know He is perfect. We cannot reach His perfectness, but we do feel our hearts, poor and feeble as they are, responding. The Father has shown us something of Christ's perfectness. The Father is communicating of His delight. "This is My beloved Son, *in whom I have found My delight,"* not in whom you ought to be well pleased (which is true, too); but His way is to communicate to them of His own love to Christ. It is a wonderful thing that the Father should tell of His affection for Christ—and that when He was here among us, the Son of man on earth among sinful men.

With the woman in the Pharisee's house, it was what was revealed in Christ to her that made her love much, not what she got from Him. The blessedness of what was in Christ had so attracted her and absorbed her mind that she found her way into the house, thinking not of the dinner or of others present. She was taken up with Him; she wept, but had nothing to say. Jesus was there. He commanded all her thoughts, her tears, her silence, her anointing of His feet—all noticed by Him, and all before she knew what He had done for her. Attracted there by what she saw in Him, she got the answer as regards peace of conscience from Himself.

W. C. Reid

The love of the Christ constrains us, having judged this: that One died for all, then all have died; and He died for all, that they who live should no longer live to themselves, but to Him who died for them and has been raised. *(2 Corinthians 5:14-15)*
For me to live is Christ, and to die gain. *(Philippians 1:21)*

Paul was in prison and yet so utterly oblivious of self that his sole desire was that Christ should be magnified in his body, whether by life or by death. Christ was the one object of his life; in all that he desired and in all that he did, everything had respect to Christ.

He was thus following the example of our blessed Lord. For Christ never sought to please Himself, but He always did those things that pleased the Father; He found His meat in doing His Father's will and in finishing His work (Jn. 4:34; 8:29). "Be ye therefore imitators of God, as beloved children, and walk in love, even as the Christ loved us, and delivered Himself up for us, an offering and sacrifice to God for a sweet-smelling savor" (Eph. 5:1-2). Christ did love the Church and did give Himself for it; yet even in this it was God who was the object before His soul; He ever sought His glory and this was the governing motive of His death.

So also should Christ alone be the object of our lives, of our thoughts, feelings, designs, occupations, activities. We are His, for He has redeemed us with His own precious blood. We should live not to ourselves, but to Him who has died for us and has risen again. What a searching, practical test does this supply! Do I purpose or desire anything? Is it for Christ? Am I busy in service? Is it for Christ? Can I look round my dwelling and say of all that I behold, "It is for Christ"? Thus, "for Christ" supplies us with a principle that can be applied to the whole of our daily lives—a principle which makes nothing of self but which makes everything of Christ. This will assure us true peace and happy fellowship with God.

L. M. Grant

Let us hear the conclusion of the whole matter: Fear God and keep His commandments, for this is man's all.

(Ecclesiastes 12:13 NKJV)

Everything in life boils down to this one simple truth, fearing God! So the all-important question is, what does it mean to fear God? For many, this would describe the feeling you get when you see a snake, go to the doctor or dentist, or when you find yourself in a time of extreme danger. It is dread of the unknown. Surely, this is not the sensation Solomon is referring to.

In our modern vernacular, the word *fear*, in the context in which it is used by Solomon, has been replaced with reverence, awe, great respect. What the writer of this book is saying is that we are to have a deep reverence and respect for the Lord. Literally, we are to be awed and humbled by His presence. Fearing God includes, but it is not limited to, respecting and reverencing Him. Holy fear gives God the place of glory, honor, reverence, thanksgiving, praise, and preeminence He deserves. But simply put, fearing God is to respect His holiness by hating what He hates and loving what He loves, with a wholesome dread of displeasing Him.

When we truly fear the Lord, we will recognize that He is the Creator and we are the creatures. He is the Master and we are the servants. He is the Father and we are the children. This attitude will manifest itself in our having a respect for God, His Word, and in our having a desire to do what He tells us to in the Bible. We can relate this kind of fear to that which a child has for his parents. If the right kind of fear is present, the child knows that his parents can punish him if there is disobedience; but overriding that fear is the knowledge that disobedience hurts the parents, and the child loves and respects his parents and does not want to hurt them. To put it simply, the fear of the Lord is a deep-seated reverence for God that causes men to want to please Him at all costs.

T. P. Hadley

The children of Israel did evil in the sight of Jehovah; and Jehovah delivered them into the hand of Midian seven years. And the hand of Midian prevailed against Israel. Because of the Midianites the children of Israel made for themselves the dens that are in the mountains, and the caves, and the strongholds.

(Judges 6:1-2)

In short, they hid themselves in the earth. God had set them in that land to be a witness for Himself. If they had walked in His ways their light would have been kept brightly shining, and other nations would have learned how good it was to have Israel's God. But they were no witness for God when hidden in the dens and caves of the earth; nor is there any light for God today in those of His people whose souls are under the power of the things of earth; their light is hidden.

God had brought His people into that land that they might enjoy it, and they found it to be a land flowing with milk and honey, where corn grew in abundance, and the cattle flourished upon its verdant hills. But when the Midianites invaded the land and made their home there, all this was lost to Israel; for the Midianites came up like grasshoppers, devouring every green thing, and the people of Israel were greatly impoverished and utterly robbed of those blessings which God had given to them.

Do you find yourself in a like situation? You have allowed the things of earth to occupy your thoughts and heart and crowd out the things that are brightest and best. The things of Christ and heaven were the joy and delight of your soul, but you have lost your taste for them; the Holy Spirit has been grieved, and your soul has become greatly impoverished. You have no time now for quiet communion with the Lord, for the Midianites have come up "with their cattle and their tents as grasshoppers for multitude; and they have entered into the land to destroy it."

J. T. Mawson

Prophets went down from Jerusalem to Antioch; and one from among them ... Agabus, rose up and signified by the Spirit that there was going to be a great famine over all the inhabited earth, which also came to pass under Claudius.   *(Acts 11:27-28)*

PROPHETS AND THEIR PROPHECIES—AGABUS (1)

While John the Baptist's ministry is mentioned repeatedly in the New Testament, Agabus is the first prophet Scripture mentions as a Christian, a part of the Church. The Church was something new in the ways of God. It was formed at Jerusalem of believing Jews on the day of Pentecost. By Acts 11 God was saving and adding Gentiles. Ephesians teaches that the Church consists of Jew and Gentile united in one body with Christ as its Head in heaven.

In the beginning, believers at Jerusalem had voluntarily sold their houses and lands and had laid the proceeds at the feet of the apostles for distribution according to the common needs. Their treasures were laid up in heaven. When persecution arose and they had to flee, they would not have been able to retain their property anyway. How wisely the Spirit of God directs!

In Acts 11 we see God-given prophets functioning in the Church. Some go from Jerusalem to Antioch, not sent by man, but moving about as the Holy Spirit directs them. One of them, Agabus, rises and by the Spirit prophesies of an approaching worldwide famine. We do not read of him asking permission or needing human authority to speak. That he was a true prophet is shown by the fact that his prophecy in due time is fulfilled (Dt. 18:21-22).

We see the result of his prophesying, too, in that what he said by the Spirit was accepted. The brethren, primarily Gentiles, impelled by the love of God poured out in their hearts by the Holy Spirit, resolve to give, each as he is able, toward the needs of their Jewish brethren at Jerusalem. They both decide to do this, and do it—a good example how we should give today!

E. P. Vedder, Jr.

July   12   Friday

Jehovah had said to Abram, Go out of thy land, and from thy kindred, and from thy father's house, to the land that I will show thee. And I will make of thee a great nation, and bless thee.

(Genesis 12:1-2)

The Bible gives no hint of how Abram came to know the true and living God in that idolatrous country of Ur, except to say, "The God of glory appeared unto our father Abraham" (Acts 7:2).

God called, in order to accomplish His purpose of blessing for mankind, and Abram responded. Because he was faithful to Him who called him, we today can rejoice in the blessings that the gospel has brought.

Notice the various areas affected by the call of Abram. He was called to leave *home*. He was called to leave *relatives* and his *native country*. In other words he was called to relinquish the most natural affections in order to fulfill a higher and divine purpose. Often it is still the same today for the one whom the Lord calls to be a missionary.

Verses 2 and 3 of Genesis 12 give us the high and holy privilege to which God was calling Abram who, of course, had no way of knowing the far-reaching consequences of his walk of faith.

Think of being called to found a *great* nation, to receive a *great* blessing, to acquire a *great* name, and in addition to be a *great* blessing to every succeeding generation. From our place in history we can see in much fuller measure than Abraham the vast scope of God's design for his life.

Have you heard God's call? Have you responded? It may be to be a missionary in some foreign land, or it may be to be a Sunday school teacher or a prayer warrior. It matters not so much to what we are called; it is the response of faith that pleases God. Who knows, save the Lord, how far-reaching the results may be.

P. E. Hall

Elijah said to her, Fear not; go, do as thou hast said; but make me thereof a little cake first; and bring it to me; and afterwards make for thee and for thy son. *(1 Kings 17:13)*

When will we Christians learn to do God's work in God's way? Elijah told the poor widow to see to it that he, the man of God was taken care of first, and afterwards "make for thee and for thy son." This was God's plan for supplying both His servant Elijah's need, and the need of the widow and her son. God has not changed. His Word for us is, "Give," give first, "and it shall be given to you" (Lk. 6:38). "Seek ye first the kingdom of God, and His righteousness, and all these things shall be added unto you" (Mt. 6:33).

Are we seeking first to advance God's work, or are we seeking first and last, and all the time, to make a living, and then, if there is a surplus, to give a pittance to support the gospel? Did we ever wake up to the fact that we are personally responsible to do our part to keep the gospel work going? My first responsibility is not to see that my personal needs are met, but to see to it that as a soldier of Jesus Christ I am doing my part to advance His cause on earth. Food and clothing shall be added unto us when we seek first the kingdom of God and His righteousness.

How ashamed you will be at the judgment seat of Christ if you have never been concerned enough about the salvation and strength-ening of other souls for whom Christ died to find out what your work is in that connection, let alone to faithfully perform it! God's ways are not our ways. Oh, may God help us to take His way of blessing, and make first a little cake for the Lord, and take it to Him for His work, and afterwards make for ourselves and our loved ones!

W. C. M.

July   **14**   Lord's Day

These things have I spoken to you that in Me ye might have peace. In the world ye have tribulation; but be of good courage: I have overcome the world.   *(John 16:33)*

The mystery of suffering is indeed great. Why should a God of love allow suffering? Human reason cannot answer it; and when it tries, it only comes to the false conclusion that there is no God, or that He does not love His creatures.

But faith looks at the suffering Son of God and exclaims, Oh, how He loves! Behold Him as He journeys as a Man of sorrows and acquainted with grief, a Stranger in the world His hands had made, and then on the cross, suffering infinitely more than any creature ever could—Oh, how He loves! And behold Him now "made perfect through sufferings," crowned with a glory gained through sufferings that could never otherwise have been His though He is Creator of all. He is there as Captain of salvation bringing many sons to glory.

And soon the God of all grace who has called us unto His eternal glory, after that we have suffered a little while, will present us in glory. He would have vessels of glory, formed in the mold of sufferings, filled with glory that even angels, who never knew sin or sorrow, could not dare aspire to. All, all is the fruit of His sufferings. What a glorious light, what solace for the heart has His suffering brought into our sorrows. Our sorrows, instead of being foreboding and warnings of eternal woe, are made by the Father of mercies and God of all comfort to work out for us a far more exceeding and eternal weight of glory. There is a joy gained in sorrow and a song learned in tears that far transcends angels' tongues to tell or angels' hearts to know. This is our portion while we look at the things not seen, and endure as seeing Him who is invisible.

> *Our times are in Thy hand;*
> *Why should we doubt or fear?*
> *A Father's hand will never cause*
> *His child a needless tear.*
>
> W. F. Lloyd

July 15 Monday

Having therefore a Great High Priest who has passed through the heavens, Jesus the Son of God, let us hold fast the confession.
(Hebrews 4:14)

Jesus the Son of God is both God and Man in the same blessed Person. We are reminded of His human, as well as His divine nature, of His compassion on the one hand, and His power on the other. His priesthood is not about our sins. Priesthood has to do with our infirmities, such as sickness, persecution, weariness, sorrow, and weakness. All these things are a source of trial for our faith for which His mercy and grace are needed. Mercy is the compassion, and grace is the strength He gives in the midst of these experiences.

The Lord Jesus exercises His priesthood in heaven, and on our behalf, after the pattern of Aaron, and according to the order of Melchisedec. The Aaronic pattern was characterized by *"compassion* on the ignorant, and on them that are out of the way" (Heb. 5:2 KJV). But whereas Aaron could not continue his priesthood by reason of death, an *everlasting* priesthood distinguishes the Melchisedec order, for Christ lives in the power of an endless life. His priesthood cannot be interrupted by death, for we read: "But this Man, because He continueth ever, hath an unchangeable priesthood" (Heb. 7:24).

In taking manhood, the Lord Jesus experienced all the trials and temptations (sin excepted) that we are facing now. "Wherefore it behoved Him in all things to be made like to His brethren, that He might be a merciful and faithful high priest ... For, in that Himself has suffered, being tempted, He is able to help those that are being tempted" (Heb. 2:17-18). With such a priest we are encouraged not only to "hold fast our confession" but also to "come boldly unto the throne of grace, that we may obtain mercy, and find grace to help in time of need" (Heb. 4:16 KJV).

R. A. Barnett

God spoke to Israel in the visions of the night and said, Jacob,
Jacob! *(Genesis 46:2)*

THE SEVEN DOUBLE CALLS OF PEOPLE (2)—JACOB

Jacob had just heard the thrilling news that his son, Joseph, was
still alive in Egypt. So with his entire household he began a journey
down to Egypt, saying that he wanted to see him before he died.
When he arrived at Beer-sheba, the last town in southern Canaan
before crossing the border, he offered sacrifices to the God of his
father (Gen. 45:25-28; 46:1).

But at this point God appeared to him in "visions of the night" and
said to him, **"Jacob, Jacob! … Fear not to go down to Egypt."**
This divine intervention is meaningful, for we see from it that Jacob
had been fearful and hesitant about going to Egypt. He had good
reason for this reluctance, because his grandfather, Abram, had got-
ten into trouble by going there and his father Isaac had been strictly
warned by the LORD not to go to Egypt (Gen. 12:9-10; 26:1-2). God
told Jacob, however, to go, and so he went.

But how Jacob had changed from his earlier years! In past times he
would have bargained with God or schemed to see Joseph in some
other way. Here we see the result of God's discipline in his life; a life
that had been a series of grievous trials. However, such is the effect
of God's chastening that it "afterwards yields the peaceable fruit of
righteousness" (Heb. 12:11). He silently submits to God's plan, with
no answer back to God as in his former days, and he manifests the
precious spirit of worship and obedience! Jacob had learned that no
matter how painful the circumstance that God had brought into his
life, it was all for "good" (Rom. 8:28). William Cowper captured
Jacob's life-lesson well when he wrote:

Judge not the Lord by feeble sense,
But trust Him for His grace:
Behind a frowning providence
He hides a smiling face.

How marvelous that the "God of Jacob" is our God too.

B. Reynolds

July **17** Wednesday

Jehovah said to Satan, Whence comest thou? And Satan answered Jehovah and said, From going to and fro in the earth, and from walking up and down in it. And Jehovah said to Satan, Hast thou considered My servant Job, that there is none like him on the earth, a perfect and an upright man, one that feareth God and abstaineth from evil? *(Job 1:7-8)*

Job was outstanding in how much better a way than Ahab, or even than Nebuchadnezzar or Solomon. God bore witness that in comparison with all others, Job was superlative in righteousness, a believer whom none could rightly accuse of bad practice.

Yet Job was brought low too, and suffered on earth more dreadfully in some respects than did the others. And it was God who gave Satan permission to afflict him. His three friends falsely accused him of some great hidden sin, for they could conceive no other reason for such tribulation. And Job was sorely perplexed. What an object lesson for those upright in character, and who trust greatly in their own righteousness!

Eventually, after Job's many bitter complaints, God spoke to him, declaring many wonders of His creation completely unexplainable by man. Then Job responded, "I had heard of Thee by the hearing of the ear, but now mine eye seeth Thee: Wherefore I abhor myself, and repent in dust and ashes" (Job 42:5-6). Now he saw, not his own conduct in comparison to others, but God's glory in contrast to his own sinful nature. The result was greater blessing than he ever knew before. Let us learn not to trust our own righteousness, but to rejoice in Christ Jesus, who is made unto us righteousness from God, so that no flesh should boast before God (1 Cor. 1:29-30).

L .M. Grant

As we stayed there many days, a certain man, by name Agabus, a prophet, came down from Judea, and coming to us and taking the girdle of Paul, and having bound his own hands and feet, said, Thus saith the Holy Spirit, The man whose this girdle is shall the Jews thus bind in Jerusalem, and deliver him up into the hands of the Gentiles. *(Acts 21:10-11)*

PROPHETS AND THEIR PROPHECIES—AGABUS (2)

Paul was on his way to Jerusalem. He and other brothers were bringing financial gifts from the assemblies in Macedonia and Achaia for the needy saints in Jerusalem. Their journey was nearly ended; they were at Caesarea, the Roman capital of the province of Judea. They were staying for some days in the home of Philip the evangelist, whom the Lord had used so signally in Samaria and in the conversion of the Ethiopian eunuch in Acts 8.

Philip, we are told, had four virgin daughters who prophesied. Yet the Holy Spirit did not use these four prophetesses on this occasion, but brought Agabus down from Judea to bring one last earnest message to Paul. All along the way on this journey the Spirit had been testifying to Paul that bonds and tribulation awaited him at Jerusalem, that he should not go up to Jerusalem (Acts 20:23; 21:4). Still Paul pressed on. His burning love for his kinsmen according to flesh (Rom. 9:1-5) drove him on. No one could persuade him, so they said, The will of the Lord be done!

In Acts 11 Agabus ministered prophetically to the assembly at Antioch. Here we see the Holy Spirit using him to speak to Paul personally, dramatically warning the apostle once more against going up to Jerusalem. Some of the Old Testament prophets too were used to bring messages from God through their activities as well as through their words. Whether he speaks to individuals, to crowds, or in the assembly, whether they will hear him or not, it is vital for a prophet to speak God's Word faithfully.

E. P. Vedder, Jr.

The fear of the LORD is the beginning of wisdom: and the knowledge of the Holy is understanding. *(Proverbs 9:10 KJV)*

The term *"fear of the LORD"* appears 14 times in Proverbs. According to this book, the fear of the Lord will produce certain benefits in your life and mine. When we fear the Lord, we will find certain things to be true.

First of all, the fear of the Lord is the beginning of wisdom. It has been said that wisdom is knowledge rightly applied. But another thought is that wisdom is seeing things through the eyes of God and responding the way God would respond. Proverbs 1:7 tells us, "The fear of the LORD is the beginning of knowledge: but fools despise wisdom and instruction." Proverbs 15:33 says, "The fear of the LORD is the instruction of wisdom; and before honor is humility." The best place to begin the search for true wisdom is in the fear of the Lord. True fear of the Lord is born out of a knowledge of how infinitely powerful, majestic, and full of goodness God is. Before one can grow in the Lord, he must first learn to fear Him.

Secondly, the fear of the Lord motivates us to holiness. Proverbs 3:7 says, "Be not wise in thine own eyes: fear the LORD, and depart from evil." And Proverbs 16:6 tells us, "By mercy and truth iniquity is purged: and by the fear of the LORD men depart from evil."

These verses tell us that the fear of the Lord promotes holy living. The person who truly reverences and respects the Lord as he should, will not do anything that brings disgrace, dishonor, or pain to the Lord's heart. People who genuinely fear the Lord will flee from evil, even from the appearance of something that may be questionable to some. When one is living and walking in the fear of the Lord there are no "gray areas." Every area of my life will be impacted and affected! The prospect of causing the Lord pain or grieving His holy heart will be too great to bear!

T. P. Hadley

Israel was greatly impoverished because of Midian. And the children of Israel cried to Jehovah. *(Judges 6:6)*

The Midianites are a striking figure of earthly things. They robbed the Israelites of the enjoyment of their God-given inheritance, and made their lives a burden and a misery. This is precisely what earthly things do for the Christian when he is dominated by them.

Now the things of earth are not necessarily bad and grossly sinful. They are things which may be right and proper when kept in their right place, and they may include God's temporal mercies to us. But if they become our object in life they crowd out the things of Christ and heaven, and as a consequence the sunshine departs from the life and the song from the lips, and soul prosperity is at an end.

Briefly summed up, earthly things represent the *cares, riches, pleasures, and necessities* of this life. They embrace the sweet and bitter, the joy and sorrow, the prosperity and adversity of our existence here. They are found in the family, social, and business circles. If the mind becomes absorbed with them, the seed of the Word is choked in the heart, and does not bring forth fruit (Lk. 8:14). Those who know not God and whose vision is bounded by the present seek after these earthly things (Lk. 12:30).

But as the eagle spreads his broad pinions and soars above the earth and bathes himself in the fair sunlight, so has the Christian received title and power to rise above the things of earth to enjoy the bright treasures of that place where Christ is preeminent. If instead of fulfilling this high calling of God he is found burrowing in the earth, there is neither fruit for God nor light for others, for these two things are intimately linked together by the Lord (Lk. 8:15-16).

J. T. Mawson

A garden enclosed is my sister, my spouse; a spring shut up, a fountain sealed … A fountain in the gardens, a well of living waters, which stream from Lebanon. *(Song of Songs 4:12,15)*

The fountain and the well with the flowing streams were for irrigating the garden, thus providing growth for flowers and trees. A well is a depository for living water, while a fountain bubbles forth with streams. In John 4:11 we are told that "the well is deep," which points to a capacity to store up the inflow of hidden springs, while the fountain has a continuous outflow. A well speaks of depth, and a fountain tells of continuous outpouring.

The king's garden had both a well and a fountain which provided life-giving outflow to all the plants. The garden of Eden had a river which watered all the garden. In the New Jerusalem we also see a river of life—"a river of water of life, bright as crystal going out of the throne of God and of the Lamb" (Rev. 22:1). The river of life with its continual refreshing describes the work and function of the Holy Spirit in the lives of the saints. It was this flow of living waters which caused Solomon's garden to bring forth the finest fruits and the most exquisite beauty. The waters did not originate in the garden but flowed down from the heights of Lebanon.

If the Lord Jesus had not ascended into heaven there could have been no release of the Spirit. Thus He said, "It is profitable for you that I go away; for if I do not go away, the Comforter will not come to you" (Jn. 16:7). All the spiritual refreshment which flows into the lives of believers today is the outflow of the Spirit of life from the Lord's presence as He represents us before the Father in heaven.

W. Nee

No good in creatures can be found; / All, all is found in Thee:
We must have all things and abound / Through Thy sufficiency.

J. Ryland

> Let them take a young bull with its grain offering of fine flour mixed with oil ... So you shall bring the Levites before the LORD, and the children of Israel shall lay their hands on the Levites; and Aaron shall offer the Levites before the LORD ... that they may perform the work of the LORD. *(Numbers 8:8,10-11 NKJV)*

THE SACRIFICES IN THE BOOK OF NUMBERS (3)

A living sacrifice! The Levites were servants chosen by God to assist the Levitical priests in their service, to bring animal sacrifices and with many other duties. They helped the priests in their tasks, transported the tabernacle through the wilderness, and took care of many other things. Priests and Levitical servants were marked by a special commitment to God (Dt. 33:8-10). Their other tasks were to teach Israel, to put incense before the Lord, and to present the burnt-offerings of God's people.

Israel identified with these servants by laying their hands on them as they stood before God. For their consecration the Levites brought a young bull, a meal-offering mixed with oil, and another young bull as a sin-offering. Neither they nor we would be able to function without these aspects of Christ's accomplished work. Then, Aaron presented the Levites as a sacrifice to God. Their duties then began.

A clear distinction existed between the tasks of the priests and those of the Levites. This God-given distinction had to be respected. But a Levite, Korah, rebelled, rejecting Moses' leadership, for he wanted to be a priest like Aaron (Num. 16). This kind of rebellion also has plagued the Church throughout its history. For service, cleansing, pictured by the razor of self-judgment in Numbers 8:7, is needed.

How blessed we are today: all true believers are priests, and may function as such for God's pleasure! Let us present our bodies as living sacrifices to exercise this priestly service for His delight.

A. E. Bouter

Seeing the crowds, He went up into the mountain, and having sat down, His disciples came to Him; and, having opened His mouth, He taught them. *(Matthew 5:1-2)*

In the so-called Sermon on the Mount our Lord was not preaching the gospel, but setting forth the principles of His kingdom, which should guide the lives of all who profess to be His disciples. In other words, this is the law of the kingdom; the observance of which must characterize its loyal subjects as they wait for the day when the King Himself shall be revealed. Throughout, it recognizes the existence of definite opposition to His rule, but those who own His authority are called upon to manifest the same meek and lowly spirit that was seen in Him during the days of His humiliation here on earth.

For the natural man this sermon is not the way of life, but rather a source of condemnation; for it sets a standard so high that no unsaved person can by any possibility attain to it. He who attempts it will soon realize his utter helplessness, if he is honest and conscientious. The keenest intellects of earth have recognized in the Sermon on the Mount the highest ethical teaching to men, and have praised its holy precepts even when conscious of their inability to live up to its standards. So far as the unsaved are concerned, the teaching given here becomes, as C. I. Scofield has well said, "Law raised to its nth power."

Just as the righteous requirements of the Law are fulfilled in us, who walk after the Spirit (Rom. 8:4), so the principles laid down in this sermon will find their practical expression in the lives of all who seek to walk as Christ walked. It is not for us to relegate this to the Jewish remnant or to the disciples before the Cross, though applicable to both. We need to remember that, though a heavenly people, we have earthly responsibilities, and these are defined for us in the greatest of all sermons having to do with human conduct.

H. A. Ironside

[Samson] turned aside to see the carcase of the lion; and behold, there was a swarm of bees in the carcase of the lion, and honey.

(Judges 14:8)

How interesting is a swarm of bees! They can live in a hollow tree, in a wooden box, or even in the carcass of a lion. Their city has no mayor or city manager, no city council, and no political boss. While there is a queen, she does not direct its policies or its destinies.

Nevertheless, in all the realm of nature there is hardly a more efficient community. The inhabitants are all for one and one for all. There is perfect cooperation and unity of action. There is no jealousy or strife, and they do not fight among themselves. They will fight their enemies, however, and even man must be aware of their wrath. Their system of dividing up the jobs is the best in the world. Every worker knows her precise task and does it without being told or shown by a superior, for there is no superior. In bee city there is no unemployment problem.

Perhaps God wants us to learn from these fascinating little creatures how we ought to function in the assemblies of the saints. How bright and vibrant will be the testimony of the Lord where there is close cooperation and unity among the saints; where we recognize that "the enemy is the devil," and not our fellow believers; and where each member of the body is working according to his or her God-given abilities.

Unlike the bees who act by instinct, we have a very real and very precious Superior who is in us and among us to glorify Christ and to guide us into all truth. How much nourishing "honey" is produced among the saints for the glory of God and the up-building of each other in love when we are in true submission to our Divine Superior.

G. W. Steidl

Then it seemed good to the apostles and to the elders, with the whole assembly, to send chosen men from among them with Paul and Barnabas to Antioch, Judas called Barsabas and Silas, leading men among the brethren, having by their hand written thus … Judas and Silas, being themselves also prophets, exhorted the brethren with much discourse, and strengthened them. And having passed some time there, they were let go in peace from the brethren to those who sent them. *(Acts 15:22-23,32-33)*

PROPHETS AND THEIR PROPHECIES—JUDAS AND SILAS

Paul and Barnabas and several other brothers had been sent to Jerusalem by the assembly at Antioch. They were to consider with the apostles and elders there whether or not it was necessary for salvation to circumcise those Gentiles who had believed on the Lord Jesus and to command them to keep the law of Moses. The Holy Spirit had made plain to all at this historic meeting that this was not necessary. Now the delegation from Antioch was to return home. They carried with them a letter stating the result of the meeting, and two esteemed brothers from Jerusalem, Judas and Silas, went with them to attest to these things in person.

Both of these brothers were prophets. When their errand was completed, they remained a while longer, encouraging and strengthening the brethren with many words. A prophet speaks on behalf of God, bringing His message to the people. People often assume that a prophet's task is to foretell future events. His message may look on to the future, but this is not necessarily so. According to 1 Corinthians 14:3, "he that prophesies speaks to men in edification, and encouragement, and consolation."

When Judas and Silas had accomplished their mission, they were free to go back to the brethren who had sent them. Judas seems to have gone back to Jerusalem, while Silas remained at Antioch and then accompanied Paul on his second missionary journey.

E. P. Vedder, Jr.

Brethren, I count not myself to have apprehended: but this one thing I do, forgetting those things which are behind, and reaching forth unto those things which are before, I press towards the mark for the prize of the [calling on high] of God in Christ Jesus. *(Philippians 3:13-14 KJV)*

The man born blind in John 9 knew one thing: that he had received his sight. For Mary of Bethany in Luke 10 one thing was needful: to sit at that same Person's feet and listen to His word. One leads to the other, and both lead to Paul's exercise here: pressing towards the mark for the prize of the calling on high of God in Christ Jesus.

Paul's desire in this letter of experience and joy was to focus the hearts and minds of his readers on Christ. There was a certain lack of unity among them and the antidote he prescribed for this was occupation with Christ. The treatment is the same today: as we contemplate Him we become more like Him and we are drawn together whatever our little foibles. It is bound to be the case: what is there to be proud of or to exalt us over others when we consider Christ? John the Baptist said, "He must increase, but I must decrease" (Jn. 3:30).

Paul had the same spirit but so much more light. Surely we all rejoice in the righteousness which is through the faith of Christ (v. 9). But what about the rest of what he writes: to know Christ as He is in heaven and the power of the resurrection that put Him there, the fellowship of His sufferings as a dependant and obedient Man in this world even to the point of death, what it is to pass into the Lord's presence according to His perfect will, whatever that involves. Paul discarded anything that held him back, and stretched out with every spiritual sinew for *one thing*. Christ had gained Him, and he wanted to gain Christ. This is to live Christ, and to die gain (Phil. 1:21). Are we imitators of Paul?

S. Attwood

Jehovah saw that he turned aside to see, and God called to him
out of the midst of the thorn-bush and said, Moses, Moses!

(Exodus 3:4)

THE SEVEN DOUBLE CALLS OF PEOPLE (3)—MOSES

When Moses was about forty years of age, he had it in his heart to
deliver the people of God out of their bondage (Acts 7:23). But God
had not yet called Moses to this service. Neither would God bless
his position as the "son of Pharaoh's daughter" to work deliverance
for Israel. This action of Moses was the energy of the flesh and no
flesh shall glory in God's presence.

After fleeing Egypt, Moses spent the next forty years tending his
father-in-law's flocks in the "backside of the desert" (Ex. 3:1 KJV).
All thought of serving God had by now left him, but God had not left
him. Although Moses didn't know it, the "school of God" had been
preparing him for service, teaching him his own nothingness and his
need for lowly dependence on God. Every true servant of God has his
"hidden years" during which he is learning, consciously or not, that
God is everything and that He cannot share His glory; the servant is
but a vessel. Moses' "call" to service came from the burning bush;
for when he turned aside to see this unusual sight, the voice of God
came to him "out of the midst" of the bush, **"Moses, Moses!"** God
had observed, years before, the desire of Moses to serve Him and
His people. But now, unexpectedly for Moses, the time had arrived!

How wonderful now for Moses to receive a divine visitation. He
must remove his sandals, for it is the "I AM" that speaks, Jehovah,
the Eternal One (v. 14, cf. Jn. 8:58). Moses protests that he is not
competent for the job (v. 11), but this was the very proof that *he was
now* serviceable to God. It has been said of Moses that he spent forty
years in Egypt learning to be somebody, forty years in obscurity
learning to be nobody, and forty years in the wilderness learning that
God is everything.

B. Reynolds

God having spoken in many parts and in many ways formerly to the fathers in the prophets, at the end of these days has spoken to us in the Person of the Son, whom He has established Heir of all things, by whom also He made the worlds. *(Hebrews 1:1-2)*

How much that means! How we should tread here with unshod feet! What divine fullness is there! God has spoken in His Son! The Son of God, then, is the theme. The Son of God is the One whom God has made known to us; the knowledge of the Son of God is what in infinite grace, He has given to every one of us.

Have you ever paused to thank God, to bless Him from the depths of your soul, that you are living in these last days? Would you change places with a Moses, who saw that glory which God was able to reveal in connection with law? Would you change places with an Isaiah, who in the temple saw the Lord high and lifted up, and all the glory that could be manifested in a house made with hands? Or with a David, who foresaw One who was to sit upon his throne, and all things put in His power? Ah, the feeblest child of God who lives in these last days has infinitely greater privileges. As our blessed Lord has said, "Many prophets and kings have desired to see the things which ye behold, and did not see them; and to hear the things which ye hear and did not hear them."

There is nothing greater, nothing more wonderful, than the fact that all of us, all the people of God in this Christian age, are blessed with the full revelation of the Son of God, all that God has to say. Paul in Colossians speaks of his ministry fulfilling, or completing, the Word of God, for it fully unfolded Christ.

S. Ridout

We hear the words of love; / We gaze upon the blood,
We see the mighty sacrifice, / And we have peace with God.

H. Bonar

The Father loves the Son, and has given all things to be in His hand.
(John 3:35)
The Father loves the Son and shows Him all things which He Himself does.
(John 5:20)

The Lord Jesus is the Son of God, the Son of the Father, the Son of His love; but not the child of God, for the child involves birth. In manhood He was the child of Mary, but in deity He was, and is, eternally the Son of God. Sonship involves the dignity and liberty of relationship, and this precious relationship of the Father and the Son was enjoyed in perfection from eternity.

Now the Son, He who has been manifested and who has manifested the Father, can assure all mankind that it is He whom the Father loves, for the Father has given all things into His hand, and shows Him all things that He Himself does. How it shows us that we can depend on Him fully to express absolutely all that is in the Father's heart!

There cannot be another to add to this, or to remotely compare to Him. The Father has approved Him as the full representation of all that He is. He only is worthy of knowing all that the Father does, and worthy of having all things entrusted to His hand.

> *Father, Oh, what boundless glory*
> *In Thy name of love we know,*
> *No more sweet, more wondrous story,*
> *Than Thy heart revealed below.*
> *Blessed, beauteous contemplation—*
> *Theme more full than all beside—*
> *Cause of deepest adoration—*
> *Thou, through Christ, art glorified!*

L. M. Grant

On July 29, 2011 it pleased the Lord to call our beloved brother Leslie M. Grant to Himself, for which he longed. For many years he was a faithful contributor to "The Lord is Near." His many contributions give ample testimony to his love for the Lord Jesus Christ and the Holy Scriptures. *[The Editors]*

Oh that thou hadst hearkened to My commandments! Then would thy peace have been as a river, and thy righteousness as the waves of the sea. *(Isaiah 48:18)*

CHRISTIAN MARRIAGE (1)—COMMITMENT

These words addressed by the Holy Spirit to the nation of Israel apply also to the Christian home. Why are there many homes of Christians lacking these two blessings: peace and righteousness? These two go together; there is no peace in the absence of righteousness and no righteousness where there is continuous bickering and discord. Why do we hear of many homes of believers breaking down? The answer is given in the verse quoted above.

God has given clear commandments concerning the Christian home, and men of God have written many wonderful books based on these commandments. In the last few decades, many eloquent lectures and seminars have been held that deal with this subject, and yet the rate of broken homes is rapidly increasing among those who confess to be true Christians. Why? The answer is simply this: Ignoring God's commandments concerning marriage. Many couples give priority to worldly things, and many others neglect the Word of God. Is it a wonder then that they discover that they have been building their homes on sand?

Every Christian home needs to be built on these four pillars:

COMMITMENT; MUTUAL LOVE; MUTUAL RESPECT; CHRIST'S LORDSHIP.

Commitment means a firm respect for the covenant of marriage. It is a commitment made in the presence of God; it is not just a piece of paper. Let unbelievers say what they want; after all, many of them deny that God even exists. But a believer who knows God's holiness must hold firmly to a commitment he made before God. Marriage was ordained by God, and the Lord Jesus said: "The two shall be one flesh ... What therefore God has joined together, let not man separate" (Mt. 19:5-6).

A. M. Behnam

Husbands, love your own wives, even as the Christ also loved the Assembly, and has delivered Himself up for it. *(Ephesians 5:25)*

CHRISTIAN MARRIAGE (2)—MUTUAL LOVE

The above verse is directed to husbands. Does any Christian conclude from this that wives need not love their husbands? God is love and we are exhorted to love one another. We are even told to love our enemies. Love is the main Christian characteristic, and by it, said the Lord, people shall know that we are His. Why then is the instruction to love given to the husbands? There are at least two reasons.

First, it is because a wife has a need to feel loved by her husband. This is part of her nature as a woman. She may be happy in the absence of wealth but never in the absence of love in her marriage. In her case it is especially true that "even if a man gave all the substance of his house for (i.e. instead of) love, it would utterly be contemned" (Song 8:7). That word "I love you" is music to her ears, and health to her heart. She would not mind hearing it ten times a day, and a husband should not hesitate to say it often, provided his acts prove it. This is good for her and for him. "So ought men also to love their own wives as their own bodies: he that loves his own wife loves himself" (Eph. 5:28).

Second, this exhortation is given specially to the husband because he is apt to get so busy in his work that he forgets the emotional need of his wife. Today many wives are also working, and need the same advice. Alas, that many have believed the lie that the more money they gain, the more happy they will be. Love is a greater treasure than gold. Love can withstand the trials of life where wealth and fame cannot. There are many poor people who have a happy marriage because they love one another. Their children are also happier and feel more secure, as they see and feel their parents' love to each other.

A. M. Behnam

Wives, be subject to your own husbands, as to the Lord. For the husband is the head of the wife, as Christ also is the head of the Church, He Himself being the Savior of the body ... and the wife must see to it that she respect her husband.

(Ephesians 5:22-23,33 NASB)

CHRISTIAN MARRIAGE (3)—MUTUAL RESPECT

Christian marriages should be according to the teachings of God's Word, and not according to the trends of society. Yet, alas, many marriages of Christians are in a pitiful condition because of neglecting the divine instructions. The verses quoted above teach us about the wife's role, which, needless to say, is very important for the success of the marriage and the happiness of both parents and children.

While the emphasis for the husband is to love his wife, the emphasis for the wife is to be subject to her husband and to respect him. Does that mean that the husband is to take a dictatorial role and disregard his wife's views? Not at all, for before saying to the wife to be subject to her husband, we are commanded to "be subject to one another" (v. 21). Why is the emphasis on respect given to the wife? Just as the woman by nature has a *need* to feel the love of her husband, so the husband has a *need* to feel the respect of his wife.

The Lord in His wisdom likened the right relationship between husbands and wives to His relationship with the Church. Can any Christian conclude that Christ's headship of the Church is to make her miserable? The expression "Himself being the Savior of the body" shows that He uses His headship for her good. The wise husband listens to his wife's opinion, but makes the decision and is responsible for the results. Marriage can be either a paradise or a prison, and the Christian marriage should be the former. It should be characterized by mutual love and mutual respect and a home where Christ delights to dwell.

A. M. Behnam

Everything, whatever ye may do in word or in deed, do all things in the name of the Lord Jesus, giving thanks to God the Father by Him.

(Colossians 3:17)

CHRISTIAN MARRIAGE (4)—CHRIST'S LORDSHIP

Commitment, mutual love, and mutual respect are necessary for the success of every marriage whether of Christians or pagans. And it is a sad fact that believers who ignore these divine principles may have a less peaceful marriage than some unsaved couples do. But a Christian marriage should have more than mere commitment, love, and respect. A Christian marriage cannot properly be called Christian unless it acknowledges the lordship of Christ who loved us and gave Himself for us. In the Christian home Christ should always "have the first place in all things" (Col. 1:18).

There is a story about a country preacher who said to a couple at the end of the marriage ceremony: "Now listen carefully, my friends, when the three of you go to your home," but the bride interrupted him, assuring him that her mother would not be living with them. Yet he continued saying that the three of them would go home. The husband then interrupted him, saying that there will be only the two of them. The preacher then said: "Listen carefully; you will be three whether you like it or not, and the third will be either the Lord or the devil."

This is a solemn fact; either we give the Lord His place in our homes, or the enemy of our souls will cause havoc in our families. When Christ's lordship is truly found in our homes there will be joy and peace, the singing of hymns and not the shouts of heated arguments. The family will be enabled to withstand the difficulties of life and will experience the truth of Isaiah 48:18. "Oh that thou hadst hearkened to My commandments! Then would thy peace have been as a river and thy righteousness as the waves of the sea."

A. M. Behnam

Balaam lifted up his eyes and saw Israel dwelling in tents according to his tribes; and the Spirit of God came upon him. And he took up his parable. *(Numbers 24:2-3)*

Who was Balaam? The three references to him in the New Testament leave us totally unprepared for his marvelous "oracles" recorded in the book of Numbers—for Peter warns us against his "path" (2 Pet. 2:15), Jude against his "error" (Jude 11), and John against his "doctrine" (Rev. 2:14).

How amazing that the Spirit of God should use this covetous prophet from Pethor to utter some of the most sublime words in the Bible. Such is our sovereign God, whose ways and thoughts are as high above ours as the heavens are above the earth. But what then did Balaam say?

In his first oracle (Num. 23:7-10) he describes God's sovereign purpose which prevails against all man's evil purposes; and which will separate and increase the people of Israel for His own glory and honor in spite of their enemies.

The second oracle (Num. 23:18-24) focuses on God's amazing grace which sees not as man sees. This grace declares a blessing for Israel which none can change, and beholds no iniquity in Jacob. How can this be? Because God ever has in view the finished work of Christ which removes all iniquity from His people.

The third oracle (Num. 24:3-9) describes God's almighty power which will produce blessing and fruitfulness in His people and give them victory over all their enemies.

The fourth oracle (Num. 24:15-19) describes God's anointed Man, that blessed One whom Balaam calls "A Star out of Jacob" and "A Scepter out of Israel." He is the One who will finally destroy all Israel's enemies and establish universal dominion. Balaam's oracles teach us that it is not the messenger but the message that contains the life-changing truth of God.

G. W. Steidl

August 4 Lord's Day

James, bondman of God and of the Lord Jesus Christ, to the twelve tribes which are in the dispersion, greeting. *(James 1:1)*

No greater dignity, no greater privilege, could possibly be accorded a mortal than to be called a "bondman of God and of the Lord Jesus Christ." To serve His interests on earth is surely a privilege angels might envy.

Only One could be called the Perfect Servant. To Him alone Jehovah calls attention, saying, "Behold my servant" (Isa. 42:1). In Isaiah 42:19 the question is asked: "Who is blind as He in whom I have trusted, and blind as Jehovah's Servant?" This perfect Servant had no eyes but for the glory of God. The adulation of men He sought not, but ever withdrew from popularity. It was written prophetically of Him, "He shall not cry, nor lift up, nor cause His voice to be heard" (Isa. 42:2), and in Mark, the Gospel of the Servant, we see our blessed Lord in most active service, yet ever withdrawn from the uncertain crowd. He knew what was in man.

The prerequisite of the Perfect Servant is to be obedient. The Lord became this in grace. In Isaiah 50:4 He says in spirit, Jehovah "hath given Me the tongue of the instructed, that I should know how to succor by a word him that is weary. He wakeneth morning by morning, he wakeneth Mine ear to hear as the instructed." Ever alert to hear the voice of the One He came to glorify, He could say, "I do nothing of Myself." Again, "My food is that I should do the will of Him that has sent Me and that I should finish His work." That path of obedience glorified God fully, and from the excellent glory the Father's voice was heard, "This is My beloved Son in whom I have found My delight."

J. W. H. Nichols

The same day at evening, being the first day of the week, when the doors were shut where the disciples were assembled, for fear of the Jews, Jesus came and stood in the midst, and said to them, "Peace be with you." *(John 20:19 NKJV)*

The disciples were together, but they had no peace. They had seen Jesus crucified, and although some of their number reported that He was alive, still they met only behind closed doors. But then the Lord Himself stood in their midst! His presence changed their entire outlook for that moment and, indeed, for the rest of their lives.

The Lord first desired to still their fear. Their particular fear was "fear of the Jews"—the influential religious leaders whose forcefulness prevented many from testifying openly about their faith in Christ (e.g., Jn. 7:13; 9:22; 19:38). We may feel the same fear, for there are many strident voices that seek to silence or at least ridicule Christian belief. But when we consider the risen Lord, to whom all authority in heaven and earth is given, we receive His words of comfort: "Peace be unto you."

Next, the Lord would strengthen their faith. "He showed them His hands and His side. Then the disciples were glad when they saw the Lord" (Jn. 20:20). We learn in Luke's Gospel that He even ate some fish and honeycomb in order to help them believe. The Lord Jesus desires to establish our faith, weak though it may be. He furnishes proof of His power and presence when we seek Him.

Having addressed the disciples' fears and faith, the Lord sends them forth. "As the Father has sent Me, I also send you" (Jn. 20:21). He had already told the Father that He would send them into the world just as He had been sent (Jn. 17:18), and now He tells them. His final words in John's Gospel are, "Follow Me" (Jn. 21:22). This is our calling and privilege too.

S. J. Campbell

Thus saith Jehovah of hosts: Yet once, it is a little while, and I will shake the heavens, and the earth, and the sea, and the dry land; and I will shake all nations, and the desire of all nations shall come. *(Haggai 2:6-7)*
But this Yet once, signifies the removing of what is shaken, as being made, that what is not shaken may remain. *(Hebrews 12:27)*

A WORD FOR TODAY

No one will deny that we have recently experienced an unknown degree of natural disasters. The number of forest fires, most of which have originated from lightning strikes, have been in excess of those reported in previous years. So are the number of tornados that have devastated whole towns in Alabama, Kentucky, and Ontario. Floods have covered great tracts of rural and urban land. Earthquakes that shook the Indian and Pacific Oceans a few years ago were followed by one near Japan that, through its accompanying tsunami, destroyed great swaths of land and greatly affected much of Japan's nuclear industry. Many who have felt the impact of these disasters firsthand readily agree: Both earth and heaven have been shaken.

The August 2011 earthquake in Virginia surprised many people. Who had ever expected such a strong earthquake in the eastern United States! Yet, it was felt in places well over a thousand miles from its epicenter.

Is this the hand of God, giving warning? Sad to say, most people will not even think of God, though some may cry in their distress: "Oh God, save me," yet soon forget that they ever called on the God whose existence they thus far have denied. Still, God has spoken! He has told us that "Yet once … I will shake the heavens and the earth." Those who know Him as their God and Father through the Lord Jesus Christ realize that "The desire of all nations shall come." The day is at hand! Indeed, the Lord's coming is near, at the door. Lord Jesus, come!

J. van Dijk

August 7 Wednesday

An angel of Jehovah came and sat under the terebinth that was in Ophrah, that belonged to Joash the Abi-ezrite. And his son Gideon threshed wheat in the winepress, to secure it from the Midianites. *(Judges 6:11)*

Gideon is introduced to our notice while threshing wheat in the secret place to hide it from the Midianites. This wheat was the true portion of the people, for it was the produce of the land which God had given them: for us it is a type of Christ. Israel had been robbed of their sustenance, but Gideon had been able to secure some, at least, from the thieves. He evidently valued that which he guarded so carefully, and would not be robbed of it if he could avoid it. It was to that man the Lord could reveal Himself, and he could be called a mighty man of valor, for he had started along the pathway to final victory.

Do you appreciate Christ? Is it your habit to retire into secret, away from the stress and worry of everyday life, in order to feed upon Him and His things, which are your true portion?

Is it possible that you have to confess that you have no time for His things, and that from dawn to sundown you are fully occupied with the duties of the day? Then, indeed, you are under the galling yoke of these most tyrannical foes of your soul—earthly things.

Make time to feed upon Christ in secret. You will soon realize the good of it. The days will be brighter, the loads less heavy, your spirit less fretful, and perhaps that anxious look will depart from your face. In short, a new era will dawn for you if you will but turn aside to thresh the true Wheat in the secret of God's presence. You will need to guard these quiet moments jealously, for these earthly things will intrude themselves into the most sacred hours, if permitted.

J. T. Mawson

Revelation of Jesus Christ, which God gave to Him, to show to His bondmen what must shortly take place; and He signified it, sending by His angel, to His bondman John, who testified the word of God and the testimony of Jesus Christ, all things that he saw. Blessed is he that reads, and they that hear the words of the prophecy, and keep the things written in it; for the time is near ... For the spirit of prophecy is the testimony of Jesus. *(Revelation 1:1-3; 19:10)*

PROPHETS AND THEIR PROPHECIES—
JOHN THE APOSTLE

As we consider these passages we have reached the end of the prophecies of God's Word. The Revelation once again emphasizes to us the fact that the spirit of prophecy is the testimony of Jesus. All prophecy, whatever its particulars may be, in the final analysis relates to Him and to God's firm purpose that He might be glorified. The Revelation shows us many broad details about how this will be accomplished. Indeed, Scripture would be woefully incomplete without this account of His final victory.

Persecution was fiercely raging. John, now aged and the last survivor of the Lord's apostles, had been exiled to the island of Patmos "for the Word of God, and for the testimony of Jesus." To all outward appearances it seemed that the fourth beast of Daniel's visions, "dreadful and terrible, and exceedingly strong; [with] great iron teeth" (Dan. 7:7) had won the victory.

But this was not to be the last word. This final word of God and of the Lord Jesus presents Jesus, the One who became dead and is alive to the ages of ages, as the ultimate Victor. John was told to write what he had seen that day, "the things that are" in this present dispensation, and "the things that are about to be after these." The things John saw on that marvelous Lord's Day when the Lord Himself appeared to him reveal the Lord to be in absolute control of past, present, and future. To Him be glory!

E. P. Vedder, Jr.

Do not be wise in your own eyes; fear the Lord and depart from evil. It will be health to your flesh, and strength to your bones.

(Proverbs 3:7-8 NKJV)

Self-confidence and conceit puts us on hold as far as divine guidance is concerned. When we fear the Lord and depart from evil, it means "All systems go!" It spells health to our body and strength to our bones. Literally this has the thought of drink, refreshment, or even medicine. We are brought face to face with the close connection between man's moral and spiritual condition and his physical health.

In Proverbs 10:27, we read that "The fear of the Lord prolongs days, but the years of the wicked will be shortened." This verse reminds us of what we read in Ephesians 6:1-3: "Children, obey your parents in the Lord, for this is right. Honor your father and mother which is the first commandment with promise: that it may be well with you and you may live long on the earth." It could be said that obedience is an outward sign that we fear the Lord.

This promise of long life is not a blanket promise because any number of things can happen along the road of life that can take us away in an instant. However, generally speaking, those who live in the fear of the Lord are more likely to live to a good old age than those who live for the flesh and the world.

It has been estimated that approximately 60% of human illnesses can be traced directly or indirectly to fear, sorrow, envy, resentment, guilt, hatred, or to any number of emotional stresses. Add to that the awful pain caused by alcohol (cirrhosis of the liver), tobacco (emphysema, cancer, heart disease), and immorality (venereal diseases and AIDS). We can see that a life lived in the fear of the Lord with obedience to His Word will result in a much healthier existence. May we learn to walk in the fear of the Lord!

T. P. Hadley

Jehovah came, and stood, and called as at the other times, Samuel, Samuel!
(1 Samuel 3:10)

THE SEVEN DOUBLE CALLS OF PEOPLE (4)—SAMUEL

Samuel was just a child living under the tutorship of Eli the priest at Shiloh when the Lord called him. This was a very dark time in Israel's history, characterized by the spiritual dullness of Eli and the open immorality practiced by his sons (1 Sam. 2:12-17,22). There were "prophets" before Samuel but the *prophetic office* began with him (Acts 3:24). God had initiated it as the link between Himself and His people because failure had come in through the priesthood. God raises a prophetic voice when there has been departure from Him.

The Lord came to Samuel and "stood" and called, **"Samuel, Samuel!"** This call came to Samuel at a time when, "the word of the LORD was precious (*rare* JND) … there was no open vision" (1 Sam. 3:1 KJV). The word *vision* here is not a visual experience but a divine revelation. It means a spiritual revelation that comes to us from God. The meaning of this word from the Hebrew is *prophetic vision*. This is what Samuel would bring to his discouraged and troubled nation.

There is no such thing as a *spiritual vacuum*, for when God is rejected the enemy will come in to fill the void. This is what happened in Israel through the malfeasance of the priesthood. But God sent a remedy in Samuel. When he grew into manhood, his ministry was remarkably effective. All Israel heard his sermons from Dan in the north, to Beersheba in the south (3:19-21; 4:1). His prophetic preaching wrought repentance in the heart of the people (1 Sam. 7:3-6).

The Irish have a saying, "Cometh the hour, cometh the man." This certainly has been true in the history of the world's politics, but it also has been true in the history of God's people. How faithful of the Lord to send a man of God just when he was most needed!

B. Reynolds

I know thy works and thy labor, and thine endurance, and that thou canst not bear evil men. *(Revelation 2:2)*

At this early stage of the Church's history, represented by **Ephesus,** there were no outward signs of departure. Christ is still seen as the One who holds the seven stars in His right hand, and walks in the midst of the churches. Does this not indicate that those in subordinate authority under the guidance of the Lord to represent *His* interests in the assembly were still held in His power and under His direction? There was still much that the Lord could approve, too. The saints were marked by endurance in the Lord's service. They had resisted every attack of Satan to corrupt the Church by false pretension and evil deeds.

Nevertheless, while outwardly blameless, the Lord, who knows the heart, says, "I have against thee, that thou hast left thy first love"—the root of all failure in the Church. One has said, "What injures and finally ruins is invariably from within, not from without."

Having lost their first love for Christ, the Lord has to pronounce the solemn words, "Thou art fallen." The warning follows that unless there was repentance their candlestick would be removed. If the first love for Christ was lost the light before men would fail.

What is true of the Church as a whole is surely true of any local assembly and of each individual believer. The root of all failure is in the heart, and unless there is repentance the outward testimony will cease to have any power. Nevertheless, it was possible for individuals to overcome this inward failure and to maintain first love for Christ. To such the Lord would reveal Himself as the Tree of Life— the hidden source of spiritual sustenance in the paradise of God, where no enemy will ever intrude to draw our hearts from Christ.

H. Smith

Father, I will that they also, whom Thou hast given Me, be with Me where I am.
(John 17:24 KJV)
Who for the joy that was set before Him endured the cross.
(Hebrews 12:2 KJV)

ONE THING REMAINS

He has finished everything, accomplished everything, glorified His Father in everything, and only one thing remains, and that is, to have us with Himself. Love never tolerates absence; it may bear it, but it is impatient of it; and therefore when you look at Him, how blessed to know that He longs to have us to be forever with Himself.

Do we believe that? Do we believe that there is that one (shall I say it with reverence) unsatisfied yearning in the heart of Christ, to have the people of His love with Him? *"I will that they also, whom Thou hast given Me, be with Me where I am; that they may behold My glory."* How much is it in ours; how much is there of that longing of heart with us, that divine affection in our souls, that we long to be with Him? We have Him with us now; of course that is blessedly true, as we walk through the world, we cannot get on without Him, but to be with Him, and to be like Him when we see Him, how much is that before us? I shall see Him as He is, but I shall be like Him when I see Him, and shall be with Him, and that is what He waits for; that is the yearning of His heart at this present moment. He cheers us along the waste with the sustainment of His presence, and the comfort of His love; but the thing that is in Christ's affection with respect to us is, He wants to have us with Himself.

How wonderful to think of it! There is one thing that remains, *"Father, I will that they also, whom Thou hast given Me, be with Me where I am."* *It is the one thing that remains*: He owes one service to His Father and God, and He owes it to us, the people of His love, and He will perform it!

W. T. Turpin

August **13** Tuesday

It is better to trust in Jehovah than to put confidence in man; it is better to trust in Jehovah than to put confidence in nobles.
(Psalm 118:8-9)

A broken tooth, and a tottering foot, is confidence in an unfaithful man in the day of trouble.
(Proverbs 25:19)

Trials, troubles, difficulties of many kinds will test us. How urgently is faithfulness needed then! It is with very real reason that Paul tells Timothy, "The things thou hast heard of me in the presence of many witnesses, these entrust to faithful men, such as shall be competent to instruct others also" (2 Tim. 2:2). When things are not right, we need much grace from God to speak rightly of Him and for Him and to act wisely in His fear. For these things are tests. They will prove whether we are faithful in continuance, stable and solid in the face of storms, maintaining unshaken faith in the living God by which others may be encouraged and strengthened.

If one has confidence in us, and finds that in the acid test we withdraw, give up, become lax or weakened, resort to human reasoning in place of wholesome faith; he will find this confidence of his to be "a broken tooth." A broken tooth with its nerve exposed is significant of a distressing hindrance to feeding upon the truth of God. Along with this, it becomes "a tottering foot," a condition of painful inability for a decisive walk with God.

On the one hand, therefore, let us be faithful, dependable, that we may not let others down in times of trouble. On the other hand, let us be most careful, if we are going to have confidence in any man, to be sure he is a faithful man, consistently steadfast in the path of obedience to the Word of God. Great gift and ability, great zeal and enthusiasm, will be no substitute for simple faithfulness.

L. M. Grant

August 14 Wednesday

Faith is the substantiating of things hoped for, the conviction of things not seen. For in the power of this the elders have obtained testimony.
(Hebrews 11:1-2)

Faith is the essential in which God can take pleasure. It rests on the death of Another, and controls the life and walk of the believer, for the just shall live by faith. To move in our own strength will land us beneath the waters of despair and disappointment. Therefore, one must refuse the works of the flesh and the influences of this present evil world, all of which are energized by Satan, and rather trust in the living God. Hebrews 10:35 would instruct us: "Cast not away therefore your confidence, which has great recompense."

Further, the believer is not only to have personal faith in God through our Lord Jesus Christ, but he has been called to a path of faith which is illustrated by the following from Hebrews 11: "By faith Abel offered to God a more excellent sacrifice than Cain" (v. 4), which speaks of *approach and redemption by faith.* "By faith Enoch was translated that he should not see death ... for before his translation he has the testimony that he had pleased God" (v. 5). This is an example of one having *a walk of faith.* "By faith, Noah ... prepared an ark for the saving of his house; by which he condemned the world" (v. 7). This suggests *a confession of faith* in a world that is hastening on to judgment because of lack of faith in the One who is able to save.

"By faith Abraham, being called, obeyed" (v. 8)—*the obedience of faith,* a feature which is pleasurable to God.

Every believer, like these men of old, is to act on the principle of faith in every circumstance of his sojourn down here! That will give pleasure to the heart of God!

R. J. Costen

I will give power to My two witnesses, and they shall prophesy a thousand two hundred and sixty days, clothed in sackcloth ... These have power to shut the heaven that no rain may fall during the days of their prophecy; and they have power over the waters to turn them into blood, and to smite the earth as often as they will with every plague. *(Revelation 11:3,6)*

PROPHETS AND THEIR PROPHECIES—
THE TWO WITNESSES

These two witnesses are the last of God's prophets mentioned in Scripture. They have not yet lived, but will live and serve God during the time of dreadful tribulation that will come upon this earth after the Lord returns to take His people home to Himself.

These witnesses, like so many of God's prophets down through the course of history, will face tremendous opposition. The Spirit of God, who according to the Lord's promise in John 14:16-17 is *with us* Christians forever and *abides in us*, will no longer be present as a Divine Person upon earth at this time. Yet these witnesses, clothed in sackcloth, will be protected by God a full 3½ years until their ministry here on earth is completed.

These two witnesses will prophesy and have miraculous powers reminding us of those once granted to Moses and Elijah, faithful men of God at crucial points in Israel's history in the Old Testament. Fire coming out of their mouths will devour their enemies; they can shut the heavens that it will not rain, turn the waters into blood; and smite the earth with every plague.

Yet the time will come when the beast that comes out of the abyss will make war on them, conquer them, and kill them. Their bodies shall lie on the street, and the world will rejoice and gloat over them, full of delight. But after 3½ days they will rise, stand on their feet, and be called up to heaven in the cloud in full view of their enemies. God will be glorified and their enemies filled with fear. The victory is ever the Lord's!

E. P. Vedder, Jr.

Thy servant smote both the lion and the bear; and this uncircumcised Philistine shall be as one of them, because he has defied the armies of the living God. *(1 Samuel 17:36)*

This was the argument of faith. The hand that had delivered from one difficulty would deliver from another. David had not boasted of his triumph over the lion and the bear; no one seemed to have heard of it before; nor would he probably have spoken of it, had it not been for the purpose of showing what a solid ground of confidence he had in reference to the great work on which he was about to enter. He would fain show that it was not in his own strength he was going forth. So was it in the matter of Paul's rapture to the third heaven: for fourteen years that circumstance had remained buried as a secret with the apostle; nor would he have divulged it, had not the carnal reasonings of the Corinthians compelled him to do so.

Now, both these cases are full of practical instruction for us. With the majority of us, alas, there is too great a readiness to talk of our doings, or, at least, to think much of them. The flesh is prone to glory in anything that might exalt *self;* and if the Lord, despite the evil in us, has accomplished any little service by our instrumentality, how speedily is it communicated in a spirit of pride and self-complacency.

David, however, kept the secret of his triumph over the lion and the bear concealed in his own bosom, and did not bring it forth until the fitting occasion. *"The Lord that delivered me* out of the paw of the lion, and out of the paw of the bear, He will deliver me out of the hand of this Philistine."* Precious, self-renouncing faith!—faith that counts on God for everything, and trusts the flesh in nothing—faith which brings God into every difficulty, and leads us, with deepest thankfulness, to hide self, and give Him all the glory. May our souls know more and more of this blessed faith.

C. H. Mackintosh

Jesus answering said to her, Martha, Martha, thou art careful and troubled about many things; but there is need of one, and Mary has chosen the good part, the which shall not be taken from her.   *(Luke 10:41-42)*

THE SEVEN DOUBLE CALLS OF PEOPLE (5)—MARTHA

Among the large circle of the Lord's acquaintances and disciples there was a family in Bethany that He was especially close to. In fact, it is said that *"Jesus loved Martha, and her sister [Mary], and Lazarus"* (Jn. 11:5). Bethany was situated on the eastern slope of the Mount of Olives almost two miles from the city of Jerusalem. The Lord would often retire there after a long day in Jerusalem and find refreshment in the affections and devotion of this dear family (Jn. 12:1-3)!

It appears that it was Martha who had extended the invitation to the Lord Jesus to supper, for it is said that she *"received Him into her house"* (Lk. 10:38). But on this day, Martha, usually a most gracious and hospitable person, was becoming irritated with her sister, Mary. When the Lord Jesus arrived it would have been with a crowd of hungry disciples, and so Martha was *"distracted,"* trying to prepare everything in the kitchen. She took her complaint to the Lord, and asked Him to speak to Mary to give her help with the work. She even questioned the Lord, *"Dost Thou not care that my sister has left me alone to serve?"* Martha's trouble was not that the workload had drawn her away from hearing the Lord, but that her sister was not helping her!

The Lord Jesus responded, **"Martha, Martha,"** pointing out to her that her trouble and anxiety was due to her occupation with *"many things."* He defended Mary for having *"chosen that good part"* while at the same time graciously encouraging Martha that the food for the body could wait, but the food of His Word—the *"one"* important thing—was a priority. To serve is important, but to sit *"at the feet of Jesus"* is a necessity.

B. Reynolds

I know thy tribulation and thy poverty; but thou art rich; and the railing of those who say that they themselves are Jews, and are not, but a synagogue of Satan. *(Revelation 2:9)*

This address to **Smyrna** indicates the days of persecution the Church passed through after its declension from apostolic purity. The Lord presents Himself as the deepest encouragement to saints being persecuted, even to death. If saints are called to face death, let them remember that Christ has been into death and now lives. In Smyrna we see the fresh evils by which the Church was attacked, the tribulation the Lord allowed to arrest these growing evils, and the devotedness of individual overcomers who, in the midst of persecution, were faithful unto death.

In this period Satan's effort to corrupt the Church took a two-fold form. First there was the rise of the corrupting influence **within,** of those who sought to add Judaism to Christianity. Secondly, opposition was raised from **without** by Gentile persecutors. After the apostles' departure there arose a Judaizing party, here called the synagogue of Satan, that sought to attach the ceremonies and principles of Judaism to Christianity. This party has been at work ever since, so that today the Christian profession has lost its true heavenly character and become a great worldly system with magnificent buildings, forms, and ceremonies after the pattern of the Jewish system that appeals to the natural man.

In the presence of this great departure, the Lord allowed the Church to pass through persecution that showed those true to Him. The Lord assures them that He has set a limit to their sufferings. He will reward their faithfulness unto death with a crown of life, and He promises that, though they may pass through death, they will never "be hurt of the second death."

H. Smith

August   19   Monday

Speak to the children of Israel, saying: "If anyone of you or your posterity is unclean because of a corpse, or is far away on a journey, he may still keep the Lord's Passover. On the fourteenth day of the second month, at twilight, they may keep it."

(Numbers 9:10-11 NKJV)

THE SACRIFICES IN THE BOOK OF NUMBERS (4)

The Passover is probably the sacrifice that is most often mentioned in Scripture. In heaven we'll be reminded of it forever, for we will see the Lamb as just slain (Rev. 5:6). Christ, our Passover, has been sacrificed for us (1 Cor. 5:7), the foundation of our salvation and of all our blessings. The Old Testament types have been fulfilled in Christ's coming and His accomplished work.

The shed blood of the Lamb shelters from judgment, which came on the Lamb that was killed in our stead. The lamb was roasted in the fire, and this speaks of thorough judgment that searches and consumes. Its meat became food to those who had been sheltered by the lamb's blood. The lamb had become the very center of the household and provided security in the dark night of judgment. Many other elements are described in Exodus 12 for our instruction and encouragement. Because of its special value, God wanted this Passover feast to be kept at its set time (Num. 9:2-3,7) as a memorial for His people. He ordered it to be sacrificed in all generations (Ex. 12:42), beginning during the wilderness journey.

Many times in Numbers the wilderness is seen as a place of failure. Yet, God made provision for cases where there was failure among His people, as long as such failure was not intentional. Today's verses give details of some of such provisions. Moses had to wait for God's instructions, and we likewise need to rely on Him for guidance in applying His thoughts. The unleavened bread of self-judgment is needed, as well as the bitter herbs of a humble spirit (v. 11).

A. E. Bouter

Behold, there was a man by name called Zacchaeus, and he was chief tax-gatherer, and he was rich. *(Luke 19:2)*

Zacchaeus was in earnest. Would to God that you too were in earnest. No doubt he got up into the tree with the thought in his heart, I hope nobody will see me. That is what our hearts say till we get into the enjoyment of the grace of Christ. Then, when the love of God is enjoyed, and His salvation known, we want to tell everybody about it. That is always the way. When a man really gets to know Christ as his Savior, then he wants to let everybody know about it.

What happened next? When Jesus got to the spot, He looked up and saw him. Zacchaeus hoped nobody would see him. He sought to see Jesus, and as He moved along in the crowd his wish was gratified; he saw the Savior. Happy man! At that moment Jesus *"looked up, and saw him."* He has His eye upon you also. Then He said, *"Zacchaeus, make haste, and come down, for today I must abide at thy house."* He knew what was in Zacchaeus' heart. He knows what is in your heart; He knows exactly what you want, what you desire. He knows you want Him. Do you want to be His? Do you want to be washed in His blood? Then you will break through the press to get at Him.

"Today I must remain in thy house." That is a lovely word. *"Today"*! Do not despise it. Today! Just now, where you sit at this moment, the blessed Savior says to you, *"Today I must remain in thy house."* He wants your heart for Himself. He wants your heart filled with the knowledge of His own grace, and calls to you to *"Make haste, and come down, for today I"*—Jesus, the Savior—*"must remain in thy house."* Isn't that sweet? What did Zacchaeus do then? *"He made haste and came down, and received Him with joy."* Do not put it off. Do not delay till the morrow. Do not say, I will think about it. Stop, this will not suffice! The Lord says, Today!

W. T. P. Wolston

Jehovah said to him, Peace be unto thee: fear not; thou shalt not die. And Gideon built there an altar to Jehovah, and called it Jehovah-shalom. To this day it is yet in Ophrah of the Abi-ezrites. *(Judges 6:23-24)*

Gideon was still in ignorance as to who conversed with him. But when the right moment came, he could bring forth his offering. The Lord accepted it and said to him: "Peace be unto thee: fear not; thou shalt not die." With increasing light there was increasing faith and vigor on Gideon's part, for he built an altar unto the Lord and called it "Jehovah-shalom": "The Lord send peace." He took his stand upon God's own gracious words to himself, and claimed peace for all.

The building of that altar meant that God should have His rights—those rights of which He had been robbed. When God has His rights He can send peace.

This, then, was the man whom God could use to deliver His people. The marks of grace and faith in him are figurative of what must characterize us if we are to be delivered and deliverers. The man whose soul is fed upon the things of heaven will be a worshipper, for his heart will be filled with the things of God; and he it is who can raise the altar with a divinely-given intention to render to God what is His.

Thus far the activities and progress of Gideon had been in secret and with God; we now come to his first blow at the dominion of the enemy.

An altar to the false god, Baal, had been raised in the land. In consequence of this they were suffering under the tyranny of the Midianites. Baal was the god of the sun. The sun sets forth the influences that rule the day, and the altar of Baal in the land is typical of the things of earth having ascendancy in the hearts and minds of God's people. This altar had to go to make room for God's altar, for the two could not stand together.

J. T. Mawson

Ye are fellow-citizens of the saints, and of the household of God, being built upon the foundation of the apostles and prophets, Jesus Christ Himself being the cornerstone ... He has given some apostles, and some prophets, and some evangelists, and some shepherds and teachers, for the perfecting of the saints; with a view to the work of the ministry, with a view to the edifying of the body of Christ. *(Ephesians 2:19-20; 4:11-12)*

PROPHETS AND THEIR PROPHECIES—
PROPHETS IN THE CHURCH

These verses set before us the place of New Testament prophets in the Church. Throughout history prophets were messengers sent by God to His people with His message to them at that point in time. Usually the message pointed out their faults and failures and what God wanted in the way of correction and change. The prophets often gave warning of what would happen if people went on their wicked way. Many prophetic messages looked far into the future, looking on to when Messiah's kingdom would be set up. But Old Testament prophets never spoke of the Assembly, for it was a "mystery hidden throughout the ages in God" (Eph. 3:3-12).

God continued to send and use messengers to communicate His will once the Assembly had begun on the day of Pentecost. Initially the Holy Spirit empowered and used the apostles, those men who had companied with the Lord Himself. He also used prophets, holy men of God just as His prophets had been of old, messengers whom He used for specific purposes. Like Agabus, some were sent with a definite message for an individual or an assembly. To others He entrusted the responsibility of writing inspired letters or books that would become a part of the New Testament, God's Word.

We no longer have apostles and prophets among us today, but we have their writings. These form the foundation of the Assembly, taking direction from the Cornerstone, the Lord Jesus Himself.

E. P. Vedder, Jr.

August 23 Friday

In the fear of the LORD is strong confidence: and His children shall have a place of refuge. The fear of the LORD is a fountain of life, to depart from the snares of death. *(Proverbs 14:26-27 KJV)*

When we are walking in the fear of the Lord, we can have confidence that God is on our side (Rom. 8:31). The person who is walking in the fear of the Lord and is living by the Book will have fewer feelings of insecurity, abandonment, and fear. There will be far fewer times when salvation is doubted. The fear of the Lord produces a strong sense of security and close fellowship with the Father. Fearing the Lord calms the anxieties of the heart. Solomon goes on to say when a man fears the Lord it has an effect on his children. Every father wants to keep his children safe; Solomon says that our children will have a place of refuge under God's wings.

In Psalm 128 we see that fearing the Lord has a further effect on my wife and my children. The wife of a man who fears the Lord is seen as a fruitful vine in the very heart of his house. His children are like olive plants, full of vim, vigor, and vitality; real productivity for the Lord.

When we walk in the fear of the Lord we are stronger spiritually, like a fountain that continually springs up with spiritual vitality and strength. This enables the Christian to avoid the temptations and traps of the devil. One that fears the LORD departs from evil (Prov. 16:6). Evil is all around us today, in the check-out aisle at the supermarket, and even on the billboard as we drive down the road. Where do we find the strength not to let this world squeeze us into its mold? Only as we fear the Lord and walk in close fellowship with Him. Walking in the fear of the Lord brings joy to His heart and is the way to be a blessing to others in my life, my family, friends, and co-workers.

T. P. Hadley

The Lord said, Simon, Simon, behold, Satan hath desired to have you, that he may sift you as wheat: but I have prayed for thee, that thy faith fail not. *(Luke 22:31-32 KJV)*

THE SEVEN DOUBLE CALLS OF PEOPLE (6)—SIMON

In our series on the "double calls" we have looked thus far at the lives of Abraham, Jacob, Moses, and Samuel in the Old Testament. One point should be noticed as we move on, that each of these dear saints was called by *Jehovah.* The three New Testament ones, Martha, Simon Peter, and Saul of Tarsus are called by the *Lord Jesus.* This is a most remarkable but blessed confirmation that Jesus is Jehovah!

The Lord initiates an interview with Simon Peter by means of an arresting statement, "**Simon, Simon,** behold Satan hath desired to have you, that he may sift you as wheat." This talk between the Lord Jesus and His disciple would prove to be a milestone and critical turning point in the life of the latter. The Lord informs Simon that Satan's desire was to sift him and the other disciples, but that He had prayed for him, Simon. He prayed not that he would *not fail* (for He knew that he would), but that his **"faith fail not."** How sweet to consider that the Lord Jesus knows all about us, our weakness, our propensity to failure, and yet intercedes for us that our faith may not fail.

The Lord also prayed for Simon that when he was "restored" he should "strengthen" his brethren. Peter's problem had been overconfidence in his *own strength* and in his love for the Lord. His lack of self-judgment led him to boast of his own bravery (v. 33). The lesson he deeply learned through his failure was to have no confidence in himself, but to rely on the Lord's grace and sustaining power. He should have boasted in the Lord's grace and not in his spiritual prowess. He would go on to share this lesson with his brethren and *with us* when he wrote of "the true grace of God in which ye stand" (1 Pet. 5:12).

B. Reynolds

They which heard it, being convicted by their own conscience, went out one by one, beginning at the eldest, even unto the last: and Jesus was left alone, and the woman standing in the midst.

(John 8:9 KJV)

The word "alone," is used eight times in the Gospels in connection with the Savior. It truly expresses one aspect of the cost to Him of being made sin for us, when He became incarnate, that He might accomplish our salvation. One hesitates to speak of His being "lonely": the word hardly seems reverent applied to Him.

But eight times we are told that He was *alone*. It will be profitable to consider what that implied and involved to Him. John 8:9 stresses the *moral isolation* of the sinless Son of God on His way to the cross. That day in Jerusalem, surrounded by a critical crowd of sinners, His searching words so convicted them of sin that they were literally driven, one by one, from His holy presence until *"Jesus was left alone"* with the woman.

That scene gives the clue and supplies the underlying reason why He so often *was alone,* isolated by His innate purity and holiness. From eternity He had dwelt "in the light no man can approach unto." And in His earthly life this continually compelled that moral solitude which must have been His experience through the years and which cost Him so dearly.

He had divested Himself of His *glory,* He had laid aside His *riches,* when He came to earth; but His *purity* He could not lay aside. But having "a body prepared for Him," His humanity craved human sympathy and fellowship, and this was largely denied Him. "God setteth the solitary in families," wrote the psalmist, but the Savior's *natural family* had failed Him. His *adopted family* did not really come into "the fellowship of His sufferings" till after He had gone back to heaven.

N. Deck

By much slothfulness the building decayeth; and through idleness of the hands the house droppeth through.

(Ecclesiastes 10:18 KJV)

The Church is God's house, or building. It was once a glorious structure, but it has since fallen into disrepair, as false teachers and false doctrines have eroded its foundation. And with the headship of Christ, and the hope of the Church being set aside, it is no wonder that it has begun to "drip through." Thus it is exposed to the elements. All this is a result of the indolence and lack of vigilance of those within.

"Slothfulness" is defined as being "disinclined to work or exertion, lazy." Far too many who make up the house prefer to stand idly by and let others do the working and watching. Proverbs says that "Slothfulness casteth into a deep sleep, and an idle soul shall suffer hunger" (Prov. 19:15). Without watching, working, and praying, the soul soon finds itself starving. The Lord said that it was "while men slept, His enemy came and sowed tares among the wheat, and went his way"; and again: "If the goodman of the house had known what hour the thief would come, he would have watched, and not have suffered his house to be broken through" (Mt. 13:25; Lk. 12:39). To the servant who went and hid his talent in the earth, rather than working with it, the Lord said, "Thou wicked and slothful servant" (Mt. 25:26). In the day when the Lord will bring everything to light, many who claimed to be true servants will be exposed as false. They never knew the Master of the house, and will therefore be cast into "outer darkness: there shall be weeping and gnashing of teeth" (Mt. 25:30).

There is no hope for a general recovery for the house of God, but individual recovery is always possible, when there is genuine repentance, and confession before God. "He that hath an ear, let him hear what the Spirit saith unto the churches" (Rev. 3:22).

R. A. Barnett

We shall follow on to know Jehovah: His going forth is assured as the morning dawn; and He will come unto us as the rain, as the latter rain which watereth the earth.

(Hosea 6:3)

It is true! The Lord is coming! As surely as He came once to earth in lowly grace, so will He come again. To Israel His coming will be as the beauty of the morning dawn after centuries of dismal darkness, a darkness occasioned by their refusal of Him who was the Light of the world at the time of His first coming. Wonderful it will be to the little remnant of that nation when "the Sun of Righteousness" arises "with healing in His wings" (Mal. 4:2), awakening faith, enlightening eyes, reviving hearts, strengthening hands.

But as well as bringing the light and warmth of the friendly sun, He will come as fresh showers of refreshing rain to a land that has long been parched with drought. Precious combination! He will bring no devastating downpour or searing, unalleviated heat. As gentle showers He will water a thirsty earth, and as the accompanying sunshine He will give light and warmth that causes precious fruit to spring forth and fill the earth.

Before this, however, the Church will have been caught up to meet her Lord in the air; for He will come for her as "the bright and Morning Star" (Rev. 22:16) before the rising of the Sun, to bless her in the unspeakable joy of His own presence. This will be far greater blessing than Israel enjoys, yet we shall find deep delight in witnessing from heaven the greatness and purity of the blessing that is showered upon that recovered nation, as well as seeing other nations also blessed in submission to this glorious Lord of lords and King of kings. Well might we echo the earnest prayer, "Amen; come, Lord Jesus" (Rev. 22:20).

L. M. Grant

Forever, O Jehovah, Thy word is settled in the heavens.

(Psalm 119:89)

Have you ever asked yourself, "What will the Bible do for me?" It will satisfactorily answer all those baffling questions which the heart and conscience raise as you think of your responsibility to your Maker.

The Bible is a revelation from God's heart to your heart. Regardless of who you are or what you are, it is perfectly suited to meet you in all your needs.

The Bible no more needs the help of man to convince you that it is the Word of God than the sun needs the light of a candle to convince you that it is shining. Light is its own evidence. If you want to know that the sun is shining, look at the sun. If you look at the sun and cannot see that it is shining, it is because you are blind. If you read the Bible and cannot see that it is the Word of God, it is because you are spiritually blind (1 Cor. 2:14). But if you will earnestly ask God to open your eyes, He will do so. Then you will see that it is God's Word, and you will hear God speaking to you in your very own language so that you can understand *Him*. It is a shame to be in ignorance of God when you have a revelation from Him which is as clear as the blaze of the noonday sun.

The Bible will do for you what it has done for millions of others like you down through the centuries. It will convince you of God's love for you and of your need of a Savior (Jn. 3:16). It will set the Lord Jesus Christ so attractively before your needy heart in His wonderful life, His sacrificial death on the cross for your sins, His triumphant resurrection from the dead, and His glorious ascension as a Man to heaven, that you will not be satisfied until you have trusted Him as your Savior. It will teach you how to live and how to die to the glory of God, and make you to rejoice now and forever.

F. W. C. Wurst

Jonah rose up to flee unto Tarshish from the presence of Jehovah; and he went down to Joppa, and found a ship going to Tarshish; so he paid the fare thereof, and went down into it, to go with them unto Tarshish ... But Jehovah sent out a great wind upon the sea.   *(Jonah 1:3-4)*

Jonah resigned his commission and fled to Tarshish, but God resigned it. How good to know that the Lord loves us too well to let us have our own way! Sinners seek to flee from the Lord's presence. Like Jonah they go to Tarshish—destruction—by way of Joppa—pleasant—but they pay the fare. Though it may seem pleasant at first, it costs terribly much to go to destruction, to flee from God. (What suffering sin has caused and will cause, now and through eternity!).

But thank God, though sin demands a fearful price, God's salvation is free. Jonah paid for a trip he never got but God gave him a trip for which he never paid.

No doubt everything looked very dark and dismal to Jonah with the storm raging around and the hungry sea yawning for his life. So things often look to you and me. There seems no way of escape, no refuge in the time of storm. But **God!** But God sent the storm to save him from self; through deep waters back to faith, to faithfulness, and fruitfulness. Then God sent a gourd to comfort him, and then a vehement east wind to discomfort him.

All these fortunes and misfortunes of Jonah, things pleasant and unpleasant, were links in the chain to educate him and draw him nearer to God. They were all working together to weave that exquisite pattern that will eternally evoke astonished, admiring, adoring praise for the Master-Workman. With marvelous skill and patience, and unerringly actuated by love and wisdom, our blessed Lord is weaving our lives for His own glory and our exceeding joy.

A. Van Ryn

The Word of God is living and operative, and sharper than any two-edged sword, and penetrating to the division of soul and spirit, both of joints and marrow, and a discerner of the thoughts and intents of the heart. *(Hebrews 4:12)*

Let no one suppose that thoughts are not known to the Lord, for He has a window into the closest closet of the soul, a window to which there are no shutters. As we watch bees in a glass hive, so does the eye of the Lord see us. The Bible says, "Hell and destruction are before the Lord: How much more then the hearts of the children of men?"

But some will say that they cannot help having bad thoughts: that may be, but the question is, Do they *hate* them or not? We cannot help the birds flying over our heads, but we may keep them from building their nests in our hair. Vain thoughts will knock at the door, but we must not open to them. Though sinful thoughts rise, they must not reign. He who turns a morsel over and over in his mouth does so because he likes the flavor; and he who meditates upon evil loves it and is ripe to commit it. Think of the devil and he will appear; turn your thoughts towards sin, and your hands will soon follow.

Snails leave their slime behind them, and so do vain thoughts. An arrow may fly through the air and leave no trace, but an ill thought always leaves a trail like a serpent. Where there is much traffic of bad thinking, there will be much mire and dirt; every wave of wicked thought adds something to the corruption which rots upon the shore of life.

To keep chaff out of a bushel one sure plan is to fill it full of wheat; and to keep out vain thoughts it is wise and prudent to have the mind stored with choice subjects for meditation; these are easy to find, and we should never be without them.

C. H. Spurgeon

Thou shalt remember all the way which Jehovah thy God led thee these forty years in the wilderness, to humble thee, and to prove thee, to know what was in thy heart, whether thou wouldest keep His commandments or not. *(Deuteronomy 8:2)*

As a present thing God wants our hearts to be in tune with His in our everyday life. God says, "Your heart and Mine want to have a little talk together. I am going to show you what is in your heart, and to show you that I know it." He has brought us to Himself. Do you think that if all that is in your heart is not brought out to Him it will be all right between you both?

Do you think a father likes to have his heart all different from his child's heart? He likes the whole spirit, soul, and mind of his child to be suited to his mind. God passes us through the wilderness that we may learn this.

You often see a true Christian who, at his death-bed, does not know where he is because he has not had everything out with God day by day. "For this cause I also exercise myself to have in everything a conscience without offense towards God and men" (Acts 24:16). Paul's exercise was whether his heart was in everything attuned to God's heart. Christ's heart was. He could always say, "I do always the things that are pleasing to Him" (Jn. 8:29).

Enoch walked with God, and he had this testimony, that he pleased God. He was walking in God's presence, and the effect of it was that he pleased God. You could not walk with God without having everything out with *Him*. If you have something on your conscience, you will not be happy. Every step we take we see Him better, the light gets clearer, and we find things to judge that until then we had not known must be judged according to that which we know of the glory of God. Are your hearts up to it? Supposing they are not, what is the effect of God's presence? Why, it has to set my conscience to work in order to bring me into communion.

J. N. Darby

If you wish to enjoy uninterrupted use

of

The Lord Is Near
Daily Bible Meditations

now is the time to order your copy

for

2014

Lists of distributors can be found at the end of this booklet.

He delivered Him up to them, that He might be crucified; and they took Jesus and led Him away. And He went out, bearing His cross, to the place called place of a skull, which is called in Hebrew, Golgotha; where they crucified Him, and with Him two others, one on this side, and one on that, and Jesus in the middle. *(John 19:16-18)*

The Chinese picture Confucius, the founder of one of their national religions, at the top of a deep well shouting down good advice to the poor sinner in the mire at the bottom—advice which in no wise enables him to escape from his sad predicament.

With God, how different! As the Savior expressed it in the parable of the Good Samaritan: He "came to him" (Lk. 10:33). And so He did! For when He came to die as our Sin-Bearer and Substitute, there was not erected a single cross in solitary grandeur, where on the green hill the Son of God might die. Far otherwise! Man, seeking to degrade Him, crucified Him in company, and such company! "Then were there two thieves crucified with Him," "two other, malefactors."

But surely John's account shows this was also by the determinate counsel of God. For he records: "They crucified Him, and with Him two others, one on this side, and one on that, and Jesus in the middle." Indeed, men crowned Him with thorns to express their hate, and crucified Him between two malefactors, that their shame might extend to Him. Yet really the effect was just the opposite. For God crowned Him with glory and honor (Heb. 2:9) to express His approbation, and had Him crucified in the midst of sinners that His salvation might extend to them. "In the midst" of sinners, that He might begin to resume His rightful and needful place in the human heart, the focus and center of their lives.

N. Deck

Thanks be to God, who always leads us in triumph in the Christ, and makes manifest the odor of His knowledge through us in every place. For we are a sweet odor of Christ to God.

(2 Corinthians 2:14-15)

GOD'S REMEDY FOR OUR PROBLEMS (1)

The Character of First and Second Corinthians – Paul's two epistles to the Corinthians are wilderness epistles. The saints are viewed as having been set apart from this world by a divine call. This world, which to the eye of faith has become a wilderness, furnishes nothing to sustain faith. The Christian passing through it must live a life of complete dependence and obedience to the Lord. Failure to do so is the cause of all breakups and breakdowns in family and assembly testimony. God allows this time of testing in the wilderness in order that we might learn what is in our hearts. But what is of much greater value is to learn what is in the heart of God, and that is Christ. Then, as we learn this, we turn away from ourselves to find in Christ what answers to every need.

The apostle Paul had labored eighteen months in Corinth. The Lord had much people in that city and many had turned to Him. But during the apostle's absence things were not going well in Corinth. He had heard from the house of Chloe that there were contentions among them. They were in a carnal state, and if we sow to the flesh, we shall of the flesh reap corruption. This was evident among them, and the apostle Paul addresses these problem areas in the First Epistle.

A year later Paul wrote the Second Epistle, having heard of the true repentance the first had produced in them. Joy now fills his heart as he travels about, making Christ known. Wherever Christ is made known by word or by deed, a sweet odor of Christ will rise up to God. This is what God is looking for from each of His children.

J. Redekop

September 3 Tuesday

We give thanks to God always for you all, making mention of you at our prayers, remembering unceasingly your work of faith, and labor of love, and enduring constancy of hope of our Lord Jesus Christ, before our God and Father; knowing, brethren beloved by God, your election. *(1 Thessalonians 1:2-4)*

Work, labor, and enduring constancy are most commendable. Yet without the precious motives of faith, love, and hope, their luster and vitality will disappear, and our blessed God cannot have the same delight in them.

Let us deeply cultivate that faith that both sees God, and sees ourselves as manifest in His eyes. This is no mere dormant acknowledgement of truth, but a living, active power that produces proper work. The precious Person of Christ being the object of the Thessalonians, they responded by energetic work for His sake. How can we say we believe the Lord Jesus if we are not willing to work for Him? Indeed, James says, "I from my works will show thee my faith" (Jas. 2:18).

But love is more powerful still. It "labors." It may bear long, and forbear; continuing to serve even when rebuffed, refused, and despised. It persists in caring for its object in spite of this, as Paul would continue to "spend and be utterly spent" for the Corinthians, even though, as he said, "in abundantly loving you I should be less loved" (2 Cor. 12:15). But in the Lord Jesus we see this love preeminently, love that has labored in His great sacrifice for us, and labors still to secure the greatest blessing for souls.

And hope is the sweet anticipation of seeing the Lord Jesus face to face, and His being eternally glorified in all creation. Such hope, bright and fresh in our hearts, will issue in that patient, enduring constancy that can calmly meet every circumstance, and which will delight the heart of our God and Father.

L. M. Grant

September 4 Wednesday

Unless Jehovah build the house, in vain do its builders labor in it. *(Psalm 127:1)*

The above statement is applicable to: (1) the local assembly, (2) the home, (3) society.

The Assembly. Unless the Lord builds the assembly, in vain is every human effort. The Lord Jesus said: "On this rock I will build My Assembly, and hades' gates shall not prevail against it" (Mt.16:18). Believers are God's workmen; He has given clear instructions in His Word. His servants are "fellow workmen" working together, not as competitors, but as equals having the same goal, namely, God's glory. One may be an evangelist bringing in new living stones to be added to the edifice the Lord is building. Another helps to shape the new stones so that they may fit in their place in that magnificent temple the Lord is building, "Jesus Christ Himself being the corner-stone." It is He, not you or I, who builds it.

The Home. The Word of God has many instructions concerning the believer's home. In Deuteronomy 6 and 11, parents are urged to teach God's words to their children. Blessings to the family are promised for the man who fears the Lord (Ps. 112:1-2). In the New Testament we have clear instructions in Ephesians 5:22–6:4. "Thou and thy house" should be our goal. Praying together, and feeding on the Word of God, we can trust Him who alone can build the home.

Society. God gave instructions through Moses on how He wanted the nation Israel to function. They often failed, yet whenever they obeyed Him, they were blessed. The same applies to society today; wherever God was honored and His Word was respected, these nations were blessed. Sad to say, this has been disappearing, and many are building on immoral principles. Now disaster is looming. Let us then trust Him and seek His guidance and His help for our *homes* and *assemblies*, that we may be a blessing to the *society* we live in.

A. M. Behnam

Follow after love, and be emulous of spiritual manifestations, but rather that ye may prophesy. For he that speaks with a tongue does not speak to men but to God: for no one hears; but in spirit he speaks mysteries. But he that prophesies speaks to men in edification, and encouragement, and consolation. He that speaks with a tongue edifies himself; but he that prophesies edifies the assembly … Let all things be done to edification. *(1 Corinthians 14:1-4,26)*

PROPHETS AND THEIR PROPHECIES— PROPHESYING TODAY (1)

Thank God for the problems that arose in assemblies in the days of the apostles, for we gain the instruction we need from how they were addressed by the Spirit of God through the apostles!

The Corinthians were obsessed with tongues, a valid sign-gift at that time that for all practical purposes has ceased today. This gift builds up its possessor, but unless it is interpreted does not edify—build up—anyone else. Prophecy on the other hand edifies the assembly, a good reason for it to be used despite the fact that it is not outwardly impressive or showy. But how practical this gift is—useful to build up, encourage, and comfort! The Lord has graciously given this gift to meet His people's needs! He knows each need and is well able to meet it.

God's Word, the Bible, was completed centuries ago. God warns us not to add anything to it. Yet He wants us to hear Him speaking to us. He delights to use His Word, the Bible, for this purpose today. Not only can we read it for ourselves, but as we come together in His presence He delights to use His servants to bring messages from it to give us exactly what He sees we need. May we not fail to avail ourselves of this means He gives us for our edification! Also, may each brother, who feels the Lord wants to use him to speak in a meeting of His people, make sure that the message he gives is fresh from the Lord for the occasion.

E. P. Vedder, Jr.

The mountains shall depart, and the hills be removed; but My loving-kindness shall not depart from thee, neither shall My covenant of peace be removed. *(Isaiah 54:10)*

The mountains appear to be the most stable objects in the material world; nevertheless, wind and water are wearing them down. But more enduring than the mountains of primitive granite is God's loving-kindness. Other things may change and vanish away sooner or later—the laboriously amassed money, the lovingly nurtured lawn, or the interminably paid-for house may all be taken away in one adverse moment.

But God's love is immutable and immovable! His "covenant of peace" is not to be "removed." These are glorious guarantees. Nothing can assail the believer's safety or undermine his security. God says to us, as it were, Within My fold you are safe forever. As another has said, Our cause is in the very hands of Him who can say with unimpeachable dignity: "No one shall seize them out of My hand" (Jn. 10:28). We rejoice that our cause is not in our own hands, because it would not be desirable that it would be. Why? Have we not had in our hands things that we lost, but is it not true that what we have placed in God's hands we still possess!

We rejoice in our faithful, covenant-keeping God. Anchor your soul on the rock of divine veracity. The great adversary may try to impair your confidence, shake your trust, and even question your salvation. But what are these to challenge God's promises, for just as the mountains surrounded and protected Jerusalem, so the Lord will surround and protect His people "from henceforth and forevermore" (Ps. 125:2).

J. R. MacDuff

> *We change—He changes not,*
> *Though changing years roll by;*
> *His love, not ours, the resting-place,*
> *We on His truth rely.*

H. Bonar

Saul, still breathing out threatenings and slaughter against the disciples of the Lord ... suddenly there shone round about him a light out of heaven, and ... he heard a voice saying to him, Saul, Saul, why dost thou persecute Me?   *(Acts 9:1,3-4)*

THE SEVEN DOUBLE CALLS OF PEOPLE (7)–SAUL

Saul of Tarsus had been a fast-rising star in the rabbinic circles of Judaism. He had been educated at the feet of the great Rabbi, Gamaliel (Acts 22:3). He was a member of the strictest branch of the sect of the Pharisees and was very proud of his Hebrew lineage (Acts 26:5; Phil. 3:5). All this led him into a path of violent persecution and hatred against those who were confessing Jesus as Messiah, thus fulfilling the prophetic words of Christ that in killing His disciples, such a persecutor would think "to render service to God" (Jn. 16:2; cf. Gal. 1:13; Phil. 3:6). Such a man was Rabbi Saul of Tarsus!

Saul, full of threats and violence, was on his way to Damascus to arrest believers when he himself was arrested by the Lord Jesus: **"Saul, Saul,** why dost thou persecute Me?" It is difficult to fully appreciate the effect that this Voice and the light out of heaven had on this intelligent but religiously bigoted Pharisee! In persecuting the disciples of Jesus of Nazareth he had been persecuting the Lord of glory! His conversion thus becomes a precursor of his subsequent line of ministry: the doctrine that believers are members of the body of Christ and are linked with their "Head" in heaven. This doctrine Paul would later call the "mystery of the Christ" (Eph. 3:4).

In the **"Double Calls"** we see in **Abraham,** a faith which justifies; in **Jacob,** discipline and its fruit; in **Moses,** sanctification for service; in **Samuel,** a call to prophetic ministry; in **Martha,** the priority of hearing the Lord's Word; in **Simon,** sifting and restoration; in **Saul,** the salvation of an "elect vessel." How faithful is our God in His dealings with His saints!

B. Reynolds

September 8 Lord's Day

When therefore it was evening on that day, which was the first day of the week, and the doors shut where the disciples were, through fear of the Jews, Jesus came and stood in the midst, and says to them, Peace be to you. *(John 20:19)*

Here is again a blessed significance in the term "in the midst." Having purchased the believer's pardon at the cost of His precious blood, Jesus could not rest there. For pardon from sin is not a terminus—it is only the starting-point for a life in Christ. More than pardon is needed. For when man sinned against God, peace with God was lost for the race. So the Savior died that peace might be regained as well as pardon purchased. These together form the legacy He bequeathed to all believers at His death. And, blessed fact, He rose again that He might become the executor of His own dying bequest; and having "made peace by the blood of His cross," He came that fateful evening to announce the tremendous fact to all believers.

But are all of us actually enjoying this peace of God in troubled days and anxious lives? This peace of God is meant for all, is needed by all, and is meant for you. Yet it can only be ensured and enjoyed by a daily life of faith.

Though God does give an absolutely freehold title to heaven to all His own, yet He only gives a leasehold of blessing for the enjoyment of salvation on the way to heaven. And some of us have not been paying the rent! So we have been evicted from the needed shelter of the peace of God till we do! Let us pay all our dues of love and devotion, and again prove our God, if He will not at once and again admit us into the safe haven of the "peace of God."

N. Deck

Oh! the peace forever flowing
From God's thoughts of His own Son,
Oh, the peace of simply knowing,
On the cross that all was done.

A. P. Cecil

I, brethren, have not been able to speak to you as to spiritual, but as to fleshly; as to babes in Christ. I have given you milk to drink, not meat, for ye have not yet been able, nor indeed are ye yet able; for ye are yet carnal. For whereas there are among you emulation and strife, are ye not carnal, and walk according to man?
(1 Corinthians 3:1-3)

GOD'S REMEDY FOR OUR PROBLEMS (2)

Carnality—The Root of Our Problems—In reflecting on this portion of Scripture we must bear in mind the great object the apostle had before him. He longed to see the Corinthian saints lifted up out of their low spiritual condition as he described it in the First Epistle. He therefore says: "I, brethren, have not been able to speak to you as to spiritual, but as to fleshly." Their carnal condition had led to worldliness and moral laxity, which further opened the door to assembly disorder and doctrinal error. It left them with little spiritual discernment and no spiritual strength to cope with their problems.

This is much of what we are facing today. This condition, exposed in the First Epistle, is addressed in the Second Epistle in order to show us God's way of transforming us into the moral likeness of our Lord Jesus Christ. As this is being accomplished by the Spirit working out *in* us subjectively what God has purposed *for* us (in Christ) objectively, problems are solved in a God-honoring way. Self is set aside in all its varied forms, and in its place Christ is seen in all His moral beauty.

It is not our intent to be occupied with difficulties and problems, but to see God's remedy for them. That does not mean that we try to escape the problems, for we all know that none of us can run away from them. But rather we would see God's provision to meet every need; and that provision is in Christ.

J. Redekop

September **10** Tuesday

Answer not a fool according to his folly, lest thou also be like unto him. Answer a fool according to his folly, lest he be wise in his own eyes. He that sendeth a message by the hand of a fool cutteth off his own feet, and drinketh damage. *(Proverbs 26:4-6)*

A fool **will** argue for the sake of ridicule, with no real reasonableness. It is a mistake therefore to lower oneself to the same unwholesome level of argument. Heated words are likely to betray a believer into the use of the same unsound argument and ridicule. Thus we make ourselves like the one whom we so resent! A fool's objections ought to find us most careful to weigh our answers well. "But foolish and senseless questionings avoid, knowing that they beget contentions" (2 Tim. 2:23).

Yet there is a delicate balance to be observed here, as is plain from verse 5. It may on the surface appear contradictory, but it is not so, of course. Mere argument on the same basis is to be avoided. Yet it may be most necessary that a fool should be answered in such a way that his argument **will** be exposed as folly, without any resorting to argument. Titus 1:9 implies this: "That he may be able both to encourage with sound teaching and refute gainsayers."

The wisdom of the Lord Jesus in answering contentious men illustrates this beautifully. Rather than merely answering their cunning questions, He answered the men themselves. Consider His answer to the lawyer who was desirous of justifying himself in Luke 10:25-37. Remember also His answer when asked by the Pharisees and Herodians about the lawfulness of paying tribute to Caesar in Matthew 22:15-22. There could be then no argument: they were silenced.

L. M. Grant

September 11 Wednesday

Be vigilant, watch. Your adversary the devil as a roaring lion walks about seeking whom he may devour. *(1 Peter 5:8)*

Satan longs to interpose the world in some form between your soul and Christ. He cares not how little, or in what form. If you knew how little will answer his purpose, you would be alarmed. It is not by that which is gross or shameful; such is the *development*, not the *beginning* of evil. It is not by anything glaring that he seeks to ruin you, but in small and seemingly harmless trifles—trifles that would not shock nor offend anyone. Yet these constitute the deadly and insidious poison destined to ruin your testimony and withdraw you from Christ. Do you ask what are these alarming symptoms, and where are they seen? The question alone shows the character of Satan's opiate at work.

You are being infected with the spirit of the world. There is a dead weight, a restraint, a lack of power, that reveals itself in the meetings as plainly as if your heart were visibly displayed and its thoughts publicly read.

A form of godliness without power is seen among you, as plainly as in Christendom generally. As surely as you tamper with the world, so surely will you drift away to its level. It must be so. If you tamper with the world, the privileged place you occupy, instead of shielding you, will only expose you to greater condemnation. It must be Christ or the world. It cannot be Christ and the world. God's grace in drawing you out of the world in your ignorance is one thing, but God will never permit you to prostitute His grace and play fast and loose when you have been separated from the world.

Remember, if you take the place and claim the privilege of one whose eyes have been opened; and if on the one hand this is unspeakably blessed (and it is), on the other hand it can be the most dreadful position in which a human being can be found. Unless you are genuinely the Lord's, it is to be at the wedding feast without the wedding garment.

J. N. Darby

What is it then, brethren? Whenever ye come together ... Let all things be done to edification ... And let two or three prophets speak, and let the others judge ... For ye can all prophesy one by one, that all may learn and all be encouraged. And spirits of prophets are subject to prophets. For God is not a God of disorder but of peace, as in all the assemblies of the saints. *(1 Corinthians 14:26-33)*

PROPHETS AND THEIR PROPHECIES— PROPHESYING TODAY (2)

While we recognize that the time of God giving fresh revelations through prophets is past, we can see from passages like these that God still wishes to edify—to build up—His people. We have before us here a meeting sometimes called *the open meeting*, a meeting not prearranged, but open to the Holy Spirit's leading. Such a meeting can be an avenue of real blessing if the Spirit's direction is not usurped by the energy of the flesh.

Scripture lays down some basic ground rules for such a meeting. While assuming that all will come together with something on their hearts, God's Assembly is not a free-for-all. In a normal assembly there may be more than one brother present through whom God may speak. Sisters are to remain silent, neither taking the lead, nor speaking aloud in the meeting. Speaking in tongues was to be limited to two or three, and these one at a time. Prophets likewise were restricted to two or three one at a time: God knows we are limited in what our minds can absorb on any one occasion.

The others—those who God uses in such ministry—are responsible to judge, to see to it that all is indeed edifying and done in godly order. Failure to do this is no doubt a major reason for complaints about meetings being unprofitable and even boring! Scripture demands that we help each other, and that we be ready to accept help one from another. As prophets we have a great responsibility to help all present to learn and be encouraged.

E. P. Vedder, Jr.

September 13 Friday

All Midian and Amalek and the children of the east were gathered together, and went over, and encamped in the valley of Jezreel. And the Spirit of Jehovah came upon Gideon, and he blew the trumpet. *(Judges 6:33-34)*

The Midianites with their allies the Amalekites (a figure of the flesh); came forth to fight against Gideon. This was natural, and is so today. If your heart is drawn heavenward, you will have to contend with these combined powers, too, for the flesh loves not the things of Christ, but finds its satisfaction in the things of earth.

But Gideon was not afraid; he blew the trumpet of warning, and gathered the people of God together. But ere he undertook to go forth to battle he had again to speak with God in secret. Gideon's request was that the fleece should be saturated with the dew of heaven, that of which the earth knew nothing.

The character of the animal is known by its fleece. The fleece represents our character in this world. Character is formed from inside—from what the heart and mind dwell upon. Are we prepared to say to God: "Let the dew be upon the fleece; let us be saturated, baptized, entirely characterized by that which the earth does not possess"? That is Christ, surely; and it is only as our hearts and minds feed upon Him that we shall bear the heavenly character and stand out distinctly from what is of the earth.

Gideon did not propose to do this thing himself, but yielded the fleece to God and asked Him to bring it about. And this is the secret: "Yield yourselves unto God," and you will prove that what is impossible with men is possible with God. It is His delight, in perfect grace and by the power of the Spirit, so to fill our hearts and minds with Christ that we may bear His character in a world which knows nothing about Him.

J. T. Mawson

I know where thou dwellest, where the throne of Satan is; and thou holdest fast My name, and hast not denied My faith.

(Revelation 2:13)

In the address to **Pergamos** we see the departure of the professing Church that followed the days of persecution. To the Christian profession of this period the Lord presents Himself as the One with "the sharp sword with two edges." The solemn condition of the Church is exposed by the cutting edge of the Word. To link Judaism with Christianity is an attempt to accommodate Christianity to the world by the adoption of that which appeals to the sight and sense of the natural man. It ends not in drawing people out of the world, but in leading the Christian profession into the world. So the Lord has to say, "I know where thou dwellest, where Satan's throne is." Where we dwell is a serious indication of what our hearts desire. To dwell where Satan's throne is would indicate a desire for the patronage and glitter of a world of which Satan is the prince.

Nevertheless, the great cardinal truths as to the person and work of Christ were still maintained, for the Lord can say, "Thou holdest fast My name, and hast not denied My faith." Yet the Church adopted the world's methods and fell under the evils that marked Balaam of old. There arose a class of men who, like Balaam, turned ministry into a profitable profession and linked the Church with the world and robbed it of its position as a chaste virgin espoused to Christ. This opened the door to Nicolaitanism, which held the practical life of godliness to be of little account, seeing the believer is justified by faith. This was turning the grace of God into lasciviousness.

The overcomer who refused the world's ways would be rewarded with the secret approval of the Lord, and be sustained by Christ, "the hidden manna," who in this world was a stranger.

H. Smith

John bears witness of Him, and he has cried saying, This was He of whom I said, He that comes after me is preferred before me for He was before me … He it is of whom I said, A Man comes after me, who takes a place before me, because He was before me. *(John 1:15,30)*

John the Baptist is one of the great figures of the New Testament, indeed one of the greatest men in the entire Bible. The Lord Jesus could say of him that "among them that are born of women" there was no greater prophet than John (Lk. 7:28). But John's only desire was to emphasize the *personal dignity* of the Lord Jesus, and that his own ministry should wane in light of that dignity. He would say that he was not worthy even to untie the sandals of the One he was presenting to Israel and that "He must increase, but I must decrease" (Jn. 3:30).

This comes strikingly before us in John's statement that the One coming after him would necessarily be "preferred" before him due to the fact that He was "before" him. But what do these words of John actually mean? A literal translation will help us in understanding this: **"After me comes a Man who has a higher rank than I, for He existed before me"** (Jn. 1:30 NASB). We know that John was born about six months before the Lord Jesus (Lk. 1:36) and hence the statement that "a Man comes after me." But when this Man was born into the world and subsequently entered His public ministry He of necessity had "a higher rank" than John. The reason for this is obvious, "for He existed before me."

He is God and as a divine Person entering into this world, He takes the first place in rank. This helps us to understand the doctrine that He is the "Firstborn of all creation" (Col. 1:15-17). He was the Creator and as such He existed "before all" things and hence He has the preeminence when coming into His own creation. John "leaped with joy" in his mother's womb in the presence of that Greatness (Lk. 1:43-44).

B. Reynolds

Speak to the children of Israel, and say to them: When you have come into the land you are to inhabit … and you make an offering by fire to the LORD, a burnt offering or a sacrifice, to fulfill a vow or as a freewill offering or in your appointed feasts, to make a sweet aroma to the LORD, from the herd or the flock, then he who presents his offering to the LORD shall bring a grain offering of one-tenth of an ephah of fine flour mixed with one-fourth of a hin of oil.

(Numbers 15:2-4 NKJV)

THE SACRIFICES IN THE BOOK OF NUMBERS (5)

Israel was on a journey to the Promised Land, but there was failure all around. However, God's promises and provisions were secure and sufficient. The Lord's army was well organized, with priests and Levites, and their needed food and drink. Everything was there: the cloud to guide and protect; the silver trumpets to call and lead; the ark to go before and accompany them. Yet they failed in many ways—and we are not better ourselves.

The wilderness is God's testing ground to show what we are in ourselves, despite good intentions or confessions. Moses, Aaron, and Miriam failed; the people failed, despising the manna; their leaders failed, not willing to go on to the Promised Land. There was Korah's rebellion against Aaron's priesthood, and the Reubenites not willing to submit to Moses as the God-given leader.

In the midst of all these failures on the wilderness journey, God reminded them of His plans. In Numbers 15, as if no failure had happened, He speaks about the sacrifices His people would bring to Him once they would be in the land. He wanted them to look forward to that, as Zelophehad's daughters did (Num. 27), and Caleb and Joshua, who encouraged the people to keep going. May we do so as well and, on our journey, occupy ourselves with Christ's wonderful and rich sacrifice, the basis of all blessings.

A. E. Bouter

September 17 Tuesday

Better is little with the fear of the LORD than great treasure and trouble therewith. *(Proverbs 15:16 KJV)*

This verse teaches us that it is better to have limited resources and be in the will of God than it is to have plenty and the trouble that comes along with it. The bottom line here is that when you are in the Lord's will, and when you are walking in His fear, your care is His responsibility. In Matthew 6:25-33 the Lord Jesus strikes at our tendency to center our lives on food and clothing and to miss the real meaning and purpose of life. When we walk in the fear of the Lord we realize that "my God shall supply all your need according to His riches in glory by Christ Jesus" (Phil. 4:19). The life filled with *things* and riches is a trouble-filled life. The life lived in faith and in the fear of God is literally carefree. Paul put it this way, "Godliness with contentment is great gain" (1 Tim. 6:6).

Solomon also reminds us that "The fear of the LORD tendeth to life: and he that hath it shall abide satisfied; he shall not be visited with evil" (Prov. 19:23). People who live in the fear of God will be satisfied people. They will have one goal in life: pleasing the Lord. Therefore, their needs will be met, and they will be happy. When we must have other things to make us happy, we never will be happy! When we learn to be satisfied with the Lord and with the privilege of walking in His fear, we will be permanently satisfied. Nothing will matter but the "smile of God" and it will be upon our lives. The person who walks in the genuine fear of the Lord will never fear many of the things that trouble the world round about him.

Job was this type of man as we read in Job 1:1,10. He was one who was blameless and upright, one who feared God and turned away from evil. And that same God satisfied his heart.

T. P. Hadley

Satisfied with Thee, Lord Jesus, I am blest;
Peace which passeth understanding, On Thy breast.

H. Bennett

The just shall live by his faith. *(Habakkuk 2:4)*

HABAKKUK'S FAMOUS VERSE (1)

Habakkuk complained to the Lord about the sad moral and spiritual condition of God's people in his time. There was "spoiling and violence ... strife and contention" (Hab. 1:3). The Law was powerless and judgment was perverted. The Jews had been in the land for about 800 years, and God was very good to them, but their history for most of that period was one of rebellion. The Lord warned them through many prophets, but they hardened their hearts. One only needs to read Deuteronomy 28 to learn of the severe tragedies the Lord told them would happen if they continued to disobey Him.

Finally the time came for their chastening through a wicked and very cruel nation, Babylon. This was a great surprise to Habakkuk, especially when God spoke of the power of the Babylonians and their determination to "possess dwelling-places that are not theirs" (Hab. 1:6). Needless to say, this is now happening to Christendom, and it will certainly get worse. What is the believer to do? The answer is: **"But the just shall live by his faith"** (Hab. 2:4). This statement appears in the Word of God four times, thus suggesting its importance. It appears in Habakkuk, Romans, Galatians, and Hebrews.

This truth had a great effect on the Reformation. It came with great power to Martin Luther and delivered him from his useless and tiring attempts to obtain peace through his own efforts. It is not for the believer to be frightened or overly occupied with the problem. He is to trust in God and His wisdom and love. At the same time we know that God is holy, and that He rewards the nations that honor Him, while those who ignore Him must reap the fruits of their wickedness. Therefore we can have peace and joy, knowing that our citizenship is in heaven, "from whence also we look for the Savior, the Lord Jesus Christ."

A. M. Behnam

We all, looking on the glory of the Lord with unveiled face, are transformed according to the same image from glory to glory, even as by the Lord the Spirit. *(2 Corinthians 3:18)*

GOD'S REMEDY FOR OUR PROBLEMS (3)

Change Is Possible—The apostle Paul himself had been in stressful situations as expressed in 2 Corinthians 1:8-9 (KJV): "Pressed out of measure, above strength … we despaired even of life: but we had the sentence of death in ourselves." In spite of outward dangers, Paul does not faint or become discouraged. Instead he sees himself identified in testimony with a victorious Christ (2 Cor. 2:14-15). And by his conduct and preaching a sweet fragrance of Christ rises up to God. Paul, who called himself the chief of sinners, is now the greatest vessel God has raised up for the shining forth of the glory of God in the face of Jesus Christ (2 Cor. 4:6). Only God can bring about such a change in the life of any person.

Now, what God did in Paul He is also doing in each one of us who have believed. God by His Spirit is writing Christ upon our hearts (2 Cor. 3:3). The law could not do that. It was written on tables of stone and expressed what God righteously required of man. It could only tell man what he ought to do, what was expected of him. The law could not change him, and it gave him no strength (Rom. 8:3-4).

A Christian is one who has received new life in Christ and a new nature that delights in what is of God. The Holy Spirit now dwelling in the believer occupies the heart with Christ, where He now is in the presence of God. And as we look on the glory of the Lord— a blessed satisfying object—a transformation takes place, a moral change into the likeness of Christ as He was.

J. Redekop

Oh, to be like Thee! … Blessed Redeemer, pure as Thou art;
Come … in Thy fullness; Stamp Thine own image deep on my heart.
T. O. Chisholm

Jehovah said to Gideon, The people that are with thee are too many for Me to give Midian into their hand, lest Israel vaunt themselves against Me, saying, Mine own hand hath saved me.

(Judges 7:2)

The people were too many; and there was the danger of their taking the credit of the victory to themselves, and falling thereby into a worse state than that in which they had been. More than two-thirds of them were cowards, glad to return to their own homes. Do we shrink from exercise of soul? Do we seek ease and comfort rather than spiritual conflict, which we must have if we are to be overcomers? Ten thousand yet remained; to them was applied a further and severer test. "Bring them down to the water, and I will try them," was God's command. Water is one of the greatest of God's mercies, and in this instance an abundant supply was brought within reach of the host, and by the way they treated it, their fitness to be God's warriors was manifested. Nine thousand seven hundred stooped down to get as much as they could, and for the time seemed to forget the fight. On the other hand, three hundred took just that which would meet their present necessity, and no more: the fight of the Lord controlled them, and all else was kept in abeyance.

Here we see the true use of the mercies of God. We need food and clothing and shelter, and these are all put within our reach. If our object is to obtain as much of these things as possible we have become their servants, and cannot face the foe, for we have begun to mind earthly things. If on the contrary these things are used only as God's mercies to us, and we are content with such things as we have, remembering that we are here, not to accumulate treasure on earth, but for the testimony of the Lord, then shall we prove ourselves to be fit vessels for His service.

J. T. Mawson

September 21 Saturday

I know thy works, that thou hast a name that thou livest, and art dead. Be watchful, and strengthen the things that remain, which are about to die, for I have not found thy works complete before My God.   *(Revelation 3:1-2)*

To the church in **Sardis** the Lord is presented as the One "that has the seven Spirits of God, and the seven stars." It remains true that the fullness of power, set forth by "the seven Spirits of God," is with the Lord. However great the departure from the truth, there are those, symbolized by the seven stars, through whom He can give heavenly light to His people. This we see in the men of God in the Reformation.

But as ever, man fails in responsibility. Protestantism, which before men indeed has "a name" of standing for the truth, developed out of the Reformation. But the Lord has to say that in His sight it is dead. We may, indeed, be thankful that through it an open Bible has been won for God's people, and the great truth of justification by faith reasserted. But to the masses the Bible has become little more than a dead letter, and its truths not being received in personal faith, leave lives unchanged. One has said, "Nothing is more common among Protestants than to admit a thing to be perfectly true because it is in the Word of God, without the smallest intention of acting upon it."

Such a condition can only lead to the judgment of the Lord. Nevertheless, there is a devoted remnant, so among the dead orthodoxy of Protestantism there are "a few names" of which the Lord can say that they "have not defiled their garments, and they shall walk with me in white, because they are worthy." In the midst of a lifeless profession they personally walked with Christ, and their names will be retained in the book of life, and publicly owned before the Father and His angels.

H. Smith

September 22 Lord's Day

I saw the Lord sitting upon a throne, high and lifted up ... Seraphim were standing above Him ... And one called to the other and said, Holy, holy, holy is Jehovah of hosts ... And I said, Woe unto me! *(Isaiah 6:1-3,5)*
When I saw Him I fell at His feet as dead. *(Revelation 1:17)*

How seriously do we take the presence of the Lord? The presence of the Lord is no place for lightness. Men like Jacob (Gen. 28:16), Moses (Heb. 12:21), Joshua (Josh. 5:13-15), or Isaiah (Isa. 6) considered going into the presence of the Lord a very serious thing. Have we known Him as Jacob did? Have we seen Him as Isaiah or John? Our unique and wonderful relationship with Him as His children, because of His amazing grace, does not absolve us of the responsibility and the joy of ascribing to Him His due honor.

There were those who failed to take going into His presence as a serious matter. Men like Nadab and Abihu who offered up strange fire, unacceptable to God, and fire consumed them (Lev. 10:1-3). Men like Eli's sons, Hophni and Phinehas, who were immoral, and defiled the presence of God by their life style (1 Sam. 2). In 1 Chronicles 13 there is an account of a man name Uzza who meant good when he reached out to keep the ark (which represented the presence of God in the Old Testament) from falling off the cart it was being carried on. He was struck dead because he reached out and touched the ark, failing to discern the holiness of God. Then in the New Testament we read of Ananias and Sapphira who were dishonest in their hearts and actions. Some in Corinth were remembering the Lord in an unworthy manner and died because of it. In all these cases they had lost sight of the fact that the presence of God was something to stand in awe of, not to become familiar with. In Malachi 1:6, God asks each of us, "If then I be a Father, where is Mine honor?"

T. P. Hadley

I said unto her, Thou shalt abide for me many days; thou shalt not play the harlot, and thou shalt not be another man's, and I will also be for thee. *(Hosea 3:3)*

Since infidelity is one of the prevalent causes of marriage breakups, let us apply the principles found in the above verse to the marriage relationship.

"Thou shalt abide for me" speaks of the **permanency** of marriage. However, many marriage contracts now include a divorce clause. No longer is there a willingness to remain in a marriage when difficulties arise, and "the grass looks greener on the other side." Consider the permanent damage to the children in these situations, not to mention the dishonor done to the name of Christ. And should we wonder why so many teenagers rebel and turn to drugs and alcohol? Or why so many couples prefer to live common-law rather than marry, when they see so many marriages failing?

"Thou shalt not be for another man" speaks of the **exclusiveness** of the marriage relationship. No one else was to come between them, and yet extramarital affairs are a common thing. When one partner or both break trust, the marriage does not necessarily have to end, but it will require an abundance of grace to forgive, and to keep it going. There is no denying, however, the damage that has been done.

"So will I be for thee" speaks of the **reciprocal** nature of the relationship, with each giving and receiving love and respect. As Peter writes: "Finally, be ye all of one mind, having compassion one of another ... not rendering evil for evil, or railing for railing: but contrariwise blessing" (1 Pet. 3:8-9 KJV).

Finally, imagine that Christ has addressed these words to us who make up His bride the Church. We have to humbly confess how unfaithful we have been. But "if we confess our sins, He is faithful and just to forgive us our sins, and to cleanse us from all unrighteousness" (1 Jn. 1:9).

R. A. Barnett

It is the glory of God to conceal a thing; but the glory of kings is to search out a thing. *(Proverbs 25:2)*
As it is written, Things which eye has not seen, and ear not heard, and which have not come into man's heart, which God has prepared for them that love Him, but God has revealed to us by His Spirit; for the Spirit searches all things, even the depths of God. *(1 Corinthians 2:9-10)*

Especially when difficult times are present, it is imperative that we look beneath the surface of things. Answers to problems will not be found without real exercise of soul. God intends faith to be exercised and developed: therefore in infinite wisdom He so presents the truth in His Word that mere natural wisdom will not discern it: these things are hidden from the wise and prudent. Nor will an easy-going, complacent attitude find the precious hidden treasures of the counsels and guidance of God.

But it is a work of kingly dignity to search out the truth of God, and to ascertain His mind, especially so when truth has been trodden in the streets and treated as of no account. How deeply urgent is the responsibility of every child of God to find out the truth for himself. It is there; and only lack of faith fails to find it. Let us face this evident fact honestly, and apply ourselves to search it out. "If anyone desire to practice His will, he shall know concerning the doctrine, whether it is of God" (Jn. 7:17).

Kings were anointed with oil; and every saint of God today is anointed with the Spirit of God, by whom the understanding of "all things" is possible: let us therefore practice this kingly privilege. "Strive diligently to present thyself approved to God, a workman that has not to be ashamed, cutting in a straight line the Word of Truth" (2 Tim. 2:15).

L. M. Grant

September **25** Wednesday

The circumstances in which I am have turned out rather to the furtherance of the glad tidings, so that my bonds have become manifest as being in Christ in all the praetorium and to all others.
(Philippians 1:12-13)

How could Paul's imprisonment turn out to the furtherance of the glad tidings? That imprisonment meant he was bound to a Roman soldier, who could not leave him even if he wished to. The apostle was chained to the soldier with a "coupling-chain" or handcuff, and as the guards were changed, day by day, many a solder would hear the gospel.

It is not quite certain what is meant by the "Praetorium." Probably it was not the imperial palace, but rather it almost surely meant the great "Imperial Guard," quartered in a fortified camp on the east side of Rome. It is said to have consisted of 10,000 picked men, all of Italian birth. As each guard returned to the barracks after his duty, he would tell his comrades of the strange prisoner he had been watching: not a criminal, not a political prisoner, but a prisoner solely for Christ's sake. His bonds became manifest to all as "in Christ."

Through the mercy of God, you and I are not bound to anyone with a coupling-chain, but we are daily brought into contact with many. We go to school or the shop or office; we do our shopping; the postman calls. I wonder, is it manifest to each that we belong to Christ? Are these daily contacts for the furtherance of the glad tidings? I recall a boy who was used to lead a man to Christ by giving him a tract each time he left his film to be developed. At first the man laughed at him, but he told me himself that the child was really the means of winning him to Christ. And after he was won, he used to open his shop in the evenings for gospel meetings, and who knows how many others were won?

G. C. Willis

If there arise among you a prophet ... and the sign ... come to pass that he told unto thee, when he said, Let us go after other gods ... and let us serve them—thou shalt not hearken unto the words of that prophet ... that prophet ... shall be put to death; for he hath spoken revolt against Jehovah ... to draw thee out of the way that Jehovah thy God commanded thee to walk in; and thou shalt put evil away from thy midst.

(Deuteronomy 13:1-3,5)

FALSE PROPHETS AND THEIR PROPHECIES— DETECTING FALSE PROPHETS

Satan is a liar and a master counterfeiter. He does not hesitate to transform himself into an angel of light (2 Cor. 11:14). So it should not surprise us that he also has false prophets serving him, seeking to lead astray God's people. Isaiah 14 and Ezekiel 28 show us how he fell from his original glorious state. He rebelled against God, and ever since he led our first parents astray, he has been trying to lead mankind to rebel against God.

Our God is a jealous God who will not share His glory with anyone. He warned His earthly people against listening to anyone trying to lead them to follow and serve other gods, even if they would do signs and wonders to back up their proposal. He termed such attempts revolt against Himself and commanded that whoever might make such efforts be put to death. Also, Deuteronomy 18:21-22 shows us that if a prophet's word did not come to pass, it was not the word of the Lord, but was the prophet's own presumption.

In 2013 we too are faced with many who try to win us away from simple obedience to God's Word, the Bible. No matter how this is presented, it is revolt against God that we must categorically refuse. Our remedy for this is to love the Lord with all our heart and soul, to fear Him, to keep His commandments, to hear His voice, to serve Him, and to cleave to Him. No matter what the wrong proposals are, we are to put evil away from our midst.

E. P. Vedder, Jr.

September **27** Friday

Let us ... run with endurance the race that lies before us, looking steadfastly on Jesus the leader and completer of faith.
(Hebrews 12:1-2)

I live by faith, the faith of the Son of God, who has loved me and given Himself for me. *(Galatians 2:20)*

Many a Christian who is thoroughly well assured in his soul that faith in Christ is the only possible way by which a sinner can find pardon, fails to believe that faith in Christ is the only way by which he himself can live to God. Such a believer has faith in Christ as his Savior from the doom of sin, but not faith in Him as his strength from the power of sin. He has faith that Christ has magnified the claims of divine righteousness respecting the sins he has committed, but not faith that the Lord works righteousness and holiness in him.

The life of faith is not simply looking once to Christ for salvation, but going on with Him hour by hour. Being justified by faith, we live day by day on the principle of faith. We do not receive life from the once crucified Lord, and then go on in our own power. Every day the believer needs Christ as his strength; and living by faith, he is living outside his own resources, and by the Son of God, who loved him and gave Himself for him.

Living by faith is, really, practical dependence. The strength of the believer vanishes when the dependence is interrupted. Samson's strength departed, and he became as another man, as soon as he was shorn of the external sign of subjection. And so it is to this hour; the believer's spiritual strength flies away immediately when he trusts in himself. Yesterday's strength is of no support in today's difficulties. Christ alone makes us strong moment by moment. He is the same yesterday, today, and forever: Christ was not different eighteen hundred years ago from what He is today; He waits to be proved by all those who trust in Him.

H. F. Witherby

September 28 Saturday

Naaman came ... and stood at the doorway of the house of Elisha. And Elisha sent a messenger to him, saying, Go and wash in the Jordan seven times, and thy flesh shall come again to thee, and thou shalt be clean. *(2 Kings 5:9-10)*

Washing in the Jordan is very significant. The waters of Jordan speak of the death and resurrection of the Lord Jesus, and washing in those waters speaks of believing in the death and resurrection of the Lord Jesus and accepting that the work of redemption He did was *for me*. He died *for me!* Children can understand that. If we do not go by the death and resurrection of the Lord Jesus, we are still dead in our sins; we are still lost.

But the instructions to Naaman also specified that he was to wash "seven times." The number seven speaks of that which is complete. The work which the Lord Jesus did for our salvation is complete. He didn't do ninety-five percent of it and leave us to do five percent. No, He did it all, and did it perfectly. It was very humbling for a great man like Naaman to act like a child and dip himself seven times in the Jordan River, but he did it. Likewise, it is very humbling for those who think that they are pretty good, with plenty of commendable deeds and merits, to confess their helpless and hopeless condition and turn to a despised Savior who died for them and rose again.

The result of Naaman humbling himself and dipping himself seven times in the Jordan River was that "his flesh came again like unto the flesh of a little child, and he was clean" (v. 14). *Now* Naaman had flesh and skin like that of a newborn child! What a beautiful illustration of the words of the Lord Jesus when He said, "Ye must be born again." Salvation through faith in Christ, through faith in the efficacy of His death and resurrection, produces a new birth and a new life. A new life begins which is wonderful and eternal.

S. Labelle

September 29 Lord's Day

We have contemplated His glory. *(John 1:14)*

The apostle John had "contemplated" the glory of the Lord Jesus for three years and we too can contemplate His glory through the testimony that he has left to us. John chapter 1 presents a rich compendium of *personal names and titles* of the Lord Jesus:

1. The Word (v. 1) – As the Word He is "the expression of the whole mind that subsists in God" (J. N. Darby). "In the beginning was the Word" does not mean that He had a beginning but that His existence is eternal. He was with God and was God!

2. The True Light (v. 9) – This Light "shed its light upon" man but man preferred the darkness. He was the "universal light … there never was spiritual light apart from Christ" (W. Kelly).

3. The Only Begotten Son (v. 18) – The term "only begotten" does not have the thought of birth, but that He is "unique"; there is no other like Him. Only He can make known the Father.

4. The Prophet (v. 21) – Moses wrote of a prophet that would come; to Him they must give heed or God would "require it" of them (Dt. 18:15-19). The Lord Jesus is that Prophet.

5. The Lamb of God (v. 29) – He is the true Passover Lamb; indeed He would even be crucified during the Passover (1 Cor. 5:7).

6. The Messiah (v. 41) – This word is from the Hebrew and means "anointed" ("Christ" comes from the Greek and has the same meaning). He is God's *anointed* Prophet, Priest, and King.

7. The King of Israel (v. 49) – The guileless Israelite, Nathanael, confessed Jesus as the "Son of God" and the "King of Israel." His confession is according to Psalm 2 that the King in Zion is Jehovah's Son! (Ps. 2:6-7,12).

8 The Son of Man (v. 51) – There will be "greater things" than Christ reigning over the earth; His rule will extend also over the heavens, for in the Millennium, the Son of Man will be the object of angelic service. Nathanael had not considered this when "under the fig tree" thinking about Messiah! *B. Reynolds*

Behold, I have seen a son of Jesse the Bethlehemite, who is skilled in playing, and he is a valiant man and a man of war, and skilled in speech, and of good presence, and Jehovah is with him.
(1 Samuel 16:18)

In chapter 16 Samuel is sent of Jehovah to anoint this His chosen one. All glorying in the flesh and its birthright are here set aside; and the youngest, despised and forgotten of all, who kept the sheep, is chosen of God; for Jehovah "seeth not as man seeth" (v. 7 KJV). Samuel, taught of God, does not hesitate in his decision, and can accept none of the seven who are at home. "Are here all thy children?" At length he anoints David, brought in from the field.

God does not set David at once in the height of power, as He did in the case of Saul. He must make his way by grace and faith through all kinds of difficulties; and, although filled with the Holy Spirit, he must act in the presence of a power devoid of the Spirit, Saul, whom God has not yet set aside. He must be subject and be humbled, he must feel his entire dependence on God, and that God is sufficient in all circumstances; and his faith must be developed by trial in which God is felt to be all. Beautiful type of One who, without sin, journeyed through far more painful circumstances!

And not only a type, but at the same time a vessel prepared by God for the Holy Spirit, who could fill him with sentiments describing so touchingly, in the Psalms, the sufferings of Christ Himself and His sympathy. For one cannot doubt that the trials of David gave rise to the greater part of the beautiful psalms. The Psalms depict the circumstances, the trials, and the complaints of the remnant of Israel in the last days, as well as of Christ Himself. Thus they have furnished many other burdened souls with the expression and the relief of their sorrows.

J. N. Darby

October 1 Tuesday

It came to pass, after three days they found Him in the temple, sitting in the midst of the teachers and hearing them and asking them questions. And all who heard Him were astonished at His understanding and answers ... And His mother said to Him, Child, why hast Thou dealt thus with us? ... And He said to them ... did ye not know that I ought to be occupied in My Father's business? *(Luke 2:46-49)*

For three days Joseph and Mary searched for this unique 12-year-old Child before finding Him in the temple. Ought they not to have known that His Father's house was the place that would claim His deepest interest? Here they find Him listening to the doctors of the law and asking questions. Perfectly and becomingly taking the place of a boy His age, He makes no display of His own knowledge, but shows genuine interest in their expositions. They asked Him questions too, for His answers and understanding astonished them.

Here is illustrated the truth of Isaiah 7:15: "Butter and honey shall He eat, that He may know to refuse the evil, and to choose the good." Butter is churned from the cream of the milk. Typically it is *the Word of God itself* made good to the soul through exercise. Honey, gathered and digested by the worker bees before being contributed for the good of the hive, typifies *the ministry of the Word*, that which believers gather to share with others. What was truly of God in what the doctors gave was honey, and He received this; though of course the butter was first, that is, God's Word itself made good to the soul in personal exercise.

If the blessed Son of man required this, how deeply indeed we too require both the Word itself and the ministry of the Word in order to discern the distinction between good and evil, and to choose the good!

L. M. Grant

October   2   Wednesday

Seventy weeks are apportioned out upon thy people and upon thy holy city.
(Daniel 9:24)

The weeks spoken of here are weeks of seven years, not seven days. From the time that the commandment was given "to restore and to build Jerusalem" until the Messiah there would be seven weeks and sixty-two weeks, a total of sixty-nine (v. 25 cf. Neh. 2). "And after the sixty-two weeks shall Messiah be cut off, and shall have nothing" (v. 26). The Lord came as the Messiah of Israel to receive His kingdom, but His people rejected Him and sent Him back to heaven, via the cross, with nothing. At that point sixty-nine of the prophetic weeks were complete. The end of the seventieth week will bring in the kingdom (v. 24). That week is referred to in verse 27.

It will be a week of tremendous satanic activity leading the world in rebellion, generally known as the Great Tribulation. What Daniel was not told was that between weeks 69 and 70 there would be a span of time of unspecified length, which at present has lasted well over 1900 years. This is the time that we are in now, during which the Holy Spirit is down here calling out a people and making them members of Christ, the Head in heaven.

The point is that the present assembly period is completely passed over in silence in this prophecy. "Times and seasons" apply to the earth, and those saved in the present time of grace do not belong to earth; they belong to heaven. But the seventieth week applies to them "that dwell on the earth" (Rev. 13:8). Believers today are a heavenly people—if they would only realize it! They will have been called away when the count of prophetic time resumes its course.

S. Labelle

Israel's race shall now behold Thee / Full of grace and majesty;
Though they set at nought and sold Thee, / Pierced and nailed
Thee to the tree, / They in glory shall their great Messiah see.

C. Wesley

Greater love hath no man than this, that a man lay down his life for his friends. *(John 15:13 KJV)*

When nations are engaged in deadly strife, it is common for patriots to declare that he who gives his life for the defense of his country may be certain of a home in heaven because of having made the supreme sacrifice. Patriotism is a virtue of which any man may well be proud. But patriotism, praiseworthy as it is from a human standpoint, will never fit the soul for the presence of God. It can never wash away the guilt of sin.

The testimony of Edith Cavell, the brave British nurse who was killed by the Germans during the First World War, is well worth considering in this connection. From August 1914 until August 1915, Nurse Cavell helped to care for wounded French, Belgian, English, and German soldiers alike. She ministered faithfully even to those who had fallen while fighting against her own nation. She was caught conveying Allied soldiers to Britain and immediately arrested and was sentenced to face a firing squad. All her kindness to the German wounded was forgotten.

Just before the bandage was placed over her eyes, as she stood facing the soldiers who were about to take her life, she gave a message to the world. "I am glad," she said, "to die for my country. But as I stand here I realize as never before that *patriotism is not enough.*" Then she went on to give a clear, definite testimony to her personal faith in the Lord Jesus Christ and her assurance of salvation, not through laying down her life for others, but because He had laid down His life for her. In perfect composure she then submitted to the firing squad's bullets. Her words, *Patriotism is not enough*, have spoken loudly over the years—yet many forget this. "What more is needed?" you may ask. The answer is "Christ!" It is through faith in Him alone that the soul is saved and heaven assured.

H. A. Ironside

He divided the three hundred men into three companies, and he put a trumpet in every man's hand, and empty pitchers, and torches within the pitchers. And he said to them, Look on me, and do likewise; behold, when I come to the extremity of the camp, it shall be that, as I do, so shall ye do. *(Judges 7:16-17)*

They were a strangely equipped army as they went out to the fight; their weapons were contrary to all accepted ideas, and their tactics such as could not be learned in the military schools; but they were men with the single eye and obedient—all they needed to be. Their battle cry was a glorious one, and proved that they were men assured of victory.

They were single-eyed men, and their gaze was fixed upon their leader, for his command was: "Look on me." If they had looked upon the foe they would probably have been discouraged by the number of them. But to look upon the foe was no business of theirs, for their God-given captain claimed their attention and commanded their obedience. While they looked on him, "they stood every man in his place," and, standing each in his place, they became a compacted, undivided company.

In 2 Timothy we have the New Testament counterpart of this. This epistle has been called a dark one, and truly there is a dark side to it, for in it there is plainly set forth the professing Church's terrible departure from the truth, the result of first minding earthly things.

The state of things described in the third chapter of this letter could scarcely be worse, and yet we have there a true picture of the professing Church today. But Paul looked not in that direction; he looked above the scene of conflict and failure, and fixed his eye upon a risen Christ at God's right hand, and the result of this steadfast gaze was continual triumph.

J. T. Mawson

Seek the things which are above, where the Christ is sitting at the right hand of God: have your mind on the things that are above, not on the things that are on the earth. *(Colossians 3:1-2)*

In this passage the things which are above are set in contrast to "things on the earth." This world is occupied with vast schemes through which man seeks, by his own will and power, to improve the condition of the world and bring in a millennium without God or Christ. Looking above, we see it is the purpose of God to bring in a universe of bliss through Christ, and of which Christ will be the Head and Center. God has given assurance of the accomplishment of His purpose by exalting the One whom men have crucified to His own right hand. Christ on the cross is the clear witness to the failure of all men's schemes: Christ in the glory, at the right hand of God, is the sure token that God will accomplish His purpose.

The passage clearly indicates that above there is rest, where toil shall be no more, for Christ is "sitting" at the right hand of God. Then does not Psalm 16 tell us that, at God's right hand, there is "fullness of joy and pleasures forevermore"? Joys there may be on earth, but the fullness of joy is at God's right hand. On earth the pleasures are but for a season; in heaven they are forevermore.

Are not these some of the things that are above, on which we are exhorted to set our minds, in place of having them set on things on the earth? The apostle does not say things that are in the world, but things that are on the earth. Worldly things may include many things that are absolutely evil, and for the mind to dwell on such things would be defiling. Earthly things include natural things which, in their place, are not wrong, and yet if our minds are over-occupied with them they will spoil our taste for heavenly things.

H. Smith

I will declare Thy name unto My brethren, in the midst of the congregation will I praise Thee. *(Psalm 22:22)*

How sweet to see the Lord leading the praises of the congregation, the poor remnant whom He gathered by His death and quickened unto joy by His resurrection (cf. Heb. 2:12). Alone while He was suffering and dying for sin, He now gathers them all to Himself for the joy He has wrought by this work.

Mark the result as to the true character of our praise. Christ, as thus risen into blessedness, having declared to His brethren the name of His God and Father, His praise must be the perfect answer and reflex of this blessing, of this blessed relationship as He as a Man enjoys it. And after the toil and pain, after being forsaken by God, oh, what to Him must have been His entering, as risen from the dead, into the ineffable light and joy of God's countenance, in the perfect place into which He had come by the path of life. "Thou wilt not leave My soul to Sheol, neither wilt Thou allow Thy Holy One to see corruption. Thou wilt make known to Me the path of life: Thy countenance is fullness of joy; at Thy right hand are pleasures forevermore" (Ps. 16:10-11).

Into this He now brings His brethren. He leads the chorus of praise. Thus our praise must be according to the fullness with which Christ knows and enjoys the blessedness of the fruit of His work, and the relationship into which He is entered as Man in virtue of it. It must answer to the name He declares to us as having been heard from the "horns of the buffaloes," and risen, so that we may join Him in praising His Father and our Father, His God, and our God. Else it is out of tune with Him who so blessedly leads these praises, or it is discord. Oh, for the heart to know and, in some measure, to rise to that place and praise!

J. N. Darby

It is the God who spoke that out of darkness light should shine who has shone in our hearts for the shining forth of the knowledge of the glory of God in the face of Jesus Christ. But we have this treasure in earthen vessels, that the surpassingness of the power may be of God, and not from us. *(2 Corinthians 4:6-7)*

GOD'S REMEDY FOR OUR PROBLEMS (4)

Looking unto Christ—After having experienced how wretched the flesh is in me, the next thing is to accept the teaching God has given in many portions of Scripture. He is teaching us to look away from self to Christ and, in so doing, we take on the moral features of Christ. Some of these are obedience and dependence upon God, patience, meekness, self-control, and many others. These are presented in Galatians 5:22-23 as the fruit the Holy Spirit is working out practically in the life of the believer. In 2 Corinthians 4:7 Paul explains that our bodies, which he calls "earthen vessels," contain this treasure—Christ dwelling in the believer. And as the vessel is broken, the light shines out.

In 2 Corinthians 5:10, the apostle Paul reminds us that we must all appear before the judgment seat of Christ. Everything we have done in our lifetime will be manifested in the light of His holy presence. Our motives, our self-seeking, even when it is mixed in with our service for the Lord, will be manifested. What was done in secret or in public, at the work place or at the home, in private counseling or in public preaching, all will be laid bare.

Oh, how searching this is! But remember, when we stand before the judgment seat of Christ, the sinful nature is no longer in us. We will then be with and like Christ and will rejoice that our old selfish, sinful nature is once and forever done with. Only what was of Christ will remain forever.

J. Redekop

October **8** Tuesday

Then you will understand the fear of the LORD, and find the knowledge of God.
(Proverbs 2:5 NKJV)

In Proverbs 2:1-4, there are eight instructions that lead up to today's verse. These instructions help us begin to understand the fear of the Lord and find the knowledge of God. It is not so much a great amount of head knowledge that helps to fear the Lord and know God, as much as it is the condition or attitude of the heart.

Receive: Means *to snatch or seize.* Ask the Lord to reveal one truth each time you open the Word of God, one truth that you can snatch up and live by!

Treasure up: This has the idea of hiding them or guarding them. This reminds us of Psalm 119:11, "Your word I have hidden in my heart, that I might not sin against You!" Treasure is valued and held dear. We ought to value the Word of God daily.

Incline your ear: Means *to lean toward.* We need to lean toward the Word of God, to have an open ear and an open heart to hear it, closing the door, removing all distraction and getting alone with the Lord (Mt. 6:6).

Apply your heart: This has the thought of giving it all I have, my time and my energy.

Cry out: Shows dependency, like a little baby who will die if it doesn't cry out for help! We too are helpless and must cry out in dependency on the Lord, recognizing our helplessness!

Lift your voice: When we cry out to the Lord, lifting our voice, we acknowledge that there is an urgent need!

Seeking and Searching: What we need is the same kind of drive that men have in mining for silver or in searching for hidden treasures. The tragedy is that too often men show more zeal in acquiring material wealth than spiritual riches.

T. P. Hadley

The just shall live by faith. *(Romans 1:17)*

HABAKKUK'S FAMOUS VERSE (2)

The main subject of the Epistle to the Romans is Justification. It explains how man, who is a guilty sinner, can be justified and counted righteous in the sight of the holy God whose eyes are purer than to behold iniquity. To be justified or counted righteous is more than to be forgiven. A thief may be forgiven but that does not change the fact that he is a thief. To be counted just or righteous means to be considered *just as if you never sinned.*

This is an absolute requirement for being accepted by God, for being admitted to our heavenly home where there is no trace of sin. The Word of God declares clearly that "there is not a righteous man, not even one," and that "by works of Law no flesh shall be justified before Him" (Rom. 3:10,20). At the same time this epistle declares the glad tidings, or the gospel, which is the power of God unto salvation to everyone that believes. This indeed is the good news, "according as it is written, but **the just** shall live **by faith.**" This is the beginning of true peace and happiness. How can the believer be anything but happy in the Lord Jesus Christ, who, though we do not see Him now, we love, and we exult with joy unspeakable and filled with glory (1 Pet. 1:8)! How marvelous are His plans for us, plans which He purposed for us before the foundation of the world. How wonderful, how glorious! He who justified us is also able to keep us from stumbling, and to make us stand in the presence of His glory blameless and with great joy (Jude 24).

I will never forget the night (60 years ago) when I shared a room with a new convert from southern Egypt. All through that night he praised God even in his sleep, and whenever he turned in bed. Though I could not sleep for a minute, it was a wonderful experience!

A. M. Behnam

Then Jehovah opened the eyes of Balaam, and he saw the Angel of Jehovah standing in the way, and His sword drawn in His hand; and he bowed and prostrated himself on his face. And the Angel of Jehovah said to him, Wherefore hast thou smitten thine ass these three times? Behold, it was I who came forth to withstand thee, for the way thou walkest in is for ruin before Me.

(Numbers 22:31-32)

FALSE PROPHETS AND THEIR PROPHECIES—BALAAM

Balaam begins Scripture's roster of false prophets. Though he evidently knew the true God, and was warned by Him against going with the ambassadors of Balak, king of Moab, he went anyway. He expected this king to reward him richly for cursing Israel. In his short book, Jude warns us against repeating Balaam's error. God is for His people. He protects them even against enemies they are entirely unaware of. What a wonderful God we have!

Thrice the Angel of the Lord blocked Balaam's way. Twice his donkey managed to avoid the Angel, but this was impossible the third time, so she lay down under Balaam. Each time he beat her. The third time the Lord enabled the donkey to speak to Balaam, rebuking him. The Angel then permitted him to continue on his way, but he was only allowed to say what God wanted him to say.

Three times Balak built seven altars and offered seven bullocks and seven rams. Each time God turned Balaam's efforts to curse Israel into blessing, angering Balak immensely. God used this wicked prophet who sought enchantments against Israel to utter wonderful prophecies about Israel, both about Israel's present and future, even proclaiming the coming rule of the Lord Jesus.

How encouraging to see that God is greater than all the power of Satan! Despite their history of rebellion, He protected Israel even when He had to chasten them. Nor can wicked men or wicked spirits frustrate His purposes of blessing His people today.

E. P. Vedder, Jr.

Jehovah has sought Him a man after His own heart, and Jehovah has appointed him ruler over His people. *(1 Samuel 13:14)*
I have found David, the son of Jesse, a man after My heart, who shall do all My will. *(Acts 13:22)*

What could cause God to call David "a man after His own heart" even though He knew of the many sins that He would commit in his lifetime? For example: he committed murder to cover up his adultery with a man's wife (2 Sam. 11:4,14-17); he was moved by Satan to number Israel and did so knowing better (1 Chr. 21:1; 2 Sam. 24:10).

Even with all his failures, David was preeminently a man of confession and repentance. When confronted with his sins, he was quick to acknowledge and confess them. Thus, when confronted by Nathan, he immediately replied, "I have sinned against Jehovah" (2 Sam. 12:13). See also his broken-hearted response in Psalm 51. In Psalm 32, he describes an occasion in which he sinned but had "kept silence" (v. 3) for a while, but when the conviction of sin took its toll on his conscience and in his body, he confessed his "transgressions unto Jehovah" (v. 5) and obtained forgiveness for his sin.

Let each of us ask himself or herself, "Am I maintaining a tender, sensitive conscience before God?" When the Holy Spirit convicts us of sin, whether by witnessing to our spirit directly or through our fellow man, how do we deal with it? Do we try to deaden the pangs of conviction by pleasures? Do we go half-way, just acknowledging our sin to God while justifying ourselves before men, or by blaming others? Or do we readily acknowledge our guilt before *both God and man*. It is only by our habitually doing the latter that God can come to regard us as men and women "after His own heart"!

P. L. Canner

We know that the whole creation groans together and travails in pain together until now.
(Romans 8:22)

The Lord Jesus taught His disciples that the Father "makes His sun rise on evil and good, and sends rain on just and unjust" (Mt.5:45). His Father's beneficence is directed towards all, His kindness is indiscriminate, for the believer and unbeliever alike equally partake of His daily mercies. But just as His goodness is towards all, the trials of life also attend the "just and the unjust." As Shakespeare, the great English bard, said, we all partake of "this mortal coil."

Everyone experiences suffering irrespective of their spiritual standing before God, and the reason is that we are all part of this groaning creation. Sickness, bereavement, poverty, and other sorrows are often experienced by both believer and unbeliever alike. Our sad world groans and travails due to man's sin at the "Fall." Paul says that even we believers groan with the rest of creation throughout the vicissitudes of this life.

But if misery fills the world, then where is it that we see God's love? If we look at this "groaning creation" we see the harsh reality of what sin has caused, but His love cannot be discerned there. We experience His manifold mercies, His sun and rain, but God's love is not found there. The marvelous wonders of creation put us in awe of His power and glory, but neither is His love observed there. It is when we turn to the cross and view the Son of God suffering for sin that we see His love, for "herein as to us has been manifested the love of God, that God has sent His only begotten Son into the world, that we might live through Him" (1 Jn. 4:9). *We know* the liberty of grace now, but this groaning creation *waits for* the "liberty of the glory" when it will be delivered from its thralldom at the revelation of the sons of God (Rom. 8:19-21).

B. Reynolds

A woman, when she gives birth to a child, has grief because her hour has come; but when the child is born, she no longer remembers the trouble, on account of the joy that a man has been born into the world. And ye now therefore have grief; but I will see you again, and your heart shall rejoice, and your joy no one takes from you. *(John 16:21-22)*

The illustration here of an expectant mother is precious. The pain and sorrow must come before the joy. How wonderful though, that the Lord Jesus speaks here of the sorrow of His own disciples, not at all of His own sorrow, which in fact was infinitely deeper than theirs. In the face of all that He knew lay before Him, He occupied Himself in tender grace on behalf of them in their sorrow. This is pure, unaffected love. And He encourages them in the knowledge that the result of the travail in the birth of a child is such joy that the sorrow is forgotten.

They now had sorrow, in being told that He would leave them. No doubt that sorrow would greatly increase in their witnessing the dread experience of His crucifixion. They little understood that fact at the time, in spite of His telling them; nor did they enter into the precious truth of His words that He would see them again and bring great joy to their hearts. For they had no idea of the marvelous fact that He would rise again from the dead, though He had told them this many times before.

Yet His comforting words assure them that their joy at that time would be such that no one could take away. Indeed this was true, though He Himself would leave them to return to His Father. For His seeing them in resurrection implies a nearness continued throughout this dispensation of grace by the power of the Spirit of God.

L. M. Grant

Bind up the testimony, seal the law among My disciples.

(Isaiah 8:16)

It was a day (like today) when man abandoned trust in God and His Word, and instead formed alliances as his source of security. Rezin, king of Syria, was joined with Pekah, the son of Remaliah, king of Israel, to go up against Judah, but could not prevail, for "The scepter will not depart from Judah" (Gen. 49:10). Furthermore, it was a day of feigned reverence for God, and of trying His patience. Ahaz, king of Judah, was invited by the Lord to ask for a sign as proof that God would preserve them, but he declined with these words: "I will not ask, neither will I tempt the Lord" (Isa. 7:12 KJV). This sounded very pious, and reverent, but in fact Ahaz had no faith. He was relying instead on the Assyrians for his protection (see 2 Ki. 17:7).

All man-made alliances, be they political, military, or economic, will end in failure. Such was the case with Israel and Syria, and so it will be for that future confederacy of which John writes: "And the ten horns which thou sawest are ten kings … These have one mind, and shall give their power and strength to the beast. These shall make war with the Lamb, and the Lamb shall overcome them" (Rev. 17:12-14). So, in spite of the incredulity of man (2 Pet. 3:4), the Lord is coming for the deliverance of His people. Therefore, they are not to fear, but to sanctify the Lord in their hearts, and to wait for Him.

His law and testimony may be rejected by the secular world and the religious world, but it is bound up and sealed *among* His disciples. Jesus prayed: "For I have given unto them the words which Thou gavest Me; and they have received them, and have known surely that I came out from Thee, and they have believed that Thou didst send Me" (Jn. 17:8). As His disciples, let us cleave to Him and His Word, regardless of what the world may say or do.

R. A. Barnett

We do not preach ourselves, but Christ Jesus Lord, and our-
selves your bondmen for Jesus' sake.   *(2 Corinthians 4:5)*
I know that in me, that is, in my flesh, good does not dwell.
(Romans 7:18)

GOD'S REMEDY FOR OUR PROBLEMS (5)

Self—The Great Hindrance—The greatest hindrance to the work of
the Spirit in the believer is **self**. Good self or bad self is still self. Self-
esteem, self-worth, self-image, self-love, are at best the occupation
with the wrong man, the very man whom God has set aside and condemned in the death of Christ. God is not attempting to improve man
in the flesh, instead He has introduced another Man, the Man Christ
Jesus. This is a hard lesson for us to learn: "Old things have passed
away; behold all things have become new" (2 Cor. 5:17).

The question may be asked, How does this teaching help solve
our problems? First of all, we have to admit that "in me, that is, in
my flesh, good does not dwell" (Rom. 7:18). The kinds of problems
which cause us so much trouble in our individual lives, in our families, and in assemblies, find their source in our flesh. If we don't learn
from God's Word that the flesh profits nothing, then God will teach
us by our own failures! How sad if we have to learn it in this way!

Yet what is more sad is that we have grieved the Holy Spirit, and
that our every failure or sin necessitated those unfathomable sufferings of Christ on the cross. Then, as I learn how wretched the flesh
in me is, I turn away from self, and turn the eye of faith toward
Christ, and find an object of supreme delight; One in whom God
finds eternal joy and satisfaction.

J. Redekop

> *Nothing save Him, in all our ways,*
> *Giving the theme for ceaseless praise;*
> *Our whole resource along the road,*
> *Nothing but Christ—the Christ of God.*

S. O'M. Cluff

Then shall appear the sign of the Son of Man in heaven; and then shall all the tribes of the land lament, and they shall see the Son of Man coming on the clouds of heaven with power and great glory.
(Matthew 24:30)

This prophecy about His return in glory was made by Christ Himself. Israel knew well that their nation was to be very great—indeed the center of greatness and blessing previously unknown to all the earth. This subject was the great subject of the prophets who labored, therefore, to bring Israel back to Jehovah, since *He alone* could accomplish this marvelous change. Messiah—Christ—will accomplish it!

The great change that we Christians look for when He returns, however, is not that of being transferred from one earthly condition to another earthly one, but from an earthly condition to a heavenly one. Therefore, how sad the state of those professing Christians who reduce Christianity to a condition of bodily health or financial prosperity!

How soothing—in the midst of the increasing groans of a groaning creation—it is to know that creation soon will not only cease to groan, but will echo and re-echo with joyful praise from one end to the other. How productive of worship it is to the Christian's heart to know that even before this great change takes place on earth, he or she will have been transferred from earth to heaven to be associated with Christ in His reign over Israel and all the earth! To be witnesses in word, ways, and character of such a calling is no trifle. Our salvation was very costly to our Lord and, to be true to Him, will cost you too. When you consider what it cost Him, is that too much?

P. J. Loizeaux

We shall behold Him, whom not seen we love;
We shall be with Him, whom we long to see;
We shall be like Him, fit for realms above,
With Him, and like Him, for eternity.

J. G. Deck

They took the bullock ... and sacrificed it, and called on the name of Baal from morning until noon, saying, O Baal, answer us! But there was no voice, and none answered. And they leaped about the altar that had been made ... they cried aloud, and cut themselves after their manner with swords and spears, till the blood gushed out upon them ... but there was neither voice, nor any that answered, nor any attention. *(1 Kings 18:26,28-29)*

FALSE PROPHETS AND THEIR PROPHECIES— JEZEBEL'S PROPHETS

Jezebel, Ahab's queen, was a Zidonian princess. Although Israel had often fallen into idolatry, this wicked couple officially introduced the worship of Baal and the Asherah into Israel. This was no matter of freedom of religion, for Jezebel attempted to cut off the prophets of Jehovah. She supported 450 prophets of Baal and 400 prophets of the Asherah who ate at Jezebel's table (ch. 18:19). Evil cannot tolerate good, as we see in the case of our Lord Jesus; we read that "They that hate Me without a cause are more than the hairs of My head; they that would destroy Me, being Mine enemies wrongfully, are mighty" (Ps. 69:4).

Elijah proposed a contest to these prophets to determine who was the true God. The horde of false prophets was given the first opportunity to sacrifice and pray to their god, but all their efforts proved futile. After a few hours Elijah began taunting them. They grew frantic in their attempts to arouse their god to send fire from heaven to consume their sacrifice. But all was in vain. Their gods were dead idols.

Before praying, Elijah doused his sacrifice, the wood, the altar, and even the ditch around it with twelve pitchers of water. Then he called upon Jehovah to vindicate him, and to show that He, Jehovah, was the only true God. God answered with fire that consumed all, even the water in the ditch! The evidence was unmistakable. Jezebel's false prophets were summarily executed.

E. P. Vedder, Jr.

I know thy works, and love, and faith, and service, and thine endurance, and thy last works to be more than the first.

(Revelation 2:19)

The address to **Thyatira** forecasts the condition of the professing Church in medieval times. The Lord is presented as the Son of God with eyes like a flame of fire, discerning all evil, and with feet like fine brass, prepared to act against the evil.

During this period the professing Church had great devotedness expressed by love, faith, service, and endurance. History confirms the Lord's words, for in spite of much ignorance and superstition there were, during the Middle Ages, a great number of individuals who denied self and patiently suffered for Christ's sake.

But despite the devotedness of individuals, during this period the professing Church reached "the depths of Satan." For then the Papacy, that system symbolized by "that woman Jezebel" came to the fore. In it we see the exaltation of the flesh, for this woman "calls herself prophetess." The Church took the place of a teacher to enunciate doctrine, leading to an unholy alliance with the world, and setting up a system of idolatry in the worship of images and saints. In time the professing Church sought to exalt itself by ruling over the world and pandering to its lusts. The outcome is a professing Church that comes under the searching judgments of the Lord and the sentence of death.

Nevertheless, the Lord still had a remnant who were free from this false teaching and strangers to Satan's depths. Such do not look for repentance or reformation of this awful system, but hold fast as individuals to the truth until the Lord comes. Then they will have their reward.

H. Smith

Was not Abraham our father justified by works?   *(James 2:21)*

Is the apostle James here teaching a "gospel of works," as some claim? Is he contradicting the apostle Paul's doctrine of justification by faith? To understand this it is important to see that the purpose of the Epistle of James is to exhort believers to practical Christian living, and so keep them from severing faith from practice. A key to understanding James are his words **"show me"** (ch. 2:18). If one professes to have faith it can only be *seen* by men through one's works, and not just by his words. When James speaks of justification he is not dealing with the justifying of the soul *before God*, but rather the justification of our faith *before men*. Paul speaks of our justification toward God; James speaks of justification before man. One has to do with our **standing**, the other with our **state**.

True faith will always be evidenced by works. Both Abraham and Rahab showed their faith by their actions (ch. 2:21-26). They were not saved by their works but their works were evidence of their faith in the living God. What is interesting about these two Old Testament heroes of faith is that their works were not those which the natural man would have considered to be such. Their works would be deemed strange by most people: Abraham offered his son as a sacrifice and Rahab betrayed her country by an act of treason! God's ways are not our ways!

It is evident from Scripture that our works follow our salvation and do not precede it (Ti. 2:11-12). Before we are saved we only produced "dead works," and in many cases "wicked works" (Col. 1:21; Heb. 6:1; 9:14). Not only do our works follow salvation but God has chosen what those works will be, "For we are His workmanship, having been created in Christ Jesus for good works, which God has before prepared that we should walk in them" (Eph. 2:10). Everyone who is born again immediately asks the question, "What shall I do, Lord?" (Acts 22:10).

B. Reynolds

[Andrew says to Peter], We have found the Messias (which being interpreted is Christ). And he led him to Jesus ... Jesus finds Philip, and says to him, Follow Me ... Philip finds Nathanael, and says to him, We have found Him of whom Moses wrote in the law, and the prophets, Jesus, the Son of Joseph ... Nathanael ... said to Him ... Rabbi, Thou art the Son of God, Thou art the King of Israel. *(John 1:41,43,45,49)*

Our Lord Jesus is twice called Rabbi (ch. 1:38,49), that is, "Teacher" (v. 38). That the Spirit records this fact cannot be without meaning for us since Jesus is this in a preeminent way. All who would learn of the Father must come to Him. He spoke "the word of God" (Lk. 5:1) and thus He taught with superior wisdom and authority, with words of grace and truth. It was commonly known that when Messias came, He would be the perfect and final Teacher (cf. Jn. 4:25), and the newly-recruited disciples recognized Him as such.

We should note that their calling Him, "Son of Joseph" means that Joseph was known and recognized to be of David's line, for they said that Jesus, Son of Joseph, was the One who was prophesied to come in the law and the prophets.

Jesus is first called Son of God, and only later is He called "the King of Israel," for it is God's Son who is "His Anointed" whose coming is prophesied in Psalm 2. However, in response to Nathanael's proclamation, He asserts His title, "Son of man" (v. 51). It must never be lost sight of that it is as Son of man that He is heir to man's dominion, and that because of man's forfeiture of it through sin, He must first redeem it.

Through this redemption wrought by Him, He will in due time enter upon His inheritance, the dominion over all things, and indeed He will share this with us who are redeemed through His precious blood.

J. Bloore

They bring you a red heifer without blemish, in which there is no defect and on which a yoke has never come. You shall give it to Eleazar the priest, that he may take it outside the camp.

(Numbers 19:2-3 NKJV)

THE SACRIFICES IN THE BOOK OF NUMBERS (6)

Our blessed Lord Jesus, who never sinned, came to meet and over-come the power of death. That power had come into the world through sin (Rom. 5:12), but Christ, the Sinless One, was going to meet it through death! The Lord Jesus is usually prefigured by male sacrifices, focusing on their strength, commitment, steadiness, ma-turity, or other qualities. The male often displays special energy and actions: the focus is on the *activity*. With the red heifer, a female, there is specific focus on its *condition*.

The color, red, links it with the earth. Thus, the Second Man, our Lord, had a close relationship with the earth, as born of a woman (Gal. 4:4). The first Adam was taken out of this earth, earthy (1 Cor. 15:47) and innocent, but he failed and took the whole human race with him in his fall. On the other hand, the last Adam, also called the Second Man, had a relationship with this earth through Mary and His virgin birth, but yet is from eternity (Mic. 5:2).

Human beings will never fully grasp the mystery of the incarnation: God revealed in flesh. Christ's perfections are summarized by three expressions pertaining to the heifer: "without blemish, in which there is no defect, and on which a yoke has never come." Christ voluntarily undertook to do God's will and to accomplish His work (Jn. 4:34).

A. E. Bouter

> *Lord, e'en to death Thy love could go,*
> *A death of shame and loss,*
> *To vanquish for us every foe,*
> *And break the strong man's force.*

H. L. Rossier

We are confident, I say, and pleased rather to be absent from the body and present with the Lord. Wherefore also we are zealous, whether present or absent, to be agreeable to Him. For we must all be manifested before the judgment-seat of the Christ, that each may receive the things done in the body, according to those he has done, whether it be good or evil. *(2 Corinthians 5:8-10)*

GOD'S REMEDY FOR OUR PROBLEMS (6)

Christ Really Is the Remedy—If we, like Paul, lived our lives in the light of "that day," what a difference it would make. It is far easier to sing, "Nothing but Christ as on we tread," than to live it. For to live it means that it will govern what I wear, how I spend my money, where I take my vacation, how I speak to my spouse, and my attitude towards my children. Moreover it will affect relationships in the home, at the workplace, and in the world. But what is most important, it will introduce an atmosphere in the assembly which is Christ-honoring; indeed this is the mind of Christ.

Having the mind of Christ equips us to face all dangers. It enables us to make the right spiritual decisions. We will then understand with whom we can fellowship, and when associations are unscriptural and defiling. True separation and holy living is found only when it is coupled with affection for Christ and obedience to His Word. Then we will not ask, "What's wrong with this or that?" but, "What is pleasing to Christ?"

Paul concludes this section with a word of encouragement: "Having therefore these promises" (2 Cor. 7:1). If we allow God to work this out in our lives, we will experience the deep peace and joy of fellowship with the Father. This will make all the suffering or sorrow which we pass through well worthwhile. Faith looks beyond the present and evaluates everything in the light of eternity.

J. Redekop

That by law no one is justified with God is evident, because the just shall live on the principle of faith. *(Galatians 3:11)*

HABAKKUK'S FAMOUS VERSE (3)

In Romans the Holy Spirit, through the apostle Paul, taught clearly and emphatically that we are justified by faith alone, and not by faith and the works of the Law. Yet there were false teachers who opposed this cardinal truth, telling believers that they must be circumcised and observe certain days and other Jewish traditions. As sad as this is, we are grateful that the Lord allowed it to happen in the days of the apostles so that we may have the answer in the inspired Word of God. And what a marvelous answer we have in the Epistle to the Galatians!

It is regrettable that many do not study Galatians, thinking that it is too hard to understand. Martin Luther called Galatians his "beloved lady friend." What a joy it is to read the divine defense of this cardinal truth, namely, that **the just** shall live **by faith.** "If righteousness is by law" said the inspired apostle, "then Christ has died for nothing." It would be in essence setting aside the grace of God (Gal. 2:21)! Galatians emphasizes the fact that the believer is not only justified by faith, but that faith is the rule of his life. As believers we are saved by grace through faith, and we live by that same faith in the Lord Jesus Christ, the Son of God.

It is a hazardous thing for anyone to put himself under the Law. What a severe warning we have in Galatians 3:10: "For as many as are on the principle of works of law are under curse. For it is written, Cursed is everyone who does not *continue* in *all* things which are written in the book of the Law to do them." Notice the two words: "continue" and "all." That means everything—99% will not do! It brings a curse. Thank God, for He has delivered us from the curse of the Law. We have been brought into a new relationship, that of children of God.

A. M. Behnam

Jehovah said, Who shall entice Ahab that he may go up and fall at Ramoth-Gilead? … There came forth a spirit, and stood before Jehovah, and said, I will entice him. And Jehovah said unto him, Wherewith? And he said, I will go forth, and will be a lying spirit in the mouth of all his prophets. And He said, Thou shalt entice him, and also succeed: go forth, and do so. *(1 Kings 22:20-22)*

FALSE PROPHETS AND THEIR PROPHECIES— AHAB'S PROPHETS

Jezebel's prophets of Baal and of the Asherah had come to an inglorious end. But false prophets are still readily found. They are numerous in today's society, too! In the presence of King Jehoshaphat, the otherwise godly king of Judah, these 400 false prophets used Jehovah's name in their prophecies (vv. 11-12). Such preachers are readily found in our day as well. Most people in today's world do not want to hear sound teaching, but "heap up to themselves teachers, having an itching ear; and they will turn away their ear from the truth … to fables" (2 Tim. 4:3-4).

Although he had put himself in a difficult, wrong position by allying himself with Ahab without consulting God, Jehoshaphat, to his credit, did not trust these politically-oriented prophets. He insisted on hearing a true prophet of Jehovah. So Ahab had Micah the son of Imlah summoned, a man he said he hated, "for he prophesies no good concerning me, but evil" (v. 8). The man of this world will never appreciate God's true prophet!

Though warned to agree with Ahab's prophets, Micah, when adjured to speak the truth in the name of Jehovah, did exactly that. He prophesied Ahab's death in battle and Israel's defeat. He went on to describe to both kings a most solemn scene in heaven where Jehovah had commissioned a spirit to be a lying spirit in the mouth of Ahab's 400 prophets. In 2 Thessalonians 2:11-12 we find that likewise in a coming day God will send a strong delusion to all those who refuse to believe the truth in this day of grace.

E. P. Vedder, Jr.

Without faith it is impossible to please Him. For he that draws near to God must believe that He is, and that He is a rewarder of them who seek Him out. *(Hebrews 11:6)*

While carnal men say "seeing is believing," we assure them that to us "believing is seeing." We turn their saying upside down, our faith is eye and ear, and taste and touch to us; it is so mighty in us that we do not only know that there is a God, but we regard Him as the great motive force of the universe, and daily calculate upon His mighty aid. Hence it is the Christian's habit to fall back upon God in all time of faintness, to cry to God in all time of danger. He does not pray because he thinks it a pious though useless exercise, but because he believes it to be an effectual transaction, the potent pleading of a child with its parent, rewarded with loving grants of blessing.

The believer does not look up to heaven because it is a natural instinct to hope for better days, and to cheer one's self with a pious fiction about providence; but he looks up to heaven because God is actually there, truly observant, tenderly sympathetic, and ready with a mighty arm to come to the rescue of His people.

So, then, because it is our habit to wait upon the Lord, we go to Him in troublous days as a matter of course. We do not make Him an occasional resort to be used only when we cannot help it, but we dwell in Him, and morning by morning pour out our hearts before Him. So when adversity comes, we fly to God as naturally as the dove to its dovecote, or the coney to the rock, or the weary child to its mother's bosom. The nautilus, when disturbed, folds up its sails and sinks into the depths. Even so in every hour of storm we descend into the deeps of divine love. Blessed is that man whose spirit looks to God alone at all times. Let us each one ask his own heart—is this my case?

C. H. Spurgeon

The fear of the LORD is to hate the evil; pride and arrogance and the evil way and the perverse mouth I hate.

(Proverbs 8:13 NKJV)

How do we look at sin? Often we are concerned more about the consequences of sin than committing the sin itself. Sometimes it seems that many of us try to see just how close we can get to sin without touching it, or actually getting involved with it. We'll watch it on television or on the internet without realizing the effect it has on us. In Luke 3:7 God likens sin to venomous snakes. He likens sin to the stench of a sepulcher (a place where human flesh has rotted) in Romans 3:13. In 2 Peter 2:22 He likens sin to the vomit of dogs, and in 2 Timothy 2:17 God likens sin to cancer or gangrene. These are all things that we naturally shy away from. We would not want to get close to any of these things, we run from them! Is this how we treat sin?

God hates sin so much and must deal with it, and has dealt with it at Calvary! He sent the Lord Jesus to die to pay the penalty of sin, which is death. So why would we run back to that which we have been set free from and which has cost Him so much?

Someone has once said, "What the Lord is looking for is men and women who fear God and hate sin!" These two things go together, and are illustrated for us in the life of Job. We read in Job 1:1 that Job was a blameless man, meaning that the life he lived before others was one of integrity. He was also an upright man, meaning that he sought to live his life in a way pleasing to God. But the foundation for Job's character was the fact that he feared God and shunned evil. Job sought to live out the words he later repeats, "Behold, the fear of the Lord, that is wisdom, and to depart from evil is understanding (Job 28:28 KJV).

T. P. Hadley

I became in the Spirit on the Lord's day, and I heard behind me a great voice as of a trumpet. *(Revelation 1:10)*

The apostle John was in exile on the island of Patmos, when he became in the Spirit. This was a spiritual "state into which he entered." It was an extraordinary spiritual condition, which was necessary for him in order to receive the great visions of the Revelation. Later we read that John "became in the Spirit" to stand before the throne and was carried away "in the Spirit" to see the holy city (Rev. 4:2; 21:10).

We may never have an experience of being in the Spirit similar to that of John, however there is another kind of being in the Spirit. The apostle Paul's doctrine of being "in the Spirit" is that it is something which is true of every child of God and not an ecstatic or mystical state. All believers are "in the Spirit" for this is our new standing before God and we are no longer "in the flesh" (see Rom. 8:8-9). This being so, Paul then exhorts us to "walk in the Spirit" with the result being that we will "not fulfill the lust of the flesh" (Gal. 5:16 KJV). Our *standing* is that we are "in the Spirit" but our practical *state* is that we are to be walking "in the Spirit." If we "live by the Spirit" says the apostle, then "let us walk also by the Spirit" (Gal. 5:25). These things are characteristic of God's children "for as many as are led by the Spirit of God, these are the sons of God" (Rom. 8:14).

The apostle Paul also says that we worship God "in the Spirit" (Phil. 3:3 KJV or "by the Spirit" JND). There is a "fleshly" worship, which is really "strange fire" (Lev. 10:1). This is common today: entertainment under the guise of worship, often accompanied by garish displays of the flesh. But God is seeking worshippers who will worship Him "in spirit and truth" (Jn. 4:23). Thus every Christian is in the Spirit and is to *walk* in the Spirit and *worship* in the Spirit.

B. Reynolds

The Spirit of Jehovah will come upon thee, and thou shalt prophesy with them, and shalt be turned into another man.

(1 Samuel 10:6)

The case of Saul has often perplexed anxious souls. But no one can rightly argue from this verse that Saul was a converted man who lost his salvation. The Spirit came upon him as a prophet, but this in no way proves that he was converted. At conversion a man is *born* of the Spirit, and then *indwelt* by the Spirit. But God may use a wicked man like Balaam as His mouthpiece (Num. 24:2); and Saul was thus used, not only at the beginning of his career, but even after God had rejected him as king (1 Sam. 19:23). We read of many who will say in a coming day, "Lord, Lord, have we not prophesied through Thy name?" And then He will profess to them, "I never knew you" (Mt. 7:22-23). Note, it does not say, "I knew you once," but, "I *never* knew you."

Years ago when the blessed emancipating truth of the gospel was recovered by God's grace, a dear and pious saint of God was groaning out his misery, still under the bondage of law, and ignorant of the liberty of grace. He was saying that God had withdrawn the shining of His countenance from him. The one who had been a chief instrument in God's hands of this recovery of truth replied, "God never withdraws the shining of His countenance from a true believer, for all believers are in Christ, and God cannot withdraw the light of His countenance from Christ." "Ah," replied the other, "but I turn my back upon Him." "Then," came the quick rejoinder, "God will shine upon your back."

Yes, He has made us accepted in His beloved Son (Eph. 1:6 KJV), and believers stand always in His favor (Rom. 5:2). But it remains ever true that the believer is called upon to walk consistently with the grace that has so richly blessed him. "As ye have therefore received Christ Jesus the Lord, so walk ye in Him" (Col. 2:6 KJV)

A. H. Burton

October **29** Tuesday

The marriage of the Lamb is come, and His wife has made herself ready. And it was given to her that she should be clothed in fine linen, bright and pure; for the fine linen is the righteousnesses of the saints. *(Revelation 19:7-8)*

Note that the bride is clothed in fine linen. This is the figure of the practical righteousness which is the outcome of going before the judgment seat of Christ. This fine linen, I judge, is the reward for our work and the love which we have shown to His name (Heb. 6:10), a reward that can then be given after all that was not worthy of reward has been consumed in the fire of judgment there (1 Cor. 3:12-14). Believers, however, can never be judged for their sins, because our Lord Jesus has already paid the penalty for them all.

When we appear before the Lord at His judgment seat, it will be a very blessed, though a very solemn time. We will review His grace operating in us as it worked with our unsaved souls, convicted them, and then produced fruit through the new nature imparted at the new birth. I will see my failures and faults; I will see what a fool I was here; I shall see how grace helped me, and I shall say, "Oh! what wondrous grace He has shown me!"

Who is the bride? The bride is every believing soul on earth from the day of Pentecost right on to the moment when the Lord raptures His people. The terms "bride" and "bridegroom" suggest those holy and blessed affections that befit the relationship between Christ and His blood-bought Church that began with the marriage.

When with Christ in glory, each shall say, "Oh, what wondrous grace that I am in glory!" I shall want to praise forever that blessed, loving Lord who brought me here!

W. T. P. Wolston

October **30** Wednesday

The secret of Jehovah is with them that fear Him. *(Psalm 25:14)*

A LETTER ON GUIDANCE

We do not expect any revelation, or anything extraordinary, but He, by laying on the mind what is pleasing to Him, or by some providential way, will indicate His will. This may be so distinct that it virtually amounts to a certainty in the mind, though we may not be able to prove it to another. The great thing is *nearness to the Lord,* and a subject mind, with the desire, "Show me Thy way." He sets before us an open door, with something to indicate that we may enter. We see His hand in it, recognize it, and act accordingly.

This is something we have to learn experimentally. It is not easy to teach it to another, because it is not a mere mental or intellectual operation. Some years ago I passed through a great exercise of soul as to how I could know the Lord's will to go here or go there. I spoke of it to J. N. Darby once when I met him at Alton, Illinois. The answer I got was, "The secret of the LORD is with them that fear Him." I never forgot it. And I have found since that when I could get no light, there was some cause, something in my state that hindered full communion.

Often there has been misgiving as to whether I had His mind; but generally I have found that when any step was taken in His fear, sooner or later it became manifest that He had guided. Sometimes it is "bit and bridle," some restraint, some hindrance, but this is where mere nature is working, or will work, and the eye is not clear. But the simple, normal thing is, "I will counsel thee with Mine eye" (see Ps. 32:8-9 KJV). God's Word gives us the great principles. God's Spirit forms our hearts in these principles; and the little details fall into line with them. We exercise our judgment; but it is the judgment of a "sound mind"; that is, a mind formed in its workings by the Word of God.

A. H. Rule

In one body we have many members, but all the members have not the same office. *(Romans 12:4)*

To each one of us has been given grace according to the measure of the gift of the Christ. *(Ephesians 4:7)*

Every member of the body has a ministry; and it is by each one knowing his or her function in the body and working effectively together that the growth of all is promoted. It is immensely important for each one to know his or her own proper work, or we can make one mistake after another. It is most disastrous for anyone to mistake his or her own function, since it brings failure not only on one's own work, but hinders the work of others. May the Lord give us to each know our niche and help us to fill it!

There is a distinct difference between the gift of the teacher and the gift of the evangelist. If a person has not the gift of evangelist, he is not an evangelist no matter how able he is to teach fluently. The feature of a true evangelist is an *intense* love for souls—a thirst for their salvation. The evangelist ought to confidently expect results, just as the husbandman looks for the fruit of his labor. However, one may have to exercise "long patience" while still fully counting on the Lord for results.

If the Lord calls us to a work, He will most surely sustain us in it. However, there are those who give themselves to the Lord's work, and the sequel proves in a very humiliating way that they were not called of God to enter that line of ministry. But no one can make a rule for another.

May the Lord guide us into and keep us in whatever He calls us to do, and may our earnest breathing ever be, "What shall I do, Lord?" (Acts 22:10).

C. H. Mackintosh

If you wish to enjoy uninterrupted use

now is the time to order

your copy

of

The Lord Is Near
Daily Bible Meditations

for

2014

Lists of distributors can be found at the end of this booklet.

I know thy works: behold, I have set before thee an opened door, which no one can shut, because thou hast a little power, and hast kept My word, and hast not denied My name. *(Revelation 3:8)*

To the assembly in Philadelphia the Lord presents Himself as "the Holy" and "the True." This is in keeping with the moral condition of this assembly. Amid general departure they cherished and obeyed the Lord's word, and above all jealously maintained the glory of the Person of Christ and refused every denial of His name. The Lord who holds the key can use it on their behalf. In spite of all the power of the enemy, He opens doors of service and closes doors that would lead into a path contrary to His mind.

In this letter the Lord shows that in the midst of the increasing corruptions of Christendom, a testimony would be raised to the truths of Christ's Word, and the authority and preciousness of His name. However, we are also warned that Satan will raise up a counter-testimony by a revival of Judaism with its forms and ceremonies, ritualism and superstition. Thus Satan sought to nullify the Word of Christ, draw hearts from Christ's Person, and so rob Christians of all true service and worship.

If these faithful believers are warned of opposition they will meet from Satan, they are also encouraged to patiently endure, knowing that if they are kept through present trials, they will be kept from the hour of tribulation soon coming "upon all the world." They are exhorted to "hold fast" what they have, lest they lose their reward in the day to come. To encourage such to "hold fast" the Lord sets before them His coming, for which they will have to wait but a little while, for He is coming quickly.

H. Smith

"A little while"—'twill soon be past,
Why should we shun the promised cross?
O let us in His footsteps haste, / Counting for Him all else but loss.
J. G. Deck

Ye turned to God from idols to serve a living and true God, and
to await His Son from the heavens. *(1 Thessalonians 1:9-10)*

PREMILLENNIAL DOCTRINE VS
"WAITING FOR THE SON" (1)

In a day like the present, when knowledge on every question is so
widely diffused, it is most needful to press upon the consciences of
Christians the vast distinction between merely *holding the doctrine*
of the Lord's second coming and *actually waiting* for His appearing.
Many hold and, it may be, eloquently preach, the doctrine of a second advent who really do not know *the Person* whose advent they
profess to believe and preach.

The present is an age of knowledge—even of religious knowledge,
but knowledge is not life, knowledge is not power—knowledge will
not deliver from sin or Satan, from the world, from death, from hell.
Knowledge, I mean, short of the knowledge of God in Christ. One
may know a great deal of Scripture, a great deal of prophecy, a great
deal of doctrine, and, all the while be dead in trespasses and sins.

Now, it is impossible to be living in the daily and hourly expectation of "the coming of the Son of man," if the Son of man be not
experimentally known. I may take up the prophetic record, and by
mere study, and the exercise of my intellectual faculties, discover
the doctrine of the Lord's second coming, and yet be totally ignorant
of Christ, and living a life of entire alienation of heart from Him.
How often has this been the case! How many have astonished us
with their vast fund of prophetic knowledge, and yet, in the end,
proved themselves to have been displaying unhallowed light—light
not acquired by prayerful waiting upon God!

Surely the thought of this should deeply affect our hearts and lead
us to inquire whether or not *we* know the blessed Person who announces Himself as about to "come quickly."

C. H. Mackintosh

It came to pass ... that the word of Jehovah came to Nathan, saying, Go and say to My servant, to David, Thus saith Jehovah: Wilt thou build Me a house for Me to dwell in? for I have not dwelt in a house since the day that I brought up the children of Israel out of Egypt, even to this day, but I went about in a tent and in a tabernacle. In all My going about with all the children of Israel, did I speak a word ... saying, Why build ye Me not a house of cedars? *(2 Samuel 7:4-7)*

King David had an ardent desire to build a house for the Lord. But God told him that not he but his "seed," Solomon, would build the temple (2 Sam. 7:12-16). Solomon is a type of Christ, who will ultimately build "the temple" of God, and His Kingdom will be established forever. Hence, 2 Samuel 7 has profound implications in connection with the counsels of God.

But besides this there is another touching and interesting line of meditation threaded throughout today's text. Jehovah says, **"I went about in a tent,"** and in His **"going about"** with the children of Israel, He did not at any time request **"a house of cedars."** Isaiah referred to this very thing when he said of the Lord's traveling with His people in the wilderness that "in all their affliction He was afflicted" (Isa. 63:9). In going about with them He identified Himself with all of their troubles!

How blessed to see this also in the Gospels where we learn of the One who dwelt or "tabernacled" among us. He had not where to lay His head for He had no house of cedars to call His own, but slept under the open heavens (Mt. 8:20)! His going about down here in the "days of His flesh" (Heb. 5:7) has made Him able to sympathize with us. But much more than this, He identified Himself with our sins on the cross, and rose again that we may dwell with Him in His Father's house! What grace we see in our blessed Lord!

B. Reynolds

Blessed be the God and Father of our Lord Jesus Christ, who ... has begotten us again ... to an incorruptible and undefiled and unfading inheritance, reserved in the heavens for you, who are kept guarded by the power of God through faith for salvation ready to be revealed in the last time. *(1 Peter 1:3-5)*

The inheritance God gave Israel was an earthly one, Canaan, but our inheritance is reserved in heaven and is not a temporary one that can be lost like Israel's was. Our continuing faithfulness does not depend on our own power—we cannot keep ourselves. Only if we are kept by the power of God can we get through all the dangers of our pathway in this world to go on and possess and enjoy this inheritance.

How does the power of God work to keep us? By strengthening our faith! We came to the Lord by faith, believed on Him by faith, and now we walk by faith. As a result, our eyes do not see only the things that are temporal, but we see the things that are eternal—the things of heaven, the inheritance that the Word of God reveals. Having faith, we will realize that the things that will last eternally are the things to which priority should be given. As we do, we will then be exhibiting a stronger faith.

The "salvation ready to be revealed in the last time" is different from the salvation of our *souls* (v. 9)—we already have that and therefore it is not something to be revealed. What remains to be revealed is the sum total of the work of Christ. This includes receiving our new bodies and being glorified with Him, the deliverance of the earth from bondage by the removal of Satan and his hosts from the earth, and our reign with Christ in His kingdom of righteousness and peace. Meanwhile, we wait, looking forward by faith to the glorious prospect Peter puts before us.

S. Labelle

Ointment and perfume rejoice the heart; and the sweetness of one's friend is the fruit of hearty counsel. *(Proverbs 27:9)*
Let Him kiss me with the kisses of His mouth; For Thy love is better than wine. Thine ointments savor sweetly; Thy name is an ointment poured forth: therefore do the virgins love Thee. Draw me, we will run after Thee! *(Song of Songs 1:2-4)*

We are so created that fragrant odors have a peculiarly pleasing effect upon us. This is certainly intended to teach us that the Creator Himself takes delight in that which is spiritually fragrant. Ointment is plainly symbolical of the worship of the heart, as Mary's anointing of the feet of the Lord Jesus shows (Jn. 12:3).

Moses was commanded to make an ointment of precise amounts of various ingredients. It was not to be poured upon man's flesh, nor was it to be imitated in any way (Ex. 30:22-33). Its use was for the anointing of the priests and the vessels of the tabernacle, that sphere in which was expressed the worship of Jehovah alone. This is followed by instructions for making perfume, and this too was entirely for God: it was not to be imitated. God cannot share His glory with man, nor can He allow anything similar to worship be accorded to any creature (Ex. 30:24-38). The spices, whether in the ointment or the perfume, speak of the many fragrances of the Person of Christ, delightful to the heart of God. The oil added for the ointment speaks of the living operation of the Spirit of God.

In our verse then, worship is the subject of the first part. Is this not followed by communion? "The sweetness of one's friend is the fruit of hearty counsel." Candid, wholehearted taking counsel together will have its effects in precious sweetness. How deeply true in reference to communion with God Himself, and true also where there is honest, hearty confidence among the saints of God.

L. M. Grant

The just shall live by faith; and, if he draw back, my soul does not take pleasure in him. *(Hebrews 10:38)*

HABAKKUK'S FAMOUS VERSE (4)

The emphasis in Hebrews is on **faith,** because "without faith it is impossible to please God" (Heb. 11:6). Unbelief resulted in many of the Israelites who came out of Egypt not getting into the Promised Land. God was not pleased with most of them, and they fell in the wilderness. Man's sins can be forgiven and he can be made righteous if he believes; but unbelief is the one sin that prevents him from being forgiven and justified.

Faith is absolute trust in God and His Word. Faith is not blind belief as some wrongly think. It is seeing Him who is unseen. There is a difference between Moses and Pharaoh who both led their people to cross the Red Sea. By **faith** Moses and the Israelites passed through the Red Sea as on dry land, but Pharaoh and his army had no faith in the God of Israel. So the sea swallowed them up (Heb. 11:29). In Hebrews 11 the many witnesses testify that God is pleased with those who have faith in Him. We learn through these many witnesses that faith pleases God. They were people with failures and shortcomings like us, but they all "obtained witness through faith" (Heb. 11:39).

In **Habakkuk 2:4** we learn that by faith we can pass through a world of turmoil, a world under the judgment of God, observing frightening events without being frightened. In **Romans** we are made perfectly righteous in the sight of God through faith in the Lord Jesus Christ who died on the cross for us. In **Galatians** we learn that we are not only justified by faith, but that the life we now live, we live by the faith of the Son of God who loved us and gave Himself for us. **Hebrews** defines faith, and gives us many examples of true living faith. Above all it tells us to look to Jesus the Author and Finisher of our faith.

A. M. Behnam

Shemaiah … said, Let us meet together in the house of God … and let us shut the doors of the temple; for they are coming to kill thee … I perceived, and behold, God had not sent him; for he pronounced this prophecy against me; and Tobijah and Sanballat had hired him … that I should be afraid, and do so, and sin, and that they might have wherewith to spread an evil report … My God, remember … also the prophetess Noadiah, and the rest of the prophets who would have put me in fear. *(Nehemiah 6:10-14)*

FALSE PROPHETS AND THEIR PROPHECIES— SHEMAIAH AND NOADIAH

It is sad indeed when prophets can be hired to intimidate true servants of God. Shemaiah shut himself up and sent Nehemiah a message telling him to do the same, and to do so in the temple which only the priests were permitted to enter. The prophetess Noadiah and other prophets also were trying to make Nehemiah afraid, and thus hinder the work of rebuilding the wall of Jerusalem – the wall that would serve as a protection to them, for it would separate them from their enemies on every side.

Satan is still firmly against the scriptural teaching that the believer should be separated from the world around him. On the one hand he uses preachers who are allied with the world to seduce, threaten, and intimidate God's people, especially God's servants. Nor does he hesitate to use those who turn scriptural separation into unscriptural isolation. The accuser of the brethren loves to find reasons of any kind to justify his wicked work! Men and women who attack scriptural teaching for personal gain, whether money or prestige, are not hard to find today!

Nehemiah spoke to the Lord about these corrupt prophets and those who were hiring them. He refused their proposals, but did not attack them. Many such preachers are our brethren in Christ though they may be doing the enemy's work. Let's not fight them, but rather let's bring all these matters to the Lord in prayer!

E. P. Vedder, Jr.

Whosoever shall do the will of God, he is My brother, and sister, and mother.

(Mark 3:35)

Our Lord Jesus assembles into this one verse a group of the tenderest of earthly relationships. But, human affection falls far short of the depth and intensity of His love. Believer! Are you solitary and desolate? Has bereavement severed earthly ties and sundered your closest links of earthly affection? Our Lord Jesus is One whose presence and fellowship can compensate for all losses and can supply all emptiness. If you are orphaned, friendless, or comfortless here, remember that there is One on the throne whose love is as deep as the unfathomed ocean and as boundless as eternity!

Who can claim the blessedness spoken of in this wondrous imagery? No outward profession will purchase it—no ritual, no ordinance, no ecclesiastical position! It belongs to those who do the will of the Father in heaven (cf. Mt 7:21). It belongs to the person who reflects the mind of Jesus, who is led by the Spirit, who takes God's Word as the regulator of his daily walk, and makes his goal that of becoming a humble, Christ-like, heaven-bound Christian. Such as these can claim this wondrous promise of love as their own!

If it is a worthy object of ambition to be loved by the good and great here on earth, then what must be the worth of an eye of love beaming down upon us from the throne in heaven! Does not the love of brother, sister, or parent pale in comparison? Just think! He looks down on us "poor worms" and refers to us as His brother, sister, mother—He is not ashamed to call us "brethren" (Heb. 2:11). Have we known and believed "the love which God has to us" (1 Jn. 4:16)? How poor has been our response to this love!

J. R. MacDuff

Engrave this deeply on our hearts with an eternal pen,
That we may, in some small degree, / Return Thy love again.
J. Hutton

He who walks in his uprightness fears the Lord, but he who is perverse in his ways despises Him. *(Proverbs 14:2 NKJV)*

A man's conduct is a reflection of his attitude toward the Lord. The righteous man is guided by what he knows will please God. His deep desire is to walk closer and closer to his God no manner how long he has been walking with the Lord. The apostle Paul had been walking with the Lord for about 30 years, but he wasn't content with his past. His desire was to walk closer with Him and to know Him in a much deeper way (Phil. 3:7-10).

We cannot walk with God and walk with sin (Prov. 3:7; 8:13; 14:16; 1 Jn. 1:5-10).

We cannot walk with God and walk with pride (Prov. 22:4; Jas. 4:6-10).

We cannot walk with God and walk with the world (Prov. 23:17; Jas. 4:3-4; 1 Jn. 2:15-17). In Psalm 73 we have recorded for us a man doing just what John warns us against. He looked at the world with envy. He thought he was missing out. He saw the wicked seemingly getting away with so much, and it almost cost him his faith. He almost compromised with the world he envied. It would seem that he might have even tried to get as close to it as he could without crossing the line! But what was the antidote for Asaph? What is the antidote for us? Psalm 73:17 tells us that Asaph went into the presence of the Lord. This helps us clean the lenses of our spiritual eyes.

I would suggest that Asaph then began to fear the Lord! Getting into the presence of the Lord helps us to realign our thinking to be in tune with God's thoughts. We begin to see things from His point of view! When we begin to fear the Lord, hate what He hates, and love what He loves, we realize what Asaph realized in Psalm 73:25-28, that He is enough the heart and mind to fill! But it all begins with whether or not I fear the Lord!

T. P. Hadley

I received from the Lord, that which I also delivered to you, that the Lord Jesus, in the night in which He was delivered up, took bread ... For as often as ye shall eat this bread, and drink the cup, ye announce the death of the Lord, until He come.

(1 Corinthians 11:23,26)

This most remarkable request received from the Lord, from the lips of the once crucified Savior but now risen and glorified Son of Man, encompasses God's thoughts concerning His Christ.

Paul had received this new revelation concerning the Lord's Supper from the Man in the glory, the One who—though God—humbled Himself and became obedient unto death, and that the death of the cross (Phil. 2:5-8). Great indeed is the mystery of piety, God is manifest in flesh! (1 Tim. 3:16). The One who created the universe by His word, and upholds all things by His power, Himself stooped down as the dependant, obedient, lowly Man with an opened ear to receive directions for the day from God His Father. That is how He would begin each day, and how He continued, walking each step of the way that led Him to that bitter cross of shame (Isa. 50:3-5). Truly, we exclaim: Hallelujah, what a Savior!

In verse 23 we are reminded that on the night of Christ's betrayal this supper was given to His redeemed people. In the world where Christ is despised and rejected, there is now a company of saints, cleansed by His blood, surrounding the Lord at His table, to remember Him. Remembering Him draws out our hearts to offer sacrifices of praise and worship to the alone worthy One, our Lord Jesus Christ. Then, what rises up to God as a sweet fragrance of Christ—the *fruit* of our lips giving thanks to His name—spreads in *testimony* to this world. Thereby we loudly and clearly proclaim the victory Christ has gained by His death on the cross. He has triumphed gloriously!

J. Redekop

Ye must be born again ... As Moses lifted up the serpent in the wilderness, even so must the Son of man be lifted up ... He must increase, but I must decrease. *(John 3:7,14,30 KJV)*

THREE DIVINE NECESSITIES

1. "Ye **must** be born again." — Because we are sinful, we need a new nature. This new nature is received at new birth through the operation of the Spirit, and the Word acting upon the heart and conscience, leading to repentance and faith in the Lord Jesus Christ. We then become partakers of God's divine nature, fitted for fellowship with God, and for entrance into His kingdom.

2. "As Moses lifted up the serpent in the wilderness, even so **must** the Son of man be lifted up." — Because of the sinful acts of the children of Israel in the wilderness, God sent fiery serpents among them which bit them, resulting in many deaths. When the people confessed their sins, God responded by telling Moses to make a serpent of brass and put it upon a pole. Anyone who was bitten, and looked upon the serpent of brass, was healed. The serpent of brass illustrates the cross of Christ by which "through death, He [destroyed] him that had the power of death, that is, the devil" (Heb. 2:14). Christ absolutely had to die on that cross, that any who look to Him "should not perish, but have eternal life" (Jn. 3:15).

3. He **must** increase, but I must decrease. — God is very jealous for the glory of His Son, and looks to see His moral features formed in us who are saved; and the more we are occupied with Him, the more we are "changed into the same image from glory to glory, even as by the Spirit of the Lord" (2 Cor. 3:18). The egotist is filled with pride, and self-absorption. In fact someone defined "ego" as, "E go, and I stay." Rather, the "I" of self must go, that Christ may remain.

R. A. Barnett

November   **12**   Tuesday

Jehovah appointed a set time.   *(Exodus 9:5)*

"Appointments are the curse of my life!" So lamented a seemingly successful man who tried to cram 36 hours into every 24-hour period. Perhaps we've all felt like that at times. However, some appointments in life are unavoidable, and those which God has made even more so. How we respond to His appointments will determine the course of our lives for time and eternity.

As a human being, I cannot avoid the appointment to death and judgment cited in Hebrews 9:27, but I can prepare for it by turning to the Lord for salvation. Then as a Christian, I can rejoice that another of God's appointments may even break my appointment with physical death. If the Lord Jesus returns during my lifetime, I shall be happily numbered among those redeemed throngs who shall be caught up to meet the Lord in the twinkling of an eye. As one appointed to salvation rather than wrath, I shall be removed from the world before He pours out His wrath upon it.

But in the meantime I still live in this trouble-filled world. Therefore, without any scheduling or effort on my part, I learn that I am appointed to afflictions (1 Th. 3:3). However, as the Word of God thus prepares me to suffer as a Christian, it also teaches me that these sufferings work together for good to them that love God. By God's grace, I can respond to my appointment with afflictions with joy rather than gloom. A passage in Luke 10 illustrates a third appointment for the Christian. "The Lord appointed seventy others also, and sent them" (v. 1). As the Lord provided everything necessary for those seventy disciples, so He provides everything for our appointment to service. And then He sends us forth.

G. W. Steidl

Our times are in Thy hand, / Father, we wish them there;
Our life, our soul, our all, we leave / Entirely to Thy care.

W. F. Lloyd

**Where is the King of the Jews that has been born? For we have
seen His star in the east, and have come to do Him homage.**

(Matthew 2:2)

PREMILLENNIAL DOCTRINE VS
"WAITING FOR THE SON" (2)

Matthew 2 furnishes us with a very striking illustration of the difference between mere prophetic knowledge of Christ—intellectual exercise on the letter of Scripture—and the Father's drawing to the Person of Christ. The wise men, who manifestly were in earnest search of Christ, could not for a moment have competed with the chief priests and scribes; yet what did the scriptural knowledge of the latter do for them? It rendered them efficient instruments for Herod, who called them together in order to use their biblical knowledge in his deadly opposition to God's Anointed. They were able to give him chapter and verse. But, while they were assisting Herod by their knowledge, the wise men were, by the Father's drawing, making their way to Jesus.

Blessed contrast! How much happier to be a worshipper at the feet of Jesus with slender knowledge, than to be a learned scribe with a heart cold, dead, and distant from Him! How much better to have the heart full of living affection for Christ than to have the intellect stored with the most accurate knowledge of the letter of Scripture!

It is not that we would undervalue scriptural knowledge, if that knowledge be found in connection with genuine discipleship. But if it be not, of what value is it? None whatever! The most extensive range of knowledge, if Christ be not its center, will avail just nothing. It will, in all probability, render us more efficient instruments in Satan's hand for the furthering of his purposes of hostility to Christ. An ignorant man can do but little mischief; but a learned man, without Christ, can do a great deal.

C. H. Mackintosh

The prophet Jeremiah said unto the prophet Hananiah, Hear now, Hananiah: Jehovah hath not sent thee; and thou makest this people to trust in falsehood. Therefore thus saith Jehovah: Behold, I will cast thee from off the face of the earth: this year thou shalt die, for thou hast spoken revolt against Jehovah. And the prophet Hananiah died in the same year in the seventh month. *(Jeremiah 28:15-17)*

FALSE PROPHETS AND THEIR PROPHECIES—HANANIAH

Earlier God had told Jeremiah to make bonds and yokes, put them on his neck, and send them to the kings of the surrounding lands with God's message to submit themselves to the king of Babylon. If they would thus submit, God said, they would be allowed to remain in their lands rather than being carried away captive. Now, at the beginning of this chapter another prophet, Hananiah, had publicly proclaimed that Jehovah had broken the yoke of the king of Babylon. He had further prophesied that within two years Jehovah would bring back Jeconiah the king with all the captives and all the vessels Nebuchadnezzar had taken from the temple.

Jeremiah publicly said, "Amen, may Jehovah do so," to that which Hananiah had spoken. All Judah wanted this to happen. He pointed out, however, that only when the word of the prophet prophesying peace would come to pass, would he be known as one whom the Lord had sent. Hananiah then took the wooden yoke from off Jeremiah's neck and broke it, again declaring that the Lord said He would thus break Nebuchadnezzar's yoke. Jeremiah quietly went his way.

A bit later the Lord had Jeremiah say to Hananiah that He would replace the wooden yokes he had broken with iron yokes. The Lord had given Nebuchadnezzar the nations, and even the beasts of the field. The Lord had not sent Hananiah; he was making the people trust in a lie. For this rebellion he would die that year, and so it happened. It is most dangerous to rebel against the Lord!

E. P. Vedder, Jr.

Because thou art lukewarm, and neither cold nor hot, I am about to spue thee out of My mouth. *(Revelation 3:16)*

In the address to **Laodicea** we learn the solemn end of the Church's failure in responsibility. The reviving grace of the Lord has been abused, His warnings little heeded. Yet amid all the failure the Lord remains His people's unchanging resource. And in the darkest day there is richest blessing for the individual believer.

In striking contrast to the great Christian profession that has been neither faithful to God nor a true witness before men, the Lord Himself is "the Amen" through whom every purpose of God will be fulfilled, the "Faithful and True Witness, the Beginning of the Creation of God."

The failure that commenced with the loss of first love ends in utter indifference to Christ. The Church is unmoved though Christ is outside the door, and deaf to every appeal by which He seeks to win their hearts. The great mass uses the truth grace had restored to them to exalt themselves and boast of their riches, their vanity blinding them to their own true condition. The self-complacent mass knows not that in the Lord's sight they are spiritually wretched, miserable, poor, blind, and naked. Their condition is nauseous to Him, and can only end in His entire rejection of the Christian profession.

Yet in these dark days, true souls whom the Lord loves will be manifested by the rebukes and chastening needed to recall them to Himself. The Lord patiently knocks at the door, seeking a place in their affections. As each opens his heart's door, the Lord says, "I will come in unto him and sup with him, and he with Me." He will enter into all their exercises and trials.

H. Smith

November **16** Saturday

David therefore departed thence, and escaped to the cave Adullam ... And everyone that was in distress, and every one that was in debt, and every one that was discontented, gathered themselves unto him ... and there were with him about four hundred men.
(1 Samuel 22:1-2 KJV)

David was the anointed King of Israel, yet he was living life as a fugitive. Saul was envious of his popularity and military prowess and sought to murder him. In these things, David is a "type" of the Lord Jesus in that He also was rejected and persecuted due to envy (Mt. 27:18). David was daily being hunted like "a partridge in the mountains" and so too, Christ, for the chief priests and elders repeatedly took counsel against Jesus that they might put Him to death (Mt. 12:14; 26:4; 27:1).

The cave of Adullam was the place where the outcasts of Saul's kingdom gathered. There was nothing attractive about the cave, nothing pleasing for their flesh; it was David's person which attracted this band of men. They came to David because they had felt their personal need: they were in distress, in debt, and discontented. Like David, Christ also gathered a small but faithful band of followers who shared in His trials (Lk. 22:28-29). And just as David in his rejection had those who **"gathered themselves unto him,"** so too, the Lord Jesus is honored when His own identify with Him in His rejection, though they be only two or three. The destinies of the four hundred men who were with David would be forever linked with him. When he came to power in his kingdom they were given places of honor. They had "suffered" with him and later they "reigned" with him.

Christ now is the attractive center for the believer. The Lord Jesus went "outside the camp" and we ought to be identified with Him there. The destinies of all believers are linked with Him and they can, with anticipation and joy, look forward to the day when they will reign with Him in His kingdom.

B. Reynolds

I John ... was in the island called Patmos, for the word of God, and for the testimony of Jesus. I became in the Spirit on the Lord's day. *(Revelation 1:9-10)*

Let us see how the Lord's Day is characterized in Scripture. This is the day on which our blessed Lord arose from the dead—the day that declared before the universe His triumph over death and the grave, and over all the power of Satan. And surely this is a fact of deepest importance for our souls.

At the cross the whole question of good and evil was brought to an issue; and the resurrection of the Lord Jesus revealed the triumph of good. It was life out of death, and the bringing in of a new creation where the old had been condemned in the judgment of God. Such was the victory of the Lord Jesus; and His resurrection on the first day of the week proclaimed the completeness of the victory.

It is the day on which the Holy Spirit descended from heaven, inaugurating the full character of Christianity. The two great characteristic truths of Christianity are redemption, and the presence of the Holy Spirit on earth, while Christ is seated at the right hand of God. The first day of the week is the witness of these two things. We know from Leviticus 23:15-16: "And ye shall count from the morning after the Sabbath, from the day that ye brought the sheaf of the wave-offering, seven weeks; they shall be complete; even unto the morning after the seventh Sabbath shall ye count fifty days; and ye shall present a new oblation to Jehovah." This was the feast of Pentecost; and it began on the "morrow after the Sabbath"; that is, on the first day of the week. Acts 2 shows that this was the day on which the Holy Spirit descended.

A. H. Rule

Sweet it is to sit before Thee, / Sweet to hear Thy blessed voice,
Sweet to worship and adore Thee, / While our hearts in Thee rejoice.
T. H. Reynolds

It shall be slaughtered before him; and Eleazar the priest shall take some of its blood with his finger, and sprinkle some of its blood seven times directly in front of the tabernacle of meeting. Then the heifer shall be burned in his sight: its hide, its flesh, its blood, and its offal shall be burned. And the priest shall take cedar wood and hyssop and scarlet, and cast them into the midst of the fire burning the heifer. *(Numbers 19:3-6 NKJV)*

THE SACRIFICES IN THE BOOK OF NUMBERS (7)

God prescribed a red heifer to be sacrificed as a means for cleansing from defilement. It prefigured many aspects of Christ's perfections and sacrifice. The high priest Eleazar—"helped of God"—foreshadowed parts of Christ's ministry. The Lord was helped by God during His life, and when He offered Himself without blemish to God through the eternal Spirit (Heb. 9:14). Also, God was in control when the Sinless One was crucified through wicked hands, accomplishing God's determined counsel (Acts 2:23). Yet, both Jews and Gentiles will be held accountable for what they have done to the Son of God.

The heifer was slaughtered "outside the camp"—a phrase used 28 times in Moses' writings. It signifies that there was no room for the Messiah among God's people (Jn. 1:11). Yet He took the sinner's place when He was made sin during the three hours of darkness, dying *for* all. Even after His unique sacrifice, resurrection, and exaltation, the nation of Israel kept rejecting Him. Since then, the believers' place should also be "outside the camp"—where judgment has taken place (Heb. 13:13).

The solemn description "slaughtered before him" indicates how terrible this and its completely being burned must have been: something never to forget. The value of the blood is seen in its being sprinkled seven times: a perfect testimony of its efficacy.

A. E. Bouter

I pursue, looking towards the goal, for the prize of the calling on high of God in Christ Jesus. As many therefore as are perfect, let us be thus minded; and if ye are any otherwise minded, this also God shall reveal to you. But whereto we have attained, let us walk in the same steps. Be imitators all together of me, brethren, and fix your eyes on those walking thus as you have us for a model. *(Philippians 3:14-17)*

How sweet that God makes full allowance for individual exercise of faith. If one has been so drawn and enlightened by the Spirit of God as to see all fullness in Christ in glory, and therefore emptiness in present things, let him apply this blessed truth in practice. If some are otherwise minded, however, the apostle does not at all encourage them to remain so, nor does he demand that they conform to his thoughts; but he turns their eyes to God, who will reveal the truth to those who desire it.

Yet, to whatever level our faith may have risen, let us act fully upon the truth that has been made known to our souls. My personal responsibility is to be measured by the Word of God, not by what I may see in others, though the godly example of others may well be a means of awakening in my soul some more true realization of my own responsibility. But it is most important always to take care that only faith leads me to follow another's example. But when once a matter has been ascertained to be in truth that which God has revealed in His Word, then faith does not hesitate: it gladly obeys. And more than this, it genuinely desires to know the will of God in order to obey it.

L. M. Grant

> *O keep us, love divine, near Thee,*
> *That we our nothingness may know,*
> *And ever to Thy glory be*
> *Walking in faith while here below.*

J. N. Darby

Taste and see that Jehovah is good: blessed is the man that trusteth in Him! *(Psalm 34:8)*

Indeed how good is the God we adore! If people only knew Him they would begin to know the true meaning of life. Satan, the god of this world, blinds the minds of the unbelievers lest they see the light and the glory of our Lord. He poisoned the minds of Adam and Eve in making them think that God wanted to deprive them of happiness. And he is doing that today to billions of people.

Read the Word of God and you will see how good God is. Here are some of the facts you will find in the Bible about our God: He is the **God of hope** who fills us with joy (Rom.15:13), for in His presence is fullness of joy and pleasures forevermore (Ps. 16:11). He is the **God of encouragement** (Rom. 15:5)—what a wonderful truth! Life is full of struggles, and we need encouragement. Indeed He is the **Father of compassions and the God of all encouragement** (2 Cor. 1:3). He is the **God of love and peace** (2 Cor. 13:11). You can see now why there is not much love in this world. It is because the world does not know God. **God is love**, but He is rejected. And as to peace, the human race has not known the way of peace (Rom. 3:17). He is the **God of all grace** (1 Pet. 5:10).

Look up these references and meditate on these wonderful qualities of our God. Rejoice in Him who is the God of *hope, encouragement, compassions, peace, love, and grace.* Then you will say with Isaiah, "I will greatly rejoice in Jehovah, my soul shall be joyful in my God" (Isa. 61:10). Habakkuk, though he might lose all his possessions, could still say: "Yet I will rejoice in Jehovah, I will joy in the God of my salvation" (Hab. 3:18). Who would not rejoice in the God who loved us and gave His only begotten Son for us? We love Him because He first loved us. Hallelujah!

A. M. Behnam

Our momentary and light affliction works for us ... an eternal weight of glory; while we look not at the things that are seen, but at the things that are not seen. *(2 Corinthians 4:17-18)*

"Saved for glory, yes for glory," is a wonderful hymn we often hear sung from the redeemed hearts of the saints of God. This hymn expresses a great and valuable truth. T. H. Reynolds, the author of the hymn, was not merely expressing a truth, but his words expressed with confidence and a grateful heart that glory was his. He had placed his foot on this truth, and taken possession of it (Dt. 11:24). Unrealized to Reynolds, his words would challenge believers for years to come, saints awaiting the coming of the Lord.

Lot was a man whose righteous soul was vexed from day to day in Sodom (2 Pet. 2:8). Lot admirably left his homeland, following his uncle in quest of the land promised by God. But the true colors as to where his heart was were revealed in time. In Genesis 13, after strife between his herdsmen and the herdsmen of his uncle, he set his eyes upon the well-watered plains of Sodom. He later gave up his tent, his pilgrim character, for a house and a high position at the gate of the city. Lot depicts a believer who is saved for glory but has no savor for that glory.

Abraham, on the other hand, showed his pilgrim character when he offered Lot the first choice of the land. If Lot would go to the left, Abraham would go to the right, or if he chose the right, Abraham would go to the left. His heart was unattached to any piece of land, for he knew that his God could and would bless him, no matter where he pitched his tents. Later in the land of promise, Canaan, Abraham sojourned as in a strange country, never surrendering his tent because "he looked for a city ... whose builder and maker is God" (Heb. 11:9-10 KJV).

M. Labelle

Israel again did evil in the sight of Jehovah; and Jehovah gave them into the hands of the Philistines. *(Judges 13:1)*

There was degradation and deterioration of the spiritual power of the people. Their national faithfulness was gone, and only individual faithfulness was found. When corporate testimony is gone and you come down to the individual, you have come down to failure.

Having come down largely to individual testimony, only a wreck of what God wanted maintained was left. How can an individual maintain that which should be the testimony of God's people at large? By His grace let us never give up a sense of our responsibility to maintain a united testimony, even if Satan tries to break it in pieces!

Here we have again the same sad story—failure and sin on the part of the people, with the result that they are sold into the hands of their enemies. Note that God never allows the enemy to gain power over us unless it is a judicial result of our own failure and of departing from Him.

As we look about and view the "captivity" of God's dear people, we see the guilt of the Church today and our own departure. We must ask, What has led to this state? We must take an attitude of humility and acknowledge our share collectively and individually in the responsibility. Each one must take his or her share of the failure that has produced such a chaotic state among the saints of God, and not look for its cause somewhere else!

Let us take courage. We are in the last days and things are going to pieces, but if we take warning from the failure, we will follow at all costs, and in a spirit of obedience, the way that our God has marked out for us.

S. Ridout

November 23 Saturday

The gospel of Christ … is the power of God unto salvation to everyone that believeth. *(Romans 1:16 KJV)*

Down through the ages, and even today in some parts of the world, men will, out of fear, slavishly labor to propitiate their gods or demons. They present offerings that they hope in some way will satisfy their angry, fickle deities. What a contrast to this is the glorious gospel of Christ! Our God did not require a propitiation *from us*— indeed we had none to offer—but He Himself provided that which His holiness required. "Herein is love, not that we loved God, but that He loved us, and sent His Son a propitiation for our sins" (1 Jn. 4:10). He sent His beloved Son to the cross, out of love for us! God has provided a Savior and a salvation for all who receive Him.

But there is salvation in none other (Acts 4:12). There is no other name except Christ's by which we can be saved. Many reject this truth. A few years ago, 33 Chilean miners were trapped 700 meters underground for 69 days. A daring rescue was attempted by drilling through the solid rock and lowering down a specially designed capsule. A riveted world watched as one by one all 33 of the miners were raised to the surface. None of the miners rejected the capsule that was sent down. Neither did they think it was too "exclusive" of the engineers not to supply more rescue choices. Rather, they were thankful for their deliverance! Likewise, God has provided but one Savior.

Salvation not only has heaven in view, but is also a present power to deliver from the bondage of sin. It has been well said that salvation can be defined as "the power of God put forth for the emancipation of His creature from every force that held his soul in bondage, so that, being delivered and reestablished in new divine power, he is able to serve God in the midst of a hostile world." How wonderful God's plan of grace!

B. Reynolds

November 24 Lord's Day

On the tenth of this month let them take themselves each a lamb ... And ye shall keep it until the fourteenth day of this month.

(Exodus 12:3,6)

Ten days of the month are passed when the lamb is taken. The ten days point to the measure of human responsibility, as the Ten Commandments do. They pass in silence before the lamb is taken—a silence which answers to what seems so great a gap in the Gospels. What account have we of those thirty years in which our Lord grew up in retirement at Nazareth, and lived in the quiet fulfillment of human duties in the carpenter's house? We have a brief vision of Him at His birth; a still briefer one of His visit to the temple at twelve years old; then no more till He comes forth at thirty to take up His work among men openly.

Then, fulfilling righteousness in that baptism at the Jordan, He is sealed with the Holy Spirit, and proclaimed by the Father as His own Beloved. John announces Him as the Lamb of God; and the Father's voice, and the Spirit's act, declare Him as much more than without blemish!

The lamb being taken, immediate sacrifice does not follow, but keeping it for four days. Four speaks of testing; and this follows immediately upon the announcement of the divine satisfaction and delight in Him. Hitherto He had lived under God's eye alone; now man and the devil are to test Him as they please. To the devil He is at once exposed; led of the Spirit expressly "to be tempted:" all circumstances designedly permitted to be as adverse as to the first man in Eden they were favorable. In these forty days of temptation by the devil, He is *alone.* And this testing brought out only His perfection. The four Gospels show the result; how, as Messiah, Servant, Son of man, and Son of God, He approves Himself the same blessed One whom all circumstances only magnify.

F. W. Grant

Everyone that has this hope in Him purifies himself, even as He is pure. *(1 John 3:3)*

PREMILLENNIAL DOCTRINE VS "WAITING FOR THE SON" (3)

The believer knows the One who is coming, because He has loved him, and washed him from his sins. The believer expects the everlasting Lover of his soul. But, alas! there are very many who hold and argue about the Lord's coming who are not waiting for Him at all, who are living for themselves in the world, and "mind earthly things." How terrible to be found talking about the Lord's coming, and yet, when He does come, *to be left behind!* Oh! think of this; and if you are really conscious that you do not know the Lord, then let me entreat you to behold Him shedding His precious blood to wash you from your sins.

But if you can look up to heaven, and say, "Thank God, I do know Him, and I am waiting for Him," then let me remind you of what the apostle John says, as to the practical result of this blessed hope. "Everyone that has this hope *in Him,* purifies himself, even as He is pure." Yes, this must ever be the result of waiting for the Son from heaven; but not at all so of the mere prophetic doctrine.

It is impossible that anyone can be waiting for Christ's appearing, and not make efforts after increased holiness, separation, and devotedness of heart. Those who know the Lord Jesus Christ, and love His appearing, will daily seek to shake off everything contrary to their Master's mind; they will seek to become more and more conformed to Him in all things. Men may hold the doctrine of the Lord's coming, and yet grasp the world and the things thereof with great eagerness; but the true-hearted servant will ever keep his eye steadily fixed on his Master's return, remembering His blessed words, "I will come again and receive you unto Myself, that where I am, there ye may be also" (Jn. 14:3 KJV).

C. H. Mackintosh

Blessed is he whose transgression is forgiven, whose sin is covered! Blessed is the man unto whom Jehovah reckoneth not iniquity. *(Psalm 32:1-2)*

Although this psalm undoubtedly is looking forward to the time when the godly remnant of Israel will know full forgiveness and acceptance, it has a far wider application as describing the blessed non-imputation of guilt. It may be said to instruct us on how to be happy.

Happiness is not the result of excusing, palliating, or covering sin. When the writer of this psalm did these things, Jehovah gave him no rest (v. 3); it seemed as though whether awake or asleep, God's hand was heavily on him. Unconfessed sin and a hardened conscience can only bring unhappiness and misery of soul; but when a soul, burdened with a sense of guilt and need, draws near to God, acknowledges the sin, and confesses the transgression, forgiveness is obtained and the results are most blessed.

The child of God treads a path of faith. It leads where dangers and snares abound, but God is our resource, and His watchful eye is ever upon us. He promises: "I will instruct thee and teach thee the way in which thou shalt go; I will counsel thee with Mine eye upon thee" (v. 8). To be guided with His eye requires us to have communion and nearness to God.

How much more blessed it is to be guided in this way than to be curbed and governed just by circumstances. God can and does guide by providence, but this is *not* His preferred way. He wants to guide us by a "full knowledge of His will, in all wisdom and spiritual understanding" (Col. 1:9). We are to be like Abraham who enjoyed holy intimacy with God, and whom God could call "Abraham, My friend" (Isa. 41:8).

J. W. H. Nichols

Work out your own salvation with fear and trembling, for it is God who works in you both the willing and the working according to His good pleasure. *(Philippians 2:12-13)*

What does it mean to work out our salvation with fear and trembling? It has the thought of reverence and a deep concern for the holiness of God, with whom we have to do. To fear the Lord, conscious of His holy presence, will have a transforming effect in the life of a Christian. Isaiah 66:2 (ESV) exclaims, "This is the one to whom I will look: he who is humble and contrite in spirit and *trembles at My word.*" If we know the Lord, really know Him for who He is in the greatness of His Person, His holiness, justice and grace, we will tremble in His presence. This does not mean that I am afraid of God, but that I'm afraid to displease Him in my life.

In Matthew 10:28 we read, "Do not fear those who kill the body but cannot kill the soul. Rather fear Him who can destroy both soul and body in hell." In other words, don't fear man, fear God. Tremble at the prospect of distrusting God, not at displeasing man. Listen to the way Isaiah put it, "Do not fear what they fear, nor be in dread. But the Lord of hosts … Let Him be your fear, and let Him be your dread. And He will become a sanctuary" (Isa. 8:12-14). I as His child fear God, not as an enemy but as One infinite in power and holiness, who has reached down in His sovereign grace, snatched us from the grip of sin, and has set us free. We are justified and forgiven and we tremble—not because God is our enemy (no, He never was), but because He loved us and saved us.

How terrible it will be for all who have rejected or neglected God's great salvation when they will stand before Him in their sins! *"If You, O Lord, should mark iniquities, O Lord, who could stand? But with You there is forgiveness, that You may be feared"* (Ps. 130:3-4).

T. P. Hadley

Thus saith Jehovah of hosts, the God of Israel, concerning Ahab the son of Kolaiah, and concerning Zedekiah the son of Maaseiah, who prophesy falsehood unto you in My name: Behold, I will give them into the hand of Nebuchadnezzar king of Babylon, and he shall smite them before your eyes ... concerning Shemaiah the Nehelamite: Because that Shemaiah hath prophesied unto you, and I sent him not ... I will punish Shemaiah the Nehelamite ... because he hath spoken revolt against Jehovah.   *(Jeremiah 29:21,31-32)*

FALSE PROPHETS AND THEIR PROPHECIES— AHAB, ZEDEKIAH, SHEMAIAH

Most people today would not be able to identify these three men. Yet God devotes a number of verses in Jeremiah 29 to their activities among the Jews who had been taken captive to Babylon. We see in numerous passages of Scripture how God's eye was upon His people even in these distressing circumstances. In fact, in the first part of this chapter He has Jeremiah write a letter to those in captivity, telling them to carry on normal family lives and to seek the peace of and pray for the city where He had caused them to be led captive, for in its peace they would have peace. Their captivity was to last for 70 years, He told them.

God then stated that He knew and had been witness to the fact that Ahab the son of Kolaiah and Zedekiah the son of Maaseiah had spoken words of falsehood in Jehovah's name which He had not commanded them. King Nebuchadnezzar had roasted them in the fire for their immorality and adultery. Their names would be a curse to the Jews in captivity in Babylon. God takes seriously our attaching His name to something contrary to His Word and will!

Shemaiah the Nehelamite had written letters to tell the people and priests in Jerusalem to change priests and to have Jeremiah reproved for what he had written. God had not sent him, but was well aware of this man's doings and would punish him for them. He regarded them as revolt against Himself, a most serious sin!

E. P. Vedder, Jr.

Abide in Me and I in you. As the branch cannot bear fruit of itself unless it abide in the vine, thus neither can ye unless ye abide in Me. I am the vine, ye are the branches. He that abides in Me and I in him, he bears much fruit; for without Me ye can do nothing. *(John 15:4-5)*

How fitting that the vine should be used as a figure. Other trees may be useful apart from their fruit; with the vine it is not so. If the vine produces no fruit, it is useless.

What is the spiritual significance of fruit? *Fruit is the expression of Christ in the believer.* "The fruit of the Spirit is love, joy, peace, longsuffering, kindness, goodness, fidelity, meekness, self-control" (Gal. 5:22-23). This is a beautiful description of Christ as He passed through this world. Hence if such fruit is seen in believers, it will result in the reproduction of Christ in His people. Though Christ personally is not here, it is God's intention that Christ characteristically should still be seen in His people.

Fruit is not exactly the exercise of gift, nor service, nor work. We are indeed exhorted "to walk worthily of the Lord unto all well-pleasing, bearing fruit in every good work." This passage, while showing how closely fruit-bearing is linked with good works, yet clearly distinguishes between them. The good works are to be done in such a Christ-like manner that in the works that benefit man there will be found fruit acceptable to God. The natural man can do many good works, but in them there will be found no fruit acceptable to God. If service and work were fruit, it would largely be limited to those who possess gift and ability. But if *fruit is the character of Christ,* then it is possible and a privilege for every believer, from the oldest to the youngest, to bear fruit.

H. Smith

The sons of Ham [were] Cush and Mizraim, Phut and Canaan ... And Mizraim begot the ... Casluhim out of whom came the Philistines. *(1 Chronicles 1:8,11-12)*
Jehovah gave [Israel] into the hand of the Philistines forty years. *(Judges 13:1)*

The Philistines gave their name to the whole land, Palestine, but actually they had no right to it. They were intruders, "wanderers" who had wandered in and had settled down along the sea coast where it was easy to get into the land.

Spiritually speaking, there are Philistines today. They are people who take a place among Christ's people but who have not really identified with Christ in His death and resurrection. Thus they are wanderers or intruders into God's territory. Such a person has slipped in by means of profession without having a sense of sin met by Christ's divinely instituted sacrifice, nor experienced Christ as a personal, divinely provided sacrifice. Thus God has not won a heritage for them, and they have slipped in by a short and easy way.

Being only natural men, modern spiritual Philistines will find appealing, ritualism and ordinances, which, while they have a show of wisdom in worship, are but the puffing up of the creature. Ritualism is carnal—it contains everything that appeals to the eye, ear, and senses of natural man!

Take for instance, the gorgeous ritual of "high church" with its vestments, its incense, its rolling music, its processions, and its imposing places of worship. The feeling of reverence it produces requires no spiritual sense, no guidance by the Holy Spirit, and no new birth.

Being under the control of such Philistines prevents the people from exercising their God-given privilege of enjoying, as it were, the "whole land" that God has given us.

S. Ridout

December **1** Lord's Day

Now before the feast of the Passover, Jesus, knowing that His hour had come that He should depart out of this world to the Father, having loved His own who were in the world, loved them to the end. *(John 13:1)*

The opening verse of chapter 13 is introductory to the last discourses of our Lord. The occasion was that at last "His hour was come." In the course of our Lord's earthly path we have heard of other "hours." At Cana of Galilee He could say to His mother, "Mine hour has not yet come"—the hour of His manifestation in glory to the world. In John 5 we read, "An hour is coming, and now is, when the dead shall hear the voice of the Son of God, and they that have heard shall live"—the hour of His grace to sinners. In the presence of man's enmity we twice read that, "No man laid hands on Him, because His hour was not yet come"—the hour of His suffering. This hour—the hour that introduces the farewell words—has another character. It is the hour of His return to His glory with the Father, in the love and holiness of the Father's house.

The disciples, however, would be left behind in a defiling world that hated the Father and rejected Christ. If then they are to be kept from the evil of the world they are passing through, and yet enjoy communion with Christ in the Father's home of love and holiness, they will need this last gracious ministry with its comfort, its instruction, and its warnings.

If the Lord leaves the world, He will not forget His own, nor will He cease to love them. Alas! our hearts may grow cold towards Him, our hands may weary in well doing, our feet may wander; but of this we are assured, that He will never fail us. His love will carry us, and care for us, "unto the end"; and at the end love will receive us into love's eternal home where there are no cold hearts, nor hands that hang down, nor feet that wander.

H. Smith

[He] exhorted them all, that with purpose of heart they would cleave unto the Lord. *(Acts 11:23 KJV)*

A WORD ON CLEAVING TO THE LORD (1)

Barnabas exhorted the new believers that they should cleave to the Lord. Some are allowed to have a long season of joy on first believing, but God knows our hearts, and how soon we should be depending on our joy, and not on Christ. He is our object: joy is not our object. Do not let your joy lead you to forget the source of it. This joy is right and beautiful in its place; I am not saying a word against it—God forbid. But I warn you against resting in it. Do not lean on it for strength. There is danger of joy making you forget how dependent you are every moment.

Depend upon *Him*: cleave to Him with purpose of heart. I have seen many Christians so full of joy that they thought there was no such thing as sin left. It is true, sin no longer remains *on you*; but the flesh is *in you* to the end. The old stock is there, and you will find that, if you are not watchful, if divine life is not cultivated in your hearts by looking at Christ and feeding on Him, it will be putting forth its bud. No good fruit comes off the old stock. It is the *new* that bears fruit to God.

But though the flesh is in you, do not be thinking of this, but think of Christ—cleave to Him; and may your souls be maintained in this truth, that Christ is your life and He the object of that life (Gal. 2:20). As you grow in this knowledge of Him, a joy grows deeper than that of first conversion. I have known Christ between thirty and forty years, and I can say that I have ten thousand times more joy *now* than I had at first. It is a deeper, calmer joy. The water rushing down from a hill is beautiful to look at, and makes most noise; but you will find the water that runs in the plain is deeper, calmer, more fructifying.

J. N. Darby

[He] exhorted them all, that with purpose of heart they would cleave unto the Lord.
(Acts 11:23 KJV)

A WORD ON CLEAVING TO THE LORD (2)

Observe, they are exhorted with purpose of heart to cleave to the Lord. A distracted heart is the bane of a Christian. When my heart is filled with Christ, I have no heart or eye for the trash of the world. If Christ is dwelling in your heart by faith, it will not be the question, "What harm is there in this, or that?" Rather, Am I doing this for Christ? Can Christ go along with me in this? Do not let the world come in, and distract your thoughts. It makes many promises it cannot fulfill. The fact is, your hearts are too big for the world, it cannot fill them; they are too little for Christ, for He fills heaven; yet will He fill you to overflowing.

Observe again, it is to the Lord they were to cleave: not to duty, or law, but to the *Lord.* He knew how treacherous the heart was, and how soon it would put anything in *His* place. You will have to learn what is in your heart. Abide with God, and you will learn your heart with Him, and under His grace; else you will have to learn it with the devil through His successful temptations. But God is faithful, and if you have been getting away from Him, and other things have been coming in and forming a crust around your heart, and you want to get back again, God says, I must have you deal with it, and get rid of it.

However careless you may have been, however far you may have got away from Him, return to Him. Doubt not His joy in having you back; count upon His love; look with horror at the sin which led you away, but do not wrong Him by distrusting His love, any more than you would wrong an affectionate husband or wife, by throwing a doubt on their love. Hate yourself, but remember how He has loved you, and will love you until the end. Mistrust not His work: mistrust not His love.

J. N. Darby

If I have all faith, so as to remove mountains, but have not love, I am nothing ... Love never fails. *(1 Corinthians 13:2,8)*

About 60 years ago a new medical graduate, a Muslim, walked into the room of a Christian colleague and saw a small open book on his bed. He asked if he could read in it, and after reading the passage twice he said to his Christian friend, "Frankly, I never knew that your Bible has such good things. Can I read it again now? Can I also come again to read in it?" The chapter he read was 1 Corinthians 13. Many listeners to Arabic Christian radio have written asking for copies of what they call "the poem about love."

Needless to say, love is the very heart of the Christian faith. In His last discourse with His disciples the Lord emphasized to them the importance of love. First Corinthians 13 may be divided into three parts:

(1) verses 1-3: the *superiority of love* above miraculous gifts. It is superior to mere knowledge, including scriptural knowledge, for "knowledge puffs up, but love edifies."

(2) verses 4-7: the *qualities love produces in the believer*, and which are manifested in his relationships with others. This includes one's relationship with other believers, whether those with whom he has close contact or those who are believers, but who differ in certain doctrinal truths. Love is to continue in spite of differences. It also includes the family circle where daily situations may create temporary tensions. Love should prevail in the family, for its joy and security. Love should include sinners, and it is to be the motive behind evangelism. To win souls we must love them.

(3) verses 8-13: *the permanence of love*. In heaven there will be no need for the gifts of miracles. Faith will have served its purpose, for what we believed and hoped for we will have and we shall see with our eyes. But love will abide. How could it be otherwise when, as we know, **GOD IS LOVE!**

A. M. Behnam

The word of Jehovah came unto me, saying: Son of man, prophesy against the prophets of Israel that prophesy, and say unto them that prophesy out of their own heart, Hear ye the word of Jehovah. Thus saith the Lord Jehovah: Woe unto the foolish prophets, that follow their own spirit, and have seen nothing! O Israel, thy prophets have been like foxes in desert places.

(Ezekiel 13:1-4)

FALSE PROPHETS AND THEIR PROPHECIES—
FOOLISH PROPHETS

Throughout this chapter Jehovah speaks against false prophets, whether male or female, who prophesy out of their own heart. A true prophet is God's messenger who brings God's message to a people in need of it whom God is trying to reach.

Israel had many false prophets. They were popular but were of absolutely no help to God's people. In fact, they were just the opposite. God charges them with seeing lying divination and vanity, seeing a vain vision, seducing His people by saying peace when there was no peace, catching the souls of His people, profaning Him among His people for handfuls of barley and morsels of bread, grieving the heart of the righteous and strengthening the hands of the wicked that he should not return from his wicked way and save his life. God promised to deliver His people out of the hands of such prophets, so that they would know that He is Jehovah—an often recurrent refrain in Ezekiel.

Do we not have similar problems today? There are many prophets (preachers) whom God has not sent! They graduate from institutes whose basic beliefs and principles differ widely from the clear teachings of God's Word. They tickle the ears of their hearers, speak out of their own heart, and pattern their "services" after the performances of the world's celebrities. How different they are from that Lowly One who ever did His Father's will and whose life here on earth was fully consistent with the words He spoke!

E. P. Vedder, Jr.

The Angel of Jehovah appeared to the woman, and said to her … drink not wine nor strong drink, and eat nothing unclean. For lo, thou shalt conceive, and bear a son, and no razor shall come on his head; for the boy shall be a Nazarite … and he shall begin to save Israel out of the hand of the Philistines.

(Judges 13:3-5)

Because of their failure, God delivered the children of Israel into the hands of their enemies, the Philistines, for forty years. He now purposed to begin to deliver them using Samson as described in Judges 13 through 16.

The barren wife of Manoah was told that she would bear a son to be the deliverer of Israel. He was to be raised as a Nazarite—to abstain from wine, strong drink, and everything connected with the grape vine; and she herself was to keep herself from everything unclean. Also, his hair was never to be cut. These are figures for our instruction.

Wine is a figure of that which stimulates the natural man, producing joy and strength. Spiritually, it symbolizes that which stimulates and stirs up the flesh. Thus, one can be a thorough teetotaler as to wine and yet spiritually speaking be totally under its power. To be powerful for God, anything that simply imparts fleshly energy or fleshly excitement has to be scrupulously avoided. God cannot use it! The long hair is a figure which suggests that we should be aware of our weakness and have a spirit of dependence on God.

Sadly, Samson did not live up to what these externals symbolize, and this failure took away his God-given great strength. From this we learn that we have spiritual strength only as we make the truth a practical reality in our souls through submission to the Holy Spirit, not just through gift!

S. Ridout

To you is given to know the mystery of the kingdom of God; but to them who are without, all things are done in parables.

(Mark 4:11)

The Lord Jesus told His disciples that they would be given an understanding in "the mystery of the kingdom of God." He also spoke of another class of people to whom everything would be spoken in parables; these He described as, **"them who are without."** How solemn that God should speak of "them who are without"!

Who are the "without" and what does the Scripture have to say about them? Some Christians have the erroneous idea that the "without" are all those who do not belong to their particular sect. Not so—rather they are all those who are unsaved and still outside of the family of God. Paul mentioned those who are "without" in writing to the Colossians when he said, "Walk in wisdom toward **them that are without**, redeeming the time" (Col. 4:5 KJV). As Christians we ought to seek occasions to share the life-giving message of the gospel. He further exhorted Christians to work with their own hands, and to walk reputably and honestly **"towards those without"** (1 Th. 4:12). How can we be a witness to the lost if our own lives are sinful and unholy? In writing Timothy, Paul said that one of the qualifications of an "overseer" was "that he should have also a good testimony **from those without**" (1 Tim. 3:7).

The contrast between those that are "within" and those that are "without" is put even more starkly by Paul when he admonished the Corinthians that they must judge those that are "within." The assembly is to discipline Christians (the "within") who walk in a sinful manner, but not to judge those who are "without" (1 Cor. 5:11-12). Our duty, rather, is to bring them the gospel. Those that are "without" God will judge in a coming day and they will forever be without the gates of the heavenly city (Rev. 22:15). Sad and solemn reality!

B. Reynolds

December **8** Lord's Day

Jesus says to her, Mary. She, turning round, says to Him in Hebrew, Rabboni, which means Teacher. Jesus says to her, Touch Me not, for I have not yet ascended to My Father; but go to My brethren and say to them, I ascend to My Father and your Father, and to My God and your God. *(John 20:16-17)*

Her heart filled with sorrowful desolation, Mary Magdalene seemed unable to comprehend the angels' message that her Lord had risen from the dead. Because His body was not in the grave she turned away from the angels who were there. And when He Himself drew near, she had no thought of expecting Him, but supposed Him to be the gardener; and from Him also she turned away.

One word from His lips changes everything, "Mary." He calls His own sheep by name, and she knows His voice. Here is the One whom she loves, alive before her eyes! What joy unspeakable fills her heart as she no doubt involuntarily plunges forward to grasp Him.

But He tells her, "Touch Me not, for I have not yet ascended to My Father." No doubt she thought she had Him back the same as before. On the basis of that relationship, however, she can no longer touch Him. His death has set that aside. He now announces to her a new relationship, and gives her the great honor of carrying the message of this to those whom He calls "My brethren." He was to ascend to "My Father and your Father." For in resurrection He is the Head of a new creation in which God is now in a vital way Father to all who know His beloved Son. He was virtually telling Mary that, though He was all that she had on earth, yet now she was no longer to have even Him on earth; but she would have Him in heaven, in the Father's own presence. All her hopes and her blessings were now to be centered there, together with all the brethren of the Lord.

L. M. Grant

December   **9**   Monday

Jehovah appeared to him by the oaks of Mamre. And he sat at the tent-door in the heat of the day. And he lifted up his eyes and saw, and behold, three men standing near him. *(Genesis 18:1)*

The spiritual elevation of Abraham in Genesis 18 and 19 is something very peculiar. He seems to apprehend the divine Stranger and His angelic companions *at once,* needing no introduction, or revelation as Joshua, Gideon, and others in like circumstances, did. "He was accustomed to the divine presence," as one has said. The Lord does not come to regulate him in any way, either to rebuke or instruct him morally. Abraham is before Him in the place and character and attitude of one who was fully prepared for His presence.

Accordingly, the Lord makes His ways and thoughts known to Abraham, as a man would to his friend. He reveals secrets to him which do not concern himself—had they done so, in a sense Abraham would have been entitled to hear them. But he has no personal concern in the matters communicated. They are the Lord's purposes touching a city, Sodom, and a people with whom Abraham had no dealings whatever. They were strangers to him and he to them; so that the Lord now deals with Abraham as a *friend*, not as a *disciple,* much less as a *sinner,* but as a friend. And so, if the Lord invites us we should go; if He draws nigh to us, we should draw nigh to Him.

The angels, seizing on the mind of their Lord, retire; and Abraham draws near, and there intercedes for this city. He has nothing to ask for himself. He had no confession to make or requests for himself, but as the Lord had spoken to him about Sodom, he now speaks to the Lord about it. He intercedes, as one near to God, as one who was at ease concerning himself, and thus at leisure to attend to others. Every feature in this picture is full of grace and dignity—all is strength and spiritual elevation.

J. G. Bellett

Grow in grace, and in the knowledge of our Lord and Savior Jesus Christ.
(2 Peter 3:18)

God in His grace has centered every blessing for us in Christ. Without Christ we have nothing, nothing but our sins; with Christ we have all things, and therefore want nothing in addition to Christ. As the apostle says, "All are yours; and ye are Christ's; and Christ is God's" (1 Cor. 3:22-23). Hence the saying of an old writer, "If thou knowest not Christ, it matters not if thou knowest *everything* besides; but if thou knowest Christ, it matters not if thou knowest *nothing* besides."

Now it is not every believer who knows Christ. All believers—those, that is, who have peace with God—know Christ as their Savior. They know Him in this character or relationship, but it is another thing to know Him in Himself, to have such knowledge of Him as to be intimately acquainted with His mind, character, and ways. Those who thus know Him find their daily delight in feasting on His beauties and perfections. They value Him for what He is, if possible, more than for what He has done, though these two things can never be separated. The apostle John indeed teaches that to know Him who is from the beginning is the last and highest attainment the believer makes. This knowledge is the characteristic of the fathers in the family of God (1 Jn. 2:14).

Where then can I meet Christ and be in companionship with Him, so as to learn always more of Him? The answer to this question is that *the only place* where we can come into contact with Christ is in the written Word of God. We find Christ in every aspect, position, character, and office in the Scriptures—Christ in humiliation and rejection, and Christ in exaltation and glory. The more therefore I read and meditate on God's Word, the more I shall learn of Christ.

E. Dennett

December **11** Wednesday

Worship the Lord **in the splendor of holiness;** *tremble before him,*
all the earth! *(Psalm 96:9 ESV)*

In the forgiven, heaven-bound, eternally secure, Spirit-indwelt
Christian there is a proper fear and trembling that transforms everything. This fear and trembling should be felt especially in our times
of worship. Whether it be private or corporate worship, there should
be a conscious awareness that I am in the presence of God. Consider
how the Bible connects worship and the fear of the Lord.

*"Fear God and give Him glory, because the hour of His judgment
has come, and worship Him who made heaven and earth, the sea
and the springs of water"* (Rev. 14:7). *"Who will not fear, O Lord,
and glorify Your name? For You alone are holy. All nations will
come and worship You, for Your righteous acts have been revealed"*
(Rev. 15:4). Fear and trembling are not because God is our enemy,
but because He has saved us from His wrath through Christ, and
now we stand on the brink of the Grand Canyon of His holiness, justice, and grace with unspeakable wonder, knees wobbling and hands
trembling, but overcome with worship at the depth of His majesty.
The Bible says it so paradoxically, and yet, all true saints know what
these words mean. Psalm 2:11: *"Serve the LORD with fear, and rejoice with trembling."* Isaiah 11:3: *"And His delight shall be in the
fear of the LORD."* This fear is full of delight. Nehemiah 1:11: *"O
Lord, let Your ear be attentive to the prayer ... of Your servants
who delight to fear Your name."* Those who have seen and savored
the holiness, justice, and grace of God can never again trivialize
worship. There ought to be a sense of His holy presence when we
come together. Ananias and Sapphira lost this sense of His presence.
Those at Corinth also lost it and for that reason many were "fallen
asleep" (1 Cor. 11:30). A deep sense of the holiness of His presence
will transform us! May it be so for His Name's sake!

T. P. Hadley

A certain man a magician, a false prophet, a Jew, whose name was Bar-Jesus, who was with the proconsul Sergius Paulus, an intelligent man ... Elymas the magician (for so his name is by interpretation) opposed them, seeking to turn away the proconsul from the faith. But ... Paul, filled with the Holy Spirit, fixing his eyes upon him, said, O full of all deceit and all craft; son of the devil, enemy of all righteousness; wilt thou not cease perverting the right paths of the Lord? *(Acts 13:6-10)*

FALSE PROPHETS AND THEIR PROPHECIES— ELYMAS / BAR-JESUS

In the New Testament we have an outstanding example of a false prophet in whom we see many of the characteristic features of all such opponents of God and His truth. This wicked deceiver confronted Paul and Barnabas at Paphos in the court of the Roman proconsul of Cyprus, Sergius Paulus. This official, Scripture tells us, was an intelligent man who wanted to hear God's Word.

Elymas, who was also known as Bar-Jesus or Son of the Savior, was a magician, a man who worked with Satanic powers. There is no fellowship between Christ and Satan; consequently we see this man trying to turn the proconsul away from the faith. Note that the Bible speaks of Christianity as "the faith," not merely as "a faith." Like the Lord Jesus speaking to His adversaries in John 8:44, Paul called this man son of the devil rather than what his name said he was, son of the Savior. Full of all deceit and all craft, enemy of all righteousness, Elymas was perverting the right ways of the Lord. The Bible does not call every unbeliever "son of the devil," but applies the term to active opponents of the gospel. Let us be careful whom we label thus!

The Lord's power is greater than that of Satan. The Lord made this opponent of the gospel experience physical blindness that matched the blindness of his wicked heart. The proconsul, seeing what had happened, amazed at the teaching of the Lord, believed.

E. P. Vedder, Jr.

If a man or a woman have vowed the special vow of a Nazarite, to consecrate themselves to Jehovah; he shall separate himself from wine and strong drink ... neither shall he drink any liquor of grapes, nor eat grapes ... nothing that is made from the vine ... there shall no razor come upon his head ... all the days of his separation, he is holy to Jehovah. *(Numbers 6:2-5,8)*

What is a Nazarite? The very word means separation, and it applies to both men and women. True victory for God's people must be along the lines of Nazariteship, separation from all the things that the world counts as absolutely essential.

God cannot use the flesh! Sometimes you will hear it said that a strong will is a good thing and that plain speech is a good thing. I fear that in a large majority of cases they are the result of the indulgence of pride or the absence of self-control. I care not how truthfully one speaks: if it is not by the power of the Spirit of God, it is fleshly will. Nazariteship today calls for the absence of all that.

Modern day Nazariteship was learned by Paul. God taught him, "My power is perfected in weakness," and he learned that "when I am weak, than am I powerful," (2 Cor. 12:9-10). He learned that God can only use subjection to Himself, weakness in self, and dependence upon Him only.

However, there was only one person, spiritually speaking, who was a true Nazarite, and that was our Lord Jesus. He shows us that it is not a negative thing to be separated from the world but rather a positive thing that associated Him with God. Think of that blessed One who humbled Himself so that we might be associated with the Father and Himself.

S. Ridout

Faithful amidst unfaithfulness, / 'Mid darkness only light,
Thou didst Thy Father's name confess, / And in His will delight.
J. G. Deck

I am come down from heaven, not that I should do My will, but the will of Him that has sent Me.   *(John 6:38)*

The only true attitude for the Christian is that of dependence. The moment we get off the ground of dependence on God we are sure to come to grief. This is true both individually and collectively. Peter got off the ground of dependence when in self-confidence he said, "If all shall be offended in Thee, I will never be offended" (Mt. 26:33). Alas, he soon had to learn by bitter experience that he had no strength to stand when the hour of trial came. So it is with us; if we think we are strong and able to meet the enemy, it is just then we are in the most dangerous position of all. God has to allow some sifting to come to show us that we are nothing and that all our strength is in Him. But it is only in the Lord's presence and in nearness to Him that there can be that absence of self and constant dependence upon Him so needed for the Christian life and walk and service.

This need of dependence is also true collectively. The moment an assembly of Christians begins to say (or to *think,* if they do not say it), *"We are the* people, *the* testimony," failure has come in; they are off the ground of dependence. Self, and not Christ, has become the object of attention. They have, in fact, taken the first step on the sloping plane of self-occupation, which, if it is not repented of, is sure to end in disaster.

Our blessed Lord was the true example of dependence. He never deviated from the path of absolute dependence on the Father, not even for a moment. Blessed Savior, may we learn of Thee and be occupied with Thee! And thus may that wretched *self* which so clings to us be displaced and forgotten in the presence of Thy lowly grace, perfect devotedness, and humble submission to the Father's will in everything!

F. C. Blount

Ought not the Christ to have suffered these things and to enter into His glory? And having begun from Moses and from all the prophets, He interpreted to them in all the Scriptures the things concerning Himself. *(Luke 24:26-27)*

Two discouraged disciples were reasoning among themselves as they trudged along the road from Jerusalem to Emmaus. The subject of their exchange was the recent death of Christ and as they talked, the Lord Jesus drew alongside, "incognito." How precious was the Lord's dealing with their sadness and with their unbelief. He does not reveal Himself to them until He has first opened and expounded the Scriptures to their hearts!

As Jewish believers they had been influenced by a "one-sided theology." They were exclusively focused upon the coming kingdom and the deliverance of Israel from its enemies. This can be seen in their answer to the Lord, "We had hoped that He was the One who is about to redeem Israel" (v. 21; see Lk. 19:11). However they had entirely missed the fact that Christ must also first *suffer* before the glory of the kingdom could come.

This is a danger for us as well, for if our eyes are not upon Christ, we may restrict ourselves to one branch of truth instead of reading "in all the Scriptures" the things concerning Christ. He most surely would have opened to them the Scriptures relating to His sufferings such as: the Seed of the woman whose "heel" would be bruised (Gen. 3:15); the only son of a father placed upon an altar (Gen. 22:2); the saving blood of the Passover lamb (Ex. 12–13); the types and shadows of the offerings (Lev. 1-7); the serpent of brass that was lifted up (Num. 21:9); the Forsaken One whose hands and feet were pierced (Ps. 22); the "Man of Sorrows … acquainted with grief" (Isa. 53:3). All of these and more would have been unfolded to them with divine power during the course of those seven miles. What rejoicing as they listened to Him expound the **"things concerning Himself"**!

B. Reynolds

December **16** Monday

Whoever touches the body of anyone who has died, and does not purify himself ... That person shall be cut off from Israel. He shall be unclean, because the water of purification was not sprinkled on him. *(Numbers 19:13 NKJV)*

THE SACRIFICES IN THE BOOK OF NUMBERS (8)

The red heifer, with all its special qualifications, was truly unique: a beautiful type of our Lord Jesus. Yet the heifer had to be killed and totally burned, reduced to ashes: there was no other sacrifice like this! It was slaughtered and burned outside the camp, with all that was representative of the "first man."

The sacrifice and burning of the red heifer provided ashes needed for preparing the water of purification, also called water of separation. Israel, traveling through the wilderness, was exposed to death, its power and influence. So are we believers in a world under the control of the devil, marked by death. However, Christ having taken part in flesh and blood—yet without sin—has obtained victory through death. He annulled the power of him who had the power of death (Heb. 2:14), and He abolished death (2 Tim. 1:10).

Yet, for the time being, we are still living in a world under Satan, the ruler of this world. As long as we have the sin nature in us, we will be vulnerable and easily affected by sin around us. When defiled, our need for cleansing reminds us of Christ's perfections and sacrifice. Under Moses, the work was not yet finished, but now under grace, we stand on Christ's finished work, resurrection, and exaltation. The Holy Spirit and the completed Word bring in the resources needed in case of failure and defilement. Praise God: Christ's work is completed and the Holy Spirit has come to dwell in us! Yet, how solemn: when someone rejects God's provisions. Then there is no other remedy left, neither under law nor under grace.

A. E. Bouter

What shall the baptized for the dead do if those that are dead rise not at all? Why also are they baptized for them?

(1 Corinthians 15:29)

Who are "the dead," and who are those "baptized for the dead"? The next verse gives an important hint: "Why do **we** also endanger ourselves every hour?" The question is: "What motivates those who follow the Lord and serve Him, especially in the face of danger and opposition?" There has been a whole army of such followers who have faithfully served their Lord. Typically, this gave them neither comfort nor wealth; often it gave them troubles, testing, and sometimes, sorrow. And yet you would never have been able to dissuade them from doing their work for the Lord. What is perhaps even more surprising is that there are new workers entering the ranks of those who worked before, and replacing those who have retired from the army of God's workers to be "with the Lord."

In one sense, the new workers substitute for the previous ones. They follow the Lord in the place of those who followed Him before. They have been "baptized for the dead"; they have become followers in the place of those called home. They have seen the distress and difficulties, the soul exercises and sometimes the afflictions of those who took this path before them, and yet they decide to embark on the same journey.

This would be pure madness—if there was no resurrection. If there was no resurrection then Christ would not be risen, and all Christians would have believed a fable. Then why serve the Lord? Why suffer? Why lose out? Why not simply "eat and drink" (v. 32)? But, praise God, we know that "now Christ is raised from among the dead." Our faith is not in vain. The gospel is a fact. Christ is alive! The more these things are a reality for us, the more we will be willing to enter the ranks of God's servants, and to work for Christ.

M. Hardt

[Isaac] took Rebecca, and she became his wife, and he loved her. *(Genesis 24:67)*

The Holy Scriptures present Isaac as a type of Christ. God said to Abraham, "Take now thy son, thine *only son, whom thou lovest,* Isaac … and there offer him up for a burnt-offering" (Gen. 22:2). Abraham took him to the appointed mountain, built an altar and piled the wood, and bound Isaac his son, and laid him on the altar.

In all this we have a foreshadowing of what took place about two thousand years later when God offered His Only-Begotten Son, the Son of His love, at Mount Calvary. The Son of God was bound to the wood of the cross not by cords but by nails to His hands and His feet. And just as Isaac did not remain on the altar, Christ did not remain on the cross or in the grave, but was raised by the glory of the Father. Abraham received Isaac his son "in figure" (Heb. 11:19). Christ actually died and was buried, rose again, and ascended to heaven.

But the history of Isaac has another lesson for us, a lesson that is greatly needed in these days. Isaac was given a bride, Rebecca. Please notice the order in his relationship with her. She became his wife. **And he loved her**. There is great emphasis in many societies about "falling in love" with the one you will marry. It is nice to marry the one you love, but it is *mandatory* that you love the one you married. There is no commandment necessitating marrying one whom you have loved, but there is a divine commandment to love the one you married. In other words, you **must love her because you married her**. "Husbands, love your own wives, even as the Christ also loved the Church" is not a suggestion but a commandment. Today we hear of many who were in love, got married, then divorced because they don't love each other anymore. How sad! How dishonoring to God! How precious are *God's* instructions concerning marriage!

A. M. Behnam

The beast and the kings of the earth and their armies gathered together to make war against Him that sat upon the horse, and against His army. And the beast was taken, and the false prophet that was with him, who wrought the signs before him by which he deceived them that received the mark of the beast, and those that worship his image. Alive were both cast into the lake of fire which burns with brimstone. *(Revelation 19:19-20)*

FALSE PROPHETS AND THEIR PROPHECIES— THE FALSE PROPHET

In these verses we have the dreadful end of this wicked man whom Scripture here terms "the false prophet." Openly challenging the Lord Jesus on His return to earth in power and glory with His saints following Him, this wicked man is taken and cast into the Lake of Fire—Hell— alive. He and the man here referred to as "the beast," and in Revelation 13 spoken of as a beast rising out of the sea, have the distinction of being cast alive into the Lake of Fire 1000 years before anyone else. Revelation 20:10 clearly states that they are still there 1000 years later when the devil and all those judged at the Great White Throne are cast in to join them to be "tormented day and night for the ages of ages."

Revelation 13 shows us these two dreadful men rising to power through the agency of Satan, the dragon, during the Tribulation. Their description makes plain that the first beast is a Gentile, ruling in Europe, while the second beast, the false prophet, is a Jew ruling in Israel, closely allied for protection with the first beast, and serving as his lieutenant. He is called The Lawless One and The Man of Sin in 2 Thessalonians 2 and is The Willful King of Daniel 11:35-40. Both these wicked men are anti-Christ, against Christ, but this second beast is The Antichrist.

The Antichrist, this False Prophet, will have miraculous super-human powers and will tremendously oppress the saints of that day. But thank God, our Lord Jesus will have the final victory!

E. P. Vedder, Jr.

Brethren, if even a man be taken in some fault, ye who are spiritual restore such a one in a spirit of meekness, considering thyself lest thou also be tempted. Bear one another's burdens, and thus fulfill the law of the Christ. *(Galatians 6:1-2)*

The verse above enjoins spiritual ones to restore a fallen brother in the spirit of meekness, considering themselves lest they also be tempted. Thus the spiritual man, remembering his own liability to fall, is to go in all gentleness to him who has been "overtaken in a fault" or offense, and in grace so identify himself with his condition as to take his burden of sin and sorrow upon himself, with a view to his succor and restoration. Now this is exactly what Christ Himself has done—only perfectly—both in life and in death.

That which was spoken of by Isaiah the prophet, saying, Himself took our infirmities, and bore our diseases (Mt. 8:1,6,17), was fulfilled in His life. Concerning His death, Peter says, "Who Himself bore our sins in His body on the tree" (1 Pet. 2:24 KJV). He was thus, in life and death, the great Burden-Bearer. In life He took our infirmities and sicknesses in grace in order to remove them. In death He bore our sins in substitution, and was made sin for us by God, when He endured for the glory of God all that was due to us on account of our sins, that He might take them away forever.

There is a great difference between His burden-bearing in life and in death; but still He was in both the Burden-Bearer. And this is the law of Christ: "Bear one another's burdens," and so fulfill the law of Him who was the pattern Burden-Bearer. Love was undoubtedly the motive of all He did; for, as the apostle says, He "loved me, and has given Himself for me." It is certain that we shall never go and take the burdens of our brethren on ourselves, unless we are under the constraint of the love of Christ.

E. Dennett

Blessed is everyone who fears the LORD, who walks in His ways … Behold, thus shall the man be blessed who fears the LORD.

(Psalm 128:1,4 ESV)

The Lord has promised blessing to the man who fears Him. Scripture is clear that the entire family is impacted when the head of the home and family fears the Lord! As a father I should *be the kind of parent who helps my children tremble with joy in the presence of God.*

Fathers are encouraged to be the kind of father their children delight to fear or to respect, helping them know the Lord. Take your place as God's special representative in your family, and display the fullness of who God is, so that your children will delight to fear you.

If they only fear you, and there is no delight in it, it's wrong and dysfunctional. If they only delight in you and do not fear you, it's wrong and dysfunctional. In both cases you have made it very difficult for your children to embrace the true God. On the one hand, as fathers, we hear Proverbs 13:24, *"Whoever spares the rod hates his son, but he who loves him is diligent to discipline him."* Why? Because that's the way God is. Hebrews 12:6 tells us, *"The Lord disciplines the one He loves, and chastises every son whom He receives."* So when I discipline my child, I display God's judgment and His love.

But on the other hand, as fathers, we hear this word from Ephesians 6:4, *"Fathers, do not provoke your children to anger, but bring them up in the discipline and instruction of the Lord."* In our families we are in the place of the Lord. We are doing the discipline of the Lord. Our children are learning what the Lord is like. And what is He like? Psalm 103:13-14 assures us that, *"As a father shows compassion to his children, so the LORD shows compassion to those who fear Him. For He knows our frame; He remembers that we are dust."*

T. P. Hadley

December 22 Lord's Day

We have not a high priest not able to sympathize with our infirmities, but tempted in all things in like manner, sin apart.

(Hebrews 4:15)

There are those who would use the truth of the real manhood of the Lord Jesus and His gracious, sympathetic identification with our humanity as an occasion to teach the false doctrine that He could have sinned. It is important for us when looking at this topic to adhere very closely to the words of Scripture and not to lean on our own reasoning.

The apostles: Peter, Paul, and John, all have the same testimony on this subject, yet each apostle presents it with a different emphasis in keeping with his unique ministry and personality.

The **apostle Peter** was a *"doer," a man of action*, and his teaching is that Christ "**did** no sin." Peter presents Christ as the model for the believer's walk, describing Him as One "who did no sin" (1 Pet. 2:22). The Lord Jesus never, at any time, committed sin. This is a fact which no true Christian can possibly deny. Even the enemies of Christ bore witness to this. The Lord Jesus asked His inquisitors, "Which of you convinces Me of sin?" Pilate thrice declared Him to be guiltless (Lk. 23:4,15,22).

The **apostle Paul**, was a *thinker, a theologian*, and his testimony concerning Christ is, "He **knew** not sin" (2 Cor. 5:21). This statement goes further than Peter's and shows that all of Christ's thoughts and motives were absolutely without sin.

Lastly, we have the **apostle John**, who of all of the disciples, was the *most intimate with Christ.* It was he who leaned on the bosom of the Lord (Jn. 13:23) and thus, John could write, "**in Him** sin is not" (1 Jn. 3:5). This means more than "He did no sin" or He "knew no sin." Christ's very nature was sinless! Indeed, He was a pure meal offering of "fine flour" in which there was absolutely "no leaven" (Lev. 2:1,11).

B. Reynolds

December **23** Monday

He sent his brethren away, and they departed. And he said to them, Do not quarrel on the way. *(Genesis 45:24)*
Be all of one mind, sympathizing, full of brotherly love, tender hearted ... seek peace and pursue it. *(1 Peter 3:8,11)*

Every time when my way takes me through a street busy with people I am freshly amazed. So many people are moving in opposite directions and yet it is very seldom that one bumps into the other. When it does happen, there is an "Excuse me" or "I am sorry" heard almost immediately. Why is that? I subconsciously use the faculties God has given me, and I am able to change direction quickly even though there are so many people heading towards me. I am thus equipped to avoid bumping into people, to give way, and to be considerate of others.

Let us think about that for a moment, how it is with believers on their way to heaven. We are all running in the same direction and therefore we don't have to change course, and yet oftentimes we "bump" into each other much more often as compared to our example. We are God's children, brothers and sisters in the faith, underway not as a stranger among strangers and yet it is so very difficult for me to excuse myself when I have "bumped" into someone. Does that not cause me to think? Why do I at times "cut" others off and "push" them while on my way even though every one of us has a God-given place and path?

"Do not quarrel on the way" (Gen. 45:24). This I should also take to heart and kindly consider the other while we move on to the glory of the Lord, to the encouragement of our fellow believers! If we pursue peace (because this is so important for our fellowship with God and with one another), then I should not be too proud to say "Forgive me," if I through my impatience or carelessness have hurt someone!

W. Habicht

Behold, the angel of the Lord appeared unto him in a dream, saying, Joseph, thou son of David, fear not to take unto thee Mary thy wife: for that which is conceived in her is of the Holy Ghost. And she shall bring forth a Son, and thou shalt call His name Jesus: for He shall save His people from their sins.

(Matthew 1:20-21 KJV)

Observe the difference between the message to Mary, and the message to Joseph. The mother of Jesus hears of His greatness: He was to be called the Son of the Highest, to have the throne of David, to reign over the house of Jacob forever. The reputed father of Jesus hears that He is to be a Savior. And did not Joseph know that he needed a Savior? Indeed he did. And furthermore Mary knew it too, for in the first chapter of Luke she says, "My spirit hath rejoiced in God my Savior" (v. 47).

How sweet it is that before the Child was born, God should give Him this name—Jesus—Jehovah the Savior. Blessed news for sinners! Charming name: none other so sweet. Do you not love the name of Jesus? Does not your heart respond as you hear that name? It has been the resting-place of myriads of troubled, anxious souls in days gone by, and it can give rest to every such one today. Every other name will perish: the name of the mightiest man that ever appeared in this world will pass away, but the name of Jesus shall endure forever.

"Now all this was done, that it might be fulfilled which was spoken of the Lord by the prophet ... Behold, a virgin shall be with Child, and shall bring forth a Son, and they shall call His name Emmanuel, which being interpreted is, God with us." Thus we learn two things. The name Jesus, given to this unborn Child, speaks of His being the Savior, and furthermore His birth was the fulfillment of a prophecy, well known to Joseph, that in His Person God was going to visit the earth.

W. T. P. Wolston

December 25 Wednesday

Having opened their treasures, they offered to Him gifts, gold, and frankincense, and myrrh.
(Matthew 2:11)

When Jesus was born in Bethlehem, and when the tidings reached the guilty tyrant who sat upon the Jewish throne, he "was troubled and all Jerusalem with him." The men of the city had already made their choice. They were on the side of Herod—not on the Lord's side.

The scribes, intelligent in the Scriptures as far as the letter went, knew, or should have known, many things about the Coming King. The prophets had clearly pointed out:

1. When He would come (Gen. 49:10).
2. How He would come (Isa. 7:14).
3. Where He would be born (Mic. 5:2).

But if there was no heart for Him in Jerusalem, and no room for Him in Bethlehem, a testimony was to be raised up from among the Gentiles; and "wise men"—wise, surely, in every sense of the word—divinely led, seek Him, recognize His divinity, worship Him, and present to Him their threefold gift, "gold, frankincense, and myrrh." When the Queen of Sheba visited Solomon she brought "gold and spices." In a coming day, when the kings of the Gentiles come to worship the glory of the Lord in Jerusalem, they will bring "gold and incense" (Isa. 60).

In neither the historic nor the prophetic Scripture is there any mention of that which is here connected with these two things, namely, "myrrh." Why is this? Is there not a threefold meaning in their gifts? In the Babe of Bethlehem they saw the One who was "born King of the Jews," and to Him they presented the royal offering of gold. But there was the recognition in the frankincense that He was more than man—that He was the promised Savior. And myrrh spoke of that of which the wise men could have but dim vision: that before He sat upon the throne of His glory He "must suffer many things ... and be killed" (Mt. 16:21).

L. Laurenson

One of themselves, a prophet of their own, has said, Cretans are always liars ... This testimony is true; for which cause rebuke them severely, that they may be sound in the faith.

(Titus 1:12-13)

THE NON-LYING GOD (1)

Have you ever thought about one word or one phrase for an entire day, mulling it over in your mind, looking at it from different perspectives, defining it in different ways? Words or phrases like: atonement, precious blood, eternal life, God of all comfort? When the apostle Paul wrote to his young Christian helper Titus, he carefully selected a word he used only once in all his writings – *"apseudes."* In fact, it is only used once in all the New Testament. If you saw that word in a text or email, would you keep mulling it over in your mind, and would it be enough to keep you excited, "pumped," for the day?

Perhaps it is a slight exaggeration, but really, when Titus read that expression *apseudes*, it probably gave him his thrill for the day. He was a young man working for the Lord on the island of Crete in the Mediterranean. Before the good news of Jesus Christ reached this island, it seems many of the people had earned a nasty reputation. Like other sinners, these people had slipped into the practice of lying, to the extent that it had become an accepted part of their culture; apparently their norm. In fact, in the Mediterranean area, other people called these islanders 'liars' (Ti. 1:12). It is against this backdrop that Titus opens up the letter from Paul and reads: *"ho apseudes Theos."* Did he fall to his knees and thank the Lord for such a reassuring and strengthening thought for the day? That one word was probably enough to keep him going right straight through until midnight! But wait. Are you not experiencing the same thrill that Titus did? Maybe it's a language barrier. Here it is in English, "the non-lying God."

P. Ramsay

In the hope of eternal life, which God, who cannot lie, promised before the ages of time, but has manifested in its own due season His word. *(Titus 1:2-3)*

THE NON-LYING GOD (2)

I can lie. Titus could too, and so could the Cretans. But God can **not** lie. I can deceive. God *cannot* deceive. I can falsify something. God *cannot*. I can exaggerate. God *cannot*. God is 100% truthful and dependable 100% of the time. Paul writes to Titus about "eternal life, which [the non-lying God], promised before the world began" (Ti. 1:2).

Maybe you are going through a rough time. Perhaps you are filled with doubts, wondering if you can trust God or not. Remember: *ho apseudes Theos.* My eternal security is not based on my memory, or my consistency as a Christian; it is based on the assurance from the non-lying God. I have God's Word for it (see for example Jn. 5:24; Jn. 10:28). But God is not just truthful when it comes to the promise of eternal life. Dear child of God, He is the non-lying God for every promise He has ever given you from His Holy Word.

God is Truth. God loves the truth. God hates untruths, lies, and exaggerations. In fact, in John 8:44 we learn from the Lord Jesus this fact about the origins of lies, exaggerations, and untruths: "You are of your father the devil, and you want to do the desires of your father. He was a murderer from the beginning, and does not stand in the truth because there is no truth in him. Whenever he speaks a lie, he speaks from his own nature, for he is a liar and the father of lies" (NASB).

Lord, help me to tell the truth today. Help me to not mislead, lie, or exaggerate. I am so privileged that I have an eternal relationship with Thee, *ho apseudes Theos.*

P. Ramsay

The mouth of a righteous man is a fountain of life … The lips of a righteous man feed many. *(Proverbs 10:11,21)*

The Proverbs of Solomon is a record of divine wisdom which is to be applied to the various aspects of life. There is one facet of our life that is highlighted in Proverbs more than any other and that is *the words that come out of our mouth*. Again and again we read of **"the tongue," "the lips," "the mouth"** and **"the words"** of either the righteous or of the foolish.

The "mouth" of a righteous person is described as a *fountain* of life and his "lips" as that which dispense *food*. How lovely to see that our words can be like water from a **"fountain"** supplying refreshment and bringing life. God has deigned to use our mouth to declare the message of the gospel, the "words of this life" (Acts 5:20). Our words can also be **"food"** which supplies nourishment to the hearers. The faithful servant is to provide food "in due season" to the household of faith (Mt. 24:45 KJV). The apostle exhorts us to speak words of "needful edification" that may "minister grace to the hearers" (Eph. 4:29 KJV).

It has been said that the tongue is an "index of the soul." Thus the way in which we speak is often an indication of our spiritual state, even as the Lord Jesus taught, that out "of the abundance of the heart the mouth speaks" (Mt. 12:34). We will never *regret* speaking words of grace that give life and healing. But we will never *forget* when we have spoken words that wound or that are unkind: *"I am the master of my unspoken words, and I'm the slave of words that should have been left unspoken."* Solomon also wrote that "death and life are in the power of the tongue" (Prov. 18:21). The words of our mouth ought to be for the glory of God and for the blessing of man who is created in His image (Jas. 3:9). What an awesome responsibility as well as a wonderful privilege for every believer!

B. Reynolds

> When [the Lamb] took the book, the four living creatures and the twenty-four elders fell before the Lamb ... And they sing a new song, saying, Thou art worthy to take the book, and to open its seals; because Thou hast been slain, and hast redeemed to God, by Thy blood, out of every tribe, and tongue, and people, and nation.
> *(Revelation 5:8-9)*

In this chapter a beautiful scene opens up before us in heaven. That is where Christ is now seated. He once was here, where we still are, but He is here no longer. When the Lord Jesus was here in this scene, both Jews and Gentiles cast Him out and nailed Him to the accursed tree. What a dreadful deed this was, revealing on the one hand, the wretched sinful heart of man, and on the other hand, the surpassing riches of the grace of God, for where sin abounded, grace over-abounded.

During this period while Christ is in heaven, God, by the gospel, is calling out men and women of all ages and walks of life, and from every tribe, tongue, people, and nation to be associated with Christ in heaven. This is unfolding before our eyes in a remarkable way, as we hear of souls being reached to the four corners of the world. This is happening amid political conflicts, opposition, and natural calamities, but the Spirit of God is not bound. Praise His Name!

What is it that draws people of such vast cultural differences together? Nothing else and nothing less than God's chosen Lamb who once was slain. He by His precious blood has redeemed them to God. They will all sing one song, a new song that has never been sung before and will never end. It will only be sung by this large innumerable company that has been redeemed during the time of Christ's rejection. This company will be associated with Christ as His Bride throughout the countless ages of eternity. We shall be privileged to join this singing that He leads.

J. Redekop

It may be that Jehovah will look on mine affliction, and that Jehovah will requite me good for my being cursed this day. And David and his men went by the way; and Shimei went along on the hill's side over against him, and cursed as he went, and threw stones at him, and cast dust. *(2 Samuel 16:12-13)*

Human friends fail us. But our God is eternal and omnipotent; who ever trusted in Him in vain? Where is the man that can say, I looked up to Him and hoped in Him, and I am ashamed of my hope?

The beauty of David's looking alone to God came out in this, quite calmly and quietly. He said to himself: "God will get me out of this." Therefore he was not angry with Shimei; he did not want his head to be cut off, or anything of the sort. "God will do it."

If a man keeps in that frame of mind, what can disturb him? Though the mountains were cast into the midst of the sea and the earth were moved, yet still would he in patience possess his soul, and still be calm. God has given His angels charge concerning such a man to keep him in all His ways; for he dwells in the secret place of the Most High, and shall abide under the shadow of the Almighty. The Lord says of him: Because he has set his love upon Me, therefore will I deliver him. I will set him on high, because he has known My name. He has trusted in Me and Me alone; therefore will I never fail him. "Trust ye in the Lord forever: for in the Lord Jehovah is everlasting strength."

Fix all your confidence on Him. Lean not here and there—you will grow crooked in yourself, and the staff you lean on shall turn to a spear and pierce you. Lean wholly upon God, and as He is everywhere, you shall stand upright in leaning upon Him.

C. H. Spurgeon

December **31** Tuesday

There was a little city, and few men within it; and there came a great king against it, and encompassed it, and built great bulwarks against it: and there was found in it a poor wise man, who by his wisdom delivered the city; but no man remembered that poor man. Then said I, Wisdom is better than strength; but the poor man's wisdom is despised, and his words are not heard.

(Ecclesiastes 9:14-16)

How perverted are our natural thoughts! If a man set in high honor and dignity were to formulate a wise plan by which to deliver his city from a formidable attack by a great adversary, he would be highly acclaimed and should likely have a monument erected in his honor. But a poor man who shows such wisdom is forgotten!

God has wisely ordained that His own beloved Son, He who is worthy of dignity infinitely higher than the highest of men, should come into this world as a poor Man. He came in marvelous humility and great kindness to a world so small in comparison to the universe He had created, and so weak in comparison to the great forces of satanic power which had completely surrounded men.

This poor Man acted in wisdom wonderful beyond our thought, not only devising a plan by which to save the world, but sacrificing His own life to carry out this plan in perfection. His finished work will eventually liberate this world from all danger, and by it countless souls have already been eternally saved from a dreadful end.

How many are there in the world today who really remember this poor wise Man? Sadly, by the great majority He is forgotten as a dead man out of mind (Ps. 31:12). In clear contrast let every believer gladly remember Him with a full heart and in worshipping adoration.

L. M. Grant

You have come to the end
of
The Lord Is Near
Daily Bible Meditations for 2013

We trust that the Lord has used them for your blessing.
Please send your comments or suggestions to:

**The Lord Is Near
4 Elwin Cr.
DARTMOUTH, NOVA SCOTIA
CANADA B2W 3J6**

or: **E-mail: contact@thelordisnear.org**

May the Lord bless you in the days ahead.

The Editors:
Jacob Redekop, Brian Reynolds, John van Dijk, Eugene P. Vedder, Jr.

Orders should continue to be directed to your local Christian
bookstore or to one of our distributors:

**Believer's Bookshelf Canada Inc.
5205 Regional Road # 81 - Unit # 3
BEAMSVILLE, ONTARIO
CANADA   L0R 1B3**
www.bbcan.org
orders@bbcan.org

Lists of distributors can be found on the following pages.

North American Distributors

Canada

Believer's Bookshelf Canada Inc.
5205 Regional Road #81– Unit # 3
BEAMSVILLE, ONTARIO
L0R 1B3
www.bbcan.org
orders@bbcan.org

United States of America

Believers Bookshelf Inc.
P. O. Box 261
SUNBURY, PENNSYLVANIA 17801

European Distributors

United Kingdom

Chapter Two
Fountain House, Conduit Mews
WOOLWICH, LONDON   SE18 7AP
ENGLAND

Word of Truth
P. O. Box 147
BELFAST,   BT8 4TT
NORTHERN IRELAND

Germany

Gute Botschaft Verlag Dillenburg GmbH
Eiershauser Str. 54
D-35713 ESCHENBURG

Christliche Schriftenverbreitung
Postfach 10 01 53
D-42499 HÜCKESWAGEN

Switzerland

Beröa Verlag
Zellerstrasse 61
CH-8038 ZURICH

Asian Distributors

India

Words of Life Trust
3 Chuim Village Khar
400 052 MUMBAI

Trust of Assembly of Believers
PADISONPET,
TENALI, 522 201,
ANDHRA PRADESH

Philippines

Lord Is Near
P. O. Box 80
SAN PABLO CITY

African Distributors

Egypt

Brethren Bookstore
3 Anga Hanem Street
SHOUBRA, CAIRO 11231

Ghana

Christian Literature Service
P. O. Box GP 20872
ACCRA

Nigeria

Word of Truth
P. O. Box 1126
KADUNA, KADUNA
(S 13 Aliyu Makama Rd., Barnawa, Kaduna South)

Christian Literature Depot
P. O. Box 436
IJESHATEDO, SURULERE, LAGOS

Echoes of Truth
11 Post Office Road,
P. O. Box 2637
MUSHIN, LAGOS

Caribbean Distributors

Barbados

The Bible House
P. O. Box 344G
ST. GEORGE

Jamaica

Oceanview Bible Camp
Southfield P. O. Box 6
ST. ELIZABETH

Netherlands Antilles

Lord Is Near
Kaya Brasia 14
P. O. Box 8124
STA ROSA
CURAÇAO

St. Kitts

Lord Is Near
P. O. Box 777
BASSETERRE

St. Lucia

Lord Is Near
P. O. Box 65
CASTRIES

St. Vincent, W.I.

Lord Is Near
Ruthland Vale
LAYOU

Trinidad, W.I.

Lord Is Near
18/439 Balmattee Street
COUVA

Lord Is Near
11 Aquamarine Drive
DIAMOND VALE
DIEGO MARTIN

South American Distributors

Brazil

Depósito de Literatura Christã
Rua Arlindo Bétio, 117
CEP 09911-470 DIADEMA - SP
BRASIL

Guyana

Believers Book Centre
308 Quamina & East Streets
GEORGETOWN

South Pacific Distributors

New Zealand

Bible & Book Depot Foundation
12 Cullahill Street
CHRISTCHURCH 8051